The ~~~ hen

By
Kate Magic

RawLiving
Elevate Your Health

First published in the UK by Raw Living publications 2023

First edition

Copyright © Kate Magic 2023

Layout and design: Simon Earl

Proofreading and photo-editing: Sophie Gould

Photography: Kate Magic

No reproduction without permission. All rights reserved. No part of this publication may be reproduced, stored in, or introduced into a retrieval system, copied or transmitted by any form or by any means - electronically, photocopy, recording or otherwise without the permission of the copyright owners.

The right of Kate Magic to be asserted as author of this work has been asserted in accordance with Sections 77 of the Copyright, Designs and Patents act 1988.

Raw Living Publications

23 Ford Rd, Totnes, Devon, TQ9 5LE

Printed and bound in the UK by Acanthus Press.

ISBN: 978-1-9161381-3-1

Contents

Intro
What is the Magic Kitchen? 10
The Magic Plate 12
A Little Bit of Science 15
Creating Recipes 19
Magical Living 23

Dips & Dressings 27
Mystic Mayo 28
Chlorella Pesto 29
Wasabi & Broccoli Pesto Dressing 30
Bayonnaise 31
Divine Sauce of Big Love 32
Krautamolé 33
Zucchini Hummus 34
Dream Chease 35
Black Velvet 36
Muhammara 37
Middle Eastern Guacamole 38
Umamayo 39
Hey Pesto 40

Soups, Sides & Sushi 44
Reuben's Garlick Soup 45
Ecstatic Soup 46
Green Goddess Soup with Kelp Noodles 47
Soup of the Woods 48
Hot Tub Soup 49
Thai Soup 50
Simple Kale Salad 54
Sauer Slaw 55
Hemp Tabbouleh 56
Cali Rolls 57
Cauliflower Rice with Baobab & Turmeric 58
Sublime Sushi 60
Rainbow Sushi 62
Stuffed Avocado 2.0 64

Mains ... 67
Tart's Spaghetti ... 68
Shepherd's Pie ... 69
Renegade Chia ... 72
LasanYea ... 74
Kraut & Kelp Noodles ... 76
The Glorious LasanYea ... 79
Spaghetti Supernese ... 82
Thai Coconut Noodles ... 83
Nachos Nachos ... 84
Magic Bubble & Squeak ... 87
Vanilla Marinara ... 88
Ten Minute Kelp Noodles ... 91
Mexican Mushroom Chia Chilli ... 93
Golden Burritos ... 94
Kale Pizza ... 96
Nori Pizzas ... 99
Perfect Pizza ... 101
Laurie's Kale & Kelp Noodles ... 103
Spring Rolls ... 104
Enchiladas ... 107
Wrawps ... 109
Nori Tacos ... 110

Crackers, Burgers & Other Dehydrated Delights ... 114
Masala Crackers ... 115
Secret Garden Burgers ... 116
Muddy Crackers ... 117
Caraway Crackers ... 118
Chia Onion Bread ... 119
Onion Bhajis ... 120
Chia Crackers ... 121
Nori Crackers ... 123
Buckers ... 124
Beautiful Broccoli Burgers ... 126
Kale Burgers ... 128
BBQ Mushroom Breasts ... 129
Chia Toast ... 130
Coconut Bacon ... 131

Everyone Loves Onion Bread 132
Garlac Bread. 134
Kale Chips. 136
Brazilliant Kale Chips 137
Lebanese Kale Chips. 138
Tahini & Baobab Kale Chips. 139
Be Blessed 140
Dragon's Spines. 142
Smoked Paprika & Balsamic Vinegar Kale Chips 143
Kate's Kale Krisps 144
Kaleola. 145
Thai Green Curry Chips 146
The Best Salt & Vinegar Crisps in the World. 147
Sweet & Spicy Kale Chips. 148
Greener Kale Chips 149

Ferments 154
Kefir 158
Kombucha. 160
Cheese-Making. 162
I Can't Believe It's Not Boursin 164
Kimchi 166
Fat Sesame Kimchi 168
Ruby Kraut 170
Pickled Cucumbers 172
Preserved Lemons 174

Candies & Cookies. 176
Violet Visions. 177
Reishi Candi 178
Roses Grow On You 180
Spearmint Candies 181
Matcha Mucuna Mints 182
Happy Accident Candy 183
Kids' Lifesavers. 184
Baobiscuits. 186
Beyond Custard Creams 189
Marching Biscuits 190

Chocolate 193
Heartcore Chocolate 194
Deviation Chocolate 195
Jing's the Thing 196
Chiaji 197
New Jamaica 198
Rum Truffles 199
Sweet Enough. 200
The Low Down Loretta Brown 201
Chiacolate. 202
Seasonal Chocolate Truffles. 203
Easter Eggs. 204
Choc Ice. 206
Magic Bounty Bars. 207

Cakes 210
Triple Layer Chocolate Pie 212
Teddy's Apple Pie. 214
Crikey Cake. 216
Blueberry & Chocolate Chip Cupcakes 217
Blackcurrant & Lime Cupcakes 218
Be the Cupcake You Wish to See in the World. 220
Strawberry & Baobab Cupcakes. 222
Superstar Cake. 223
Mamacakeshun 224
Strawberries & Cream Pie. 226
Cherry No Bakewell. 228
Rosemary's Rose Cheesecake. 231
The Pop-Up Cake. 232
Return of the Sun Cheesecake. 234
Papaya Pie Yea. 236
Inca Redible Cake 238
Chi Lime Pie. 239
Mucunaroons. 240
Baobab Brownies. 242
Dulsilicious Chocolate Brownies. 243
Zillionaire Shortbread. 244
They Call Me Mellow Yellow 246

California Dreaming Pie 248
Chake 249
Fermented Cheesecake 250
Durian Cheesecake 252

Desserts 255
Strawberry Coconut Mousse 255
Chocolate Chia Trifles 256
Autumn Chia 258
Tequila Slimmer 259
Full of Christmas Chia 260
Red Sky at Night 261
Chia Leaders 262
Yo! Gurt 263
Just Peachy 264

Drinks 267
Kombucha Cocktails 267
The Chocolate Disco Smoothie 268
Superfood Mojitos 269
Magic Milk 270
Sweet Raspberry Milk 271
Blueberry Almond Milk 272
Secret Lemonade Drinker 273
Perfectly Magical Smoothie 274
Magic Maca Hemp Milk 274
The Bomb 275
Turmeric Latté 276
Macapuccino 277
Matcha Latté 279
Black Chaga 279

Articles:

What is Raw?	41
Hold On to the Light	51
Transition Town	65
Wise Investments	77
Sociabubble	111
Meal for 6.8 Billion, Sir?	135
The Myth of 100% Raw	150
Easy Guide to Fermentation	154 (Ferments)
Happiness is a State of Stomach	175
Simplicity & Relativity	191
On the Road	208
Life is Like a Plate of Cake	211
Value & Abundance	253
Present & Connected	265
The Mummy Bear Effect	280

Glossary **281**

Resources **290**

What is the Magic Kitchen?

Everything is energy. Everything carries a vibration, a resonance. Everything you do, say and think affects this vibration. Everyone you meet and everywhere you go. And everything you put in your mouth!

When we worry, are fearful, or scared, we lower our vibration. When we are positive, happy, and grateful, we raise our vibration. Energy is always moving and always shifting, so this is not a static thing. It's an ongoing process, which takes constant presence and awareness. It's a continual unfolding that we must pay attention to – if we don't, we can easily find ourselves getting sidetracked and waylaid in undesired directions.

I try and pay continual awareness to my thoughts, and maintain a positive frame of mind. I try and speak good and act compassionately towards others. I seek as much as I can to spend time in beautiful places with beautiful people. I make my work about upliftment and inspiration, for the good of all. But I've found the most powerful way to shift vibration is to pay attention to what goes in your mouth.

The more light energy the food holds, the more light energy will be entering our body, and the more light energy our cells will hold. As we eat this way, we experience a new quality of life that is hard to put into words. As healthy eating becomes ever more trendy, the backlash grows, of people criticising the lack of concrete science behind concepts such as alkalisation and enzymes. I say, never mind the science! When you eat this way, you know how you feel, and we can call it amazing or wonderful or energised or full of vitality, but none of those words really come close to summing up that feeling of elation and excitement that a truly healthy person knows. This feeling is not dependent on anything – your job, your partner, your surroundings, because it's in your cells. You feel like everything is possible, and you can conquer the world – because it is and you can!

Our bodies are made up of trillions and trillions of cells, more than we can count. These cells are receiving information from our environment and reacting accordingly to try and maintain homeostasis. When we put clean foods, water and air in our bodies, and are living peaceful lives, we are making it easy on our cells. When we are breathing in polluted air, drinking water full of chemicals, eating toxic foods, and living on stress, we are making it much harder. (Not to mention the onslaught of chemicals we put on our bodies. Did you know that your skin absorbs around 80% of what you put on it? You should only put on your skin what you would actually be happy to put in your mouth.)

Not only do we need to consider what our cells need to perform optimally, we also need to take note of the bacteria in our bodies. Bacteria are so infinitesimally tiny, we actually contain more bacteria than cells. That's right, we are host to more foreign organisms than we are our own organism. We are each an individual living eco-system, and it's vital that we tend to this eco-system like we would a garden, and ensure the flowers bloom and the weeds don't take over!

I believe this is why more and more people are turning to a holistic lifestyle. As the world becomes more chaotic and confusing, we go within and look for answers. It's more vital than ever that we rely on our inner peace and our inner strength to guide us through our days. And in these dark days, humanity more than ever needs people who are shifting things in positive ways, spreading love and joy and doing their bit to make the world a better place.

This is the Magic Kitchen. Eating in such a way that your cells sing for joy. You are raising your vibration, and carrying an energy that is in harmony with the universe. I believe there is a divine intelligence that runs through everything, and one of the biggest problems in the world today is the way we have become disconnected from that. Everyone worries about everything so much, and as a culture we focus on problems and difficulties rather than creating solutions and finding ways to improve. Eating this way connects us to that divine intelligence, and brings a sense of peace and harmony to our days that so many people seem to be lacking. These might seem like grandiose claims, but I have been eating this way for over three decades now, and worked with thousands of people in that time, and I can tell you hand on heart that it's true. Magic is what we are, it's in the very fabric of our being, and our hearts, minds and souls are crying out to be reunited in that magic, to swim in it every day. The more we tread this path, the more the magic intertwines with our lives, and we experience that illogical, unreasonable, ridiculous bliss that we are all seeking.

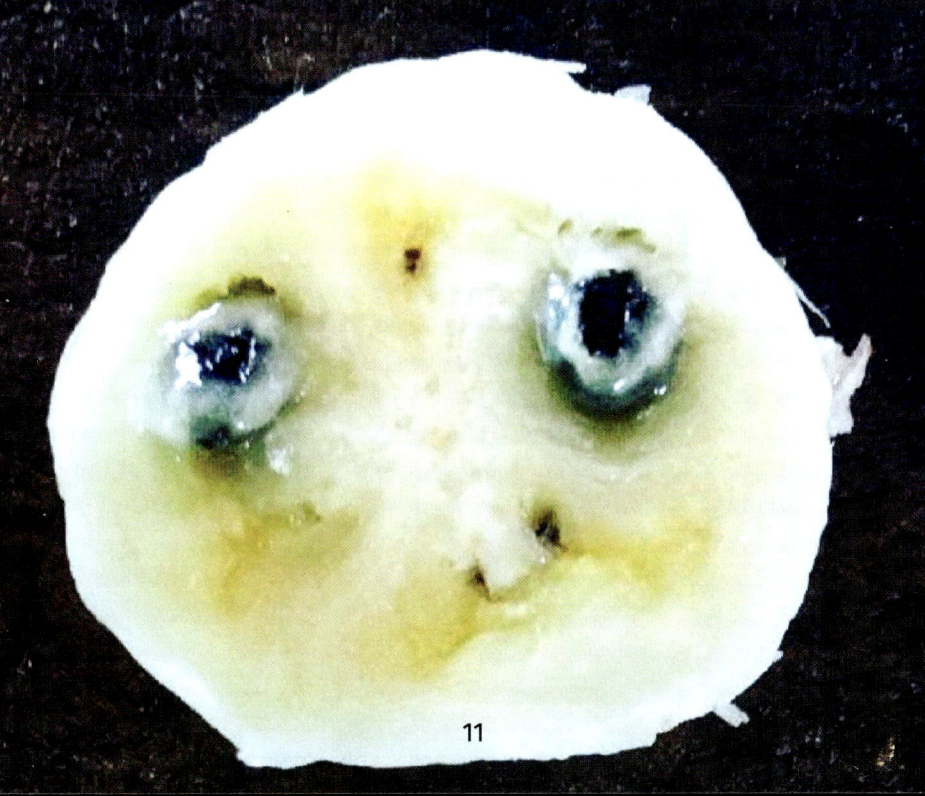

The Magic Plate

Obviously, I eat only raw vegan food, and all the recipes in this book are raw and vegan (I do use small amounts of bee products, which you can easily substitute if that is your choice). But above and beyond raw or cooked, vegan or omnivore, I consider the following to be the most important factors in health. There are certain conditions in the body that are like fertile soil to disease, and other conditions in which disease simply cannot thrive. To be in good health, and maintain good health, is a relatively simple thing when one understands these basic concepts. However to take someone who is chronically ill – with diabetes, cancer, hypothyroidism or ME, to name just a few of the prevalent illnesses these days – and try and reverse that condition with diet, lifestyle and holistic techniques is a highly complex and involved route; not impossible, but by no means straight-forward. By incorporating these simple principles we can keep disease at bay, and when we do enter those trigger situations, through overwork, stress, or environmental pollution, we can pull ourselves back into full health quickly and effectively.

Alkalisation

Ideally, we need to look at including 70-80% alkaline foods in the diet. Alkalinity promotes peace in the body – think of how calm and rejuvenated you feel with a big glass of green juice – that's alkalinity flooding the body. Stress creates acidity – it's an important and much overlooked key to vibrant health to avoid stressful situations and stop trying to do so much all the time that we don't get enough rest. Virtually all the recipes in this book are alkalising. A raw vegan alkalising diet avoids a lot of nuts and dried fruits, and focuses on the greens and the sea vegetables. Green juice (with no sweet fruits) is super alkalising, and wheatgrass and barleygrass are the two most alkalising foods.

Hydration

This, for me personally, is the number one most important factor that I believe everyone needs to prioritise. We need 250ml, or a glass of water, for every hour that we are awake – that works out at 3-4 litres a day. However, we don't want to just be drinking pure water, because that acts a flushing mechanism, and actually too much water can cause dehydration as it pulls everything out (and makes you need to pee all the time!). So we include high quality, high vibrational, high nutritional drinks such as juices, medicinal teas, superfood plant milks, coconut water, and fermented drinks. There are an abundance of drinks recipes in this book. I would recommend that you drink them as often as you can – try a juice or a hemp milk as mid-morning, mid-afternoon or early evening pick me ups and you will be surprised at how effective they are at energising and satiating you. Personally, I aim for a litre or two before lunch, a litre between lunch and dinner, and another litre or two in the evening, and my total liquid intake averages at around 4-5 litres a day.

Healthy Fats

The fats are the building blocks of the cells, they are essential for light, and I believe low-fat regimes are inherently dangerous. I intuitively follow a ketogenic diet, and have done for nearly two decades (before I knew there was a name for it!). This means, my body is very efficient at converting fats into fuel (see below p15). In terms of calorific intake, my diet is low-carb, high fat. I am liberal with seeds and their oils, avocados and olives, cacao and coconut. I find this way, I always have a ton of energy, and I never put on weight. A raw vegan diet that includes an abundance of healthy fats is far more filling and sustaining than one that tries to rely on fruits and veggies for fuel.

Oxygenation

Although you can take oxygen supplements if you feel a need (such as during and after certain respiratory illnesses that rob the body of oxygen), there are two easy ways to oxygenate that you should try and incorporate daily. Firstly, laughter, and secondly, exercise. Not a big ask in return for vibrant health. Choose standing over sitting, the stairs over the lift, and walking over getting the bus, for three easy ways to keep that oxygen circulating. It's well established that a lack of oxygen in the cells is one of the primary factors that enable cancer cells to thrive.

Low Sugar

Sugar is incredibly addictive, and a drug that most people find hard to let go of. Ask people to drop their carbs and most look at you with horror! You need to actively minimise your sugar intake or it will naturally keep creeping up, because of its addictive nature: the more we consume one day, the more we will crave the next. The good news is that your taste buds are being renewed all the time, so it's quite simple to train your palate over time to include less and less of the sweet stuff.

Fruit in itself may be a healthy choice, but the natural fruit sugars that fruit contains are still are enough to create imbalances in the body, particularly with modern-day fruits that have been bred for sweetness and appearance, and so lack the phytonutrients that fruits grown in the wild contain. Especially be wary of juices with a high sugar content such as carrot juice and beet juice, and those kind of snack bars that appear to be healthy but in actuality are mostly dates and agave. The recipes in this book are virtually all low-glycemic. For my own domestic use, my preferred sweeteners are stevia, maca, yacon, coconut nectar, and evaporated cane juice crystals. Sugar is a breeding ground for disease: it encourages candida overgrowth and a gut flora imbalance, is detrimental to the teeth, and is another major contributory factor to the growth of cancer cells. Also it creates artificial highs and then dips in our energy – the less sugar, the more stable your energy and your moods will be.

Fermented Foods

As we mentioned earlier, cultivating a healthy biome is an integral part of an energised life. The gut is a central hub in the body, passing trillions of messages around every day between the outside world, your brain, and your body. Think of it like a major airport or train station, co-ordinating a never-ending stream of traffic that has to pass through smoothly and efficiently. Including fermented foods and drinks daily will go a massive way to building this thriving eco-system, and enable the gut to ensure that there are no crashes, and that all the passengers get to where they need to go.

In my recipes, you will find I sneak in ingredients like sauerkraut as often as I can. And there is a whole section on home-fermenting that will hopefully show you how easy and accessible it is. I include fermented foods in just about every meal, even if it's only some kombucha vinegar in a dressing. I drink between half to one litre of fermented beverages in a day, usually home-made in my own kitchen.

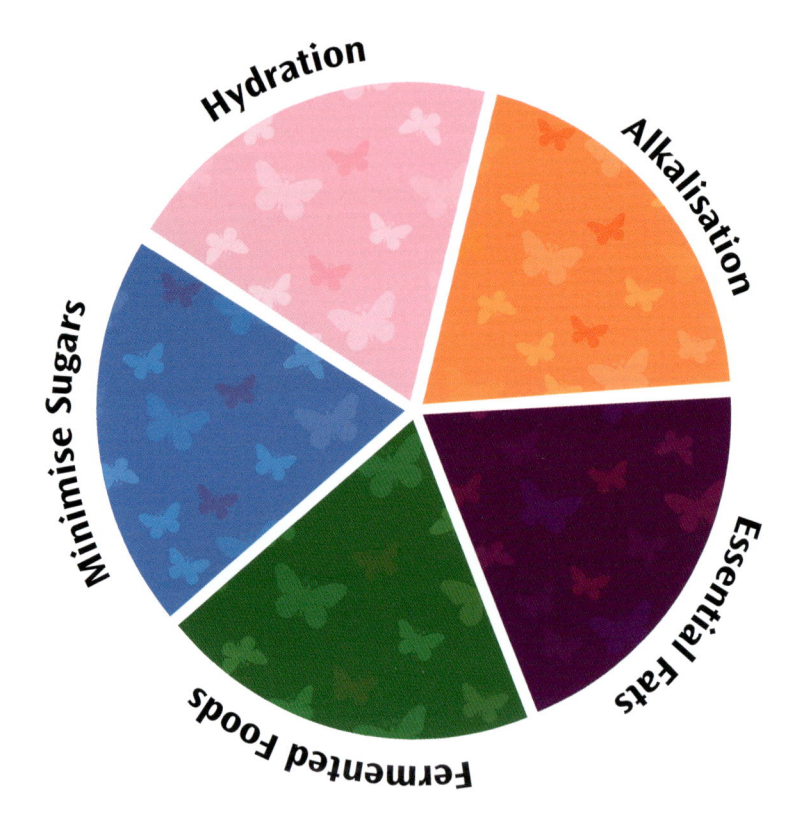

- Hydration
- Alkalisation
- Essential Fats
- Fermented Foods
- Minimise Sugars

A Little Bit of Science

To be fair, there's not a lot of robust science to back up the efficacy of a raw vegan diet. Rather than seeing this as a fault of the diet, I see it as a fault in a system that is more interested in creating a profit-making industry around sickness than coming up with any real developments in sustaining human health. And I see it as testament to the power of the diet that people don't need to understand why or how it works – they just trust their experience. No matter how many articles you read on why going vegan might be good for you or bad for you, the deciding factor on whether you go vegan or not is you; how it makes you feel and how it fits with your lifestyle. I believe the booming popularity of eating clean is down to people experiencing the enhanced energy levels it provides, and saying to themselves, "Yes! I want more of that." I know that for me, increased productivity is probably the number one factor that keeps me going on my diet: when I dip into too much sugar, or over-eating, or eating late at night, my energy wanes and I don't have the focus to handle all my responsibilities as a woman. I want to be the best mother, lover, friend, businesswoman, yogi, coach, healer, DJ, chef, writer, dancer, homemaker, that I can be. I want to juggle all these roles every day and feel fulfilled, not drained and burned out, and the way I eat provides me with the consistent resources to achieve this. What follows are some practices I adhere to, that have been recently backed up with scientific research. I hope that as time goes on, there will be increasing research into all aspects of raw veganism, so we can fully explain why this diet does wonders for us.

Ketogenics

The standard Western diet relies heavily on carbs for fuel, while neglecting the importance of healthy fats, and it's now widely recognised that this is one of the main contributory factors to obesity and diabetes. When we use carbs as our fuel source, we get a serotonin high as the sugars are released into the body (which makes them very addictive). Then as they are assimilated into the body, we get a dip in the blood sugar which makes us crave more. This up and down energy cycle is a norm for most people. The problem is that too much sugar leads to an over-production of hormones, and imbalances that prevent the body knowing its limits. When the hormonal system becomes damaged in this way, the outcome is obesity and/or diabetes, as a person stops being able to recognise their body's natural hunger signals, and instead consistently overeats.

When we limit the carbs and up our fat intake, rather than storing fats in the body, the body becomes efficient at burning them up for fuel. When we become fat-adapted in this way, our energy resources are much more stable, without the sugar highs and lows, and we become calmer. Not only this, but as disease needs to feed on sugar, by minimising sugars in your diet, you are drastically reducing your risk of most chronic illnesses, particularly cancer and diabetes. Many athletes are turning to a ketogenic diet, as they find it provides them with greater stamina and endurance levels. Our brains are mostly made of fat, so you should find your ability to focus and concentrate increase. And as your body has adjusted to burning off excess fat, rather than storing it, it is the ideal weight-loss diet, for a long-term sustainable approach to keeping fit and healthy. Personally, I am the same weight I was when I was in my 20s. I never worry about putting on weight, I always eat as much as I want, and I always feel satiated by my food.

Intermittent Fasting

The body goes through three cycles daily: the digestion cycle, between midday and 8pm, the absorption cycle, between 8pm and 4am, and the elimination cycle, between 4am and midday. When we can concentrate our food intake into the digestion cycle, our bodies become much more efficient. Everyone appreciates the wisdom of not eating a big meal in the middle of the night: the more you adhere to these natural rhythms of your body, the more you will instinctively stay away from eating outside of them. The time when the digestion is strongest is in the first half of the digestion cycle, from midday to 4pm. If you can eat your main meal of the day at this point, then that's ideal for optimizing energy, although for many of us it's not possible to relax and eat properly until the evening. If your main meal has to fall in the evening, then try and eat as early on as possible. I usually just eat one piece of fruit in the morning, and then don't eat anything else until sometime between midday and 2pm. I like to have my second meal of the day around 7-8 pm. A full meal takes around 4 hours to digest, so 5 hours between meals is optimum. Too soon and you are just piling up more food in the gut; too long and your blood sugar will start to drop. I might have a small snack outside of those optimum hours (12-8 pm), like a few squares of chocolate, a handful of olives, a flax cracker, or half an avocado, but the bulk of my intake happens in that 8 hour window, leaving the remaining 16 hours for my body to absorb, assimilate and eliminate with maximum efficiency.

It's very unnatural to be able to just eat at will, any time of the day or night, as we do nowadays. Historically, we generally had very limited windows for the consumption of food, and that's how our bodies work best, with long periods of fasting between meals. It's during those periods that the body does most of its repair work, work that it can't do when its burdened by the work of breaking down food and putting it to use in the body. Intermittent fasting is also linked to longevity, as you are putting less stress on the organs, helping them keep going for longer.

Calorie Restriction

Calorie Restriction is one of the most well researched strategies for longevity and anti-ageing. Similar to the principles of intermittent fasting, when we consume less, we reduce the burden on the organs and increase their life span. There are actually two ways that we feel full: the one most of us are familiar with is the literal, "I can't fit any more in my stomach" way. This is what people on a carb heavy diet are accustomed to: eating rice, pasta, potatoes or wheat as the bulk of the meal in order to physically feel full. But because eating this way doesn't guarantee an abundance of nutrients, it's still possible to be hungry again shortly afterwards, and "find room" for dessert. However, when we eat a nutrient dense diet, our bodies produce a hormone called leptin, which sends the signal to say that we have enough nutrients to work with and we can stop eating. Thus we become less dependent on the physical sensation of fullness, and more attuned to the body's signals in terms of what we actually need to consume.

It's almost universal that people report surprise at how much less they need to consume when eating a raw diet, and how quickly they feel satiated. It's a new type of fullness, a way of eating that satisfies the whole body, and a new experience for many people. No longer are we juggling our desires with our sensible self, and having inner battles over whether we should or should not indulge. We can fully indulge our desires to gain ecstatic pleasure from food, while simultaneously knowing that we are being as correct and sensible as it's possible to be in terms of a healthy diet. What a revelation! I would say calorie restriction is an inevitable benefit of doing a raw food diet as I have described it: high fat, low carb, low fruit, low nuts, high superfoods. If you follow this for just a few months, I would estimate your calorie intake could drop by as much as 50% (but you won't become underweight remember, because of the high fat content in the diet).

A Note On Chronic Illness

When I started teaching in 2002, I would ask people in my talks to put their hands up if they knew anyone close to them who had had cancer. Maybe 1 in 10 people would raise their hand. Did you know that when the UK Cancer Act was passed in 1939, cancer rates were 1 in 72! After a time of giving talks, I stopped asking, because it got to the point where everyone would raise their hand and it was too heart-breaking.

The normalisation of diseases like cancer, heart disease and diabetes has happened over my lifetime, and we might want to ask ourselves why the cancer industry is so hugely profitable, making billions each year for pharmaceutical companies, while a "cure" still evades them?

When someone is given a diagnosis of one of these life-threatening diseases, their bodies have got to a point of sending out loud distress signals that can no longer be sidelined or ignored. It is entirely the choice of the person who receives the diagnosis which path they want to go down from there. Everyone has to do what feels best to them personally. Some people feel the medical route is what serves them, and others choose to go holistic. Many embark on a combination of therapies. By no means would I ever suggest that someone with cancer just needs to meditate and eat more cucumbers and they will get better. They have to be ready to do some deep emotional work and make some huge lifestyle changes, and understandably, once a person is seriously ill, they might not feel that they have the bandwidth for it.

I believe ultimately, all diseases can be treated holistically, but that the patient has to be in the right place to receive that treatment, and that is a very individual thing. A patient must be willing to take complete responsibility for their own health, and that means working closely with whatever practitioners resonate with them: they could choose a Chinese or Ayurvedic practitioner, a homeopath or herbalist, a functional nutritionist or kinesiologist, or most likely use a combination of modalities.

As a qualified Functional Nutritionist, I would never dispense advice to someone about their health without first taking a detailed case history, and it shocks me when I see people handing out advice online without knowing anything about the person asking the question. As holistic therapists, I think it's entirely unethical for us to give advice outside of a professional capacity, and it also encourages the patient to think that they don't have to treat their health seriously, that they can just look up the answers online. Health is a journey, and a chronic illness will never be treatable by a quick-fix solution.

Everyone needs someone on their team! And I think that's part of the cause of the rise of disease in our culture: we've forgotten how important it is to ask for help and support. No matter if you're in the peak of fitness or chronically ill, everyone needs a regular visit to a health practitioner to keep everything tip top, even if it's just a massage therapist. In traditional Chinese medicine, you went to your doctor and you paid him a regular fee, like a subscription, and he gave you herbs to keep you well. If you fell sick, that meant he had failed in his job and he wouldn't get paid again until he made you better! How's that for an inversion of our modern healthcare system?

Creating Recipes

When I am creating recipes, there are always a few simple rules that I follow, that I wish to share with you here. These are the little tips and tricks that take your recipes to the next level; the additions that transform your dish from pedestrian to astronomical! Of course, I don't do them all every time, but they are a little mental check-list that I run through in my head to see if I've considered all the factors that will make my food as fantastic as it can be.

I've been eating a high raw diet since 1991, and to be honest, I'm as surprised as you probably are that I haven't tired of it by now. The key is to stay inventive and creative, and always be looking to broaden your horizons. I believe the universe is infinitely abundant: if I catch myself feeling restricted, or coming from a perspective of lack, I look to see how I can alter my perspective and tap back into that unending flow of abundance. If I notice myself getting stuck in a rut around food, I will seek out new books or people or places that will ignite my inspiration. Sometimes, I just go back into my old recipes, like reuniting with old friends. But once I've found something that fires up my imagination, I can play with it for weeks, loving this new discovery, and finding new layers of inspiration from it. Always be on the search for something new, and if you find yourself getting bored, know that it's not that this diet is restrictive and limiting, it's that you need to push yourself a little more to find the joy in it again.

Consider your Flavour Profiles

A lot of raw food dishes end up tasting quite bland and samey. When we cook the foods, that's what brings out the flavours. If we are not cooking, then we have to consciously consider other ways to highlight the flavours within a dish, and draw them out. I always consider four main flavour profiles in my savoury dishes:

- Salt e.g. tamari, miso, rock salt, liquid aminos
- Sweet e.g. honey, agave, coconut nectar, dates
- Spice e.g. cayenne, garlic, onion, turmeric, ginger
- Sour e.g. apple cider vinegar, lemon juice, rice vinegar, lime juice

I don't necessarily include all four in every dish, but I always think about if I may want to add them in, and make a conscious decision not to include one, if I feel that's what will work best in the recipe. You only need these ingredients in small amounts, but they will provide a depth of flavour to your dishes that will be missing otherwise.

The fifth flavour profile is "umami," and if you really want to have people raving over your dishes, this is the one to check for. Umami is a Japanese word, and what it means to me is a distinctive combination of all those flavours – a little sweet, a little salty, a little sour, a little spicy, all rolled into one. Umami ingredients make foods irresistible, and have your guests salivating. The main umami ingredients I use are balsamic vinegar, baobab powder, sun-dried tomatoes, smoked paprika, liquid aminos, miso, and nutritional yeast flakes. It's definitely fun to think about adding an umami element into each of your savoury recipes!

Consider your Textures

There is a tendency for raw foods to come out like baby food! All blitzed and puréed to a mush. Where is the crunch and the bite in your dish? This is where owning a dehydrator really comes into its own, providing that denser mouth feel that we crave. Be creative with layering, and use your machines to get different end results. For example, a simple carrot in a marinara could be:

- Blended into the sauce
- Semi-chopped into the sauce
- Grated and stirred in
- Sliced with a mandolin into ribbons and stirred in
- Spiralized
- Cut into fat chunks

All these finishes will give very different end results. Consider the other textures in the meal, and be sure to introduce variety. I think this is one of the main reasons people get bored with raw foods: if you are just making salads where everything is diced and soups and sauces where everything gets blended, we start to crave more interesting textures that will stimulate our palates in different ways.

Fats

I am a firm believer in including an abundance of healthy fats in the diet (see the section on ketogenics). I find when I eat out, often raw vegan meals can be low in fat, and this means they are not satiating. There is an abundance of nutrients in vegetables, but where are the calories? They don't provide adequate fuel. If you want to prepare a raw meal that leaves people full, consider that you have included adequate fats. I use avocados, olives, activated nuts and seeds and their oils in every meal. Otherwise the meal may be delicious, but if people leave the table hungry, they won't be convinced of the benefits of the raw food diet.

Food combining

The idea of food combining was popularised by Harvey and Marilyn Diamond in their 1985 book "Fit for Life". This was one of the first health books I ever read! Simply stated, different foods need different digestive juices in order to be correctly digested in the gut. When we incorrectly combine foods, these digestive juices will cause conflict, and that can lead to an irritable bowel, with gas and bloating. In raw foods, we don't have to worry about food combining as much, because it's a low carb diet; there's no rice, pasta, potatoes or bread involved.

However, I would still say it's important to keep dishes simple. Here are some easy rules for correct food combining on a raw food diet:

- Eat fruits on their own. Fruits only take 20 minutes to digest. They do not combine well with vegetables, and particularly not with nuts and sprouts.

- Vegetables combine well with most foods – sprouts, nuts and seeds
- Sprouted grains will not go well with sprouted pulses, or nuts and seeds. Aim to keep these three food groups separate.

What this means effectively, is that your savoury meals will be a combination of vegetables and EITHER nuts and seeds, sprouted grains, or sprouted pulses. And your desserts, if they contain fruits, should avoid nuts. Many raw food desserts are high in fruit and nuts, and loaded with sugars, which is far from optimal for gut health (not to mention the blood sugar). Coconut is the easiest fat to digest, so I do use that often in my sweet recipes.

Superfoods

First, let's start by defining superfoods. Superfoods, to me, are plant foods that heal the energy body as well as the physical body. Disease always has an emotional root as well as a physical root, and we have to examine both if we want true healing to occur. We have to look at the emotional imbalances that have created the issue, as well as the physical deficiencies. In our modern Western culture, we are very good at burying our feelings, so we can always be busy and productive capitalists, and always be ready with a smile for the camera. This creates a disconnection where people are completely unaware of what's going on under the surface for them. We create non-stop lives so we never have time to reflect and take a good look at our lives. It's a vicious cycle, because the more we stay disconnected, the more we drift from our true path, and the harder it becomes to stop and take a look, because of how far away we are from who we really would love to be. This level of disconnection will lead to chronic illness, which causes us to really stop, and gives us a chance to restructure our lives from a more authentic place. Chronic illness can actually be a great opportunity for profound healing, if we have the strength and courage to see it as such.

As I've mentioned though, it's a very complex thing to take someone who is chronically ill and try and restore good health. What is far more simple is to be committed to staying aligned and full of vitality, and if we honour that commitment without letting it slip, then we drastically reduce our chances of getting unwell. I would recommend judicious use of superfoods as one of the best ways to keep up both our physical and emotional energy. They are natural plant foods that are needed in small amounts to restore homeostasis in the body. There are three main groups of superfoods which I recommend including daily:

- Green Powders. This includes the grasses and the micro-algaes. These green powders are exceptionally nutrient dense, an important source of protein for vegans, and highly alkalising. I use barleygrass, wheatgrass, spirulina, chlorella, Klamath Lake algae.
- Adaptogens. This is a term coined by Russian scientists in the 1980s, for a plant that adapts to the individual's unique needs. These plants are calming and rebalancing. They make us feel centred and grounded, while supporting the immune system. The main adaptogens we work with are maca, ashwagandha, reishi, ginseng, suma, and aloe vera.
- Medicinal mushrooms. The mushrooms I use regularly are reishi, chaga, cordyceps and Lion's Mane, and we also do a blend of 8 Mushroom extracts that I love. Medicinal mushrooms are just about the best thing you can do for your immune system, and

are one of the most effective killers of cancer cells. As we are using extracts, they are suitable for people who avoid mushrooms usually, as they don't contain the mycelium body. Reishi is very bitter, but the others have a pleasant, yes you guessed it, mushroom flavour, which makes them a great culinary ingredient as well.

I put superfoods in all my meals! I may use ¼ teaspoon cordyceps powder in a curry for a lovely stock flavour, 1 teaspoon maca to thicken a salad dressing, or add 1 teaspoon of chlorella to a glass of green juice. You don't need to use them in large amounts, even with small doses your meal becomes so much more nutritionally dense and satisfying. I can't recommend highly enough the practice of adding a small amount of superfoods to every meal. If you include just one green powder, one adaptogen, and one mushroom extract daily, I would wager that you would notice a profound difference in your levels of energy and positivity.

Magical Living

It's not just about the food! I believe food is one of the easiest keys to use to unlock our inner magic, but there are other lifestyle practices that are just as key. In our culture, it has become normalised to be stressed and depressed, to the extent that many people don't realise how far they've deviated from being a happy and relaxed person. Indeed, if you're happy and relaxed a lot of times people will look at you like there's something wrong with you! People are surprised to see someone who is smiling and at ease with themselves when they are used to being surrounded by people who frown and shut-down in public. I often wonder what would happen to Western civilization if all the caffeine and alcohol were taken away. I think it would probably collapse, and I'm not even joking. Caffeine and alcohol are two powerful drugs which keep people operating even though they're stressed and depressed: take them away and I think a lot of people would fall apart, and not be able to cope with the pressures of modern life. We are expected to be able to toe a thin line of work, sleep, repeat, when actually being human is far more complex than that. We have so many needs that aren't met by the "9-5 until you retire" routine. Of course, feeling fulfilled by our work, and being able to support ourselves and our families are both important. But so are many other facets of life, that don't just revolve around being machines to make money. When we balance our priorities equally between work, play and rest, we find a new equilibrium that is far more healthy and rewarding. It's kind of ridiculous that we have got to the point where these things need pointing out, let alone are in question. But I believe, like all the best techniques for healthy living, these simple and inexpensive principles can make an enormous difference to your well-being.

Instead of relying on substances that are detrimental to our health in the long term, there are many simple things we can do to keep us feeling human. Some of these things are almost mind-blowingly obvious, but sadly it's also incredibly common that people aren't making sure they get these kind of needs met. Think of them as nutrients, and pay them attention as you would your Vitamin D or B12!

Fresh Air

It's so unnatural to spend time inside all day and all night, yet in our long winter months in the Northern Hemisphere, that's often what we end up doing. If we don't get exposed to all that good healthy bacteria that's found in the air in a forest or by the ocean, it's inevitable we will start feeling depressed and disconnected. Make it a priority to get out into nature and breathe deeply in clean air, at least twice a week. It might sound simplistic, but I believe it's as key to our health as showering or cleaning our teeth, yet so easily overlooked.

Earthing

Another devastatingly obvious concept, that can prove life-changing. We are electrical beings, and the earth is our battery. We need to be in physical contact with the earth in order to recharge. Time spent in nature is recharging, but even more so is physically connecting to the earth by walking barefoot, swimming in the ocean, or yes, hugging trees! If you can't do one or other of these things on a daily basis, then it's imperative you get yourself some grounding devices. These devices use silver as a conductor, and either by inserting a rod into the earth, or plugging them into a grounded socket, when you come in contact with the silver fabric, it provides that earthing energy. Nature is so much stronger than man, and it's a major weakness of Western culture to fail to see that: man thinks he can control and dominate the natural forces and it's simply not true. The more time we spend earthed, the more we are connected to the stronger forces of nature, and the more prosperous we will be. There are many different earthing devices to choose from: my personal favourite is my grounding bag, which is like a sleeping bag. You can also get sheets, mats for your feet, shoes, and more. Again, it may sound too simple to be truly effective, but most people that try grounding devices are amazed at the difference in the quality of their sleep, myself included. You can view a documentary online called Grounding, where a Vietnam veteran walks after decades in a wheelchair, just from using grounding devices for an extended period.

In the 2020-21 lockdowns, I made sure to walk barefoot daily in my local park, and it was a true medicine. Doesn't matter if it's raining! The earth is more conductive when it's wet. Doesn't even matter if it's snowing – then you're getting some cold therapy as well!

EMF Protection

I am deeply concerned about the effects on our health of the EMF soup that we live in. Let's use gluten intolerance as an example to help us understand the problem that EMFs pose. When a person becomes gluten intolerant, it means they cannot eat any gluten without suffering a reaction. Before they become intolerant, they would be able to eat half a loaf of bread with no obvious ill effect. But due to over exposure over an extended period of time, the body starts to reject the gluten. Once the body has decided that the gluten is a poisonous substance that it wants to get rid of, even a mouthful of bread can set symptoms off.

EMF sensitivity develops in the same way. A person may be exposed to EMFs in their workplace or home for hours every day, they may sleep with their phone on next to their head, or they might carry it on their body 24/7. Any of these things over an extended period of time could trigger EMF sensitivity, and once that happens, it means that person will not be able to go anywhere with EMFs without getting symptoms: maybe splitting headaches or extreme lethargy. Think about the implications for our culture! We have become so dependent on this technology, what will happen when large numbers of people can't tolerate it? People will be losing their jobs and unable to leave their homes. At the moment, it's just a small amount of people who have EMF sensitivity (maybe around 5% of the population), but you can bet as time goes on, the numbers will increase exponentially. If you want to avoid being one of the victims, I can't recommend highly enough investing in some electro-magnetic shielding devices. There are many different types on the market, but my favourite is Tachyon. I have a Tachyon disk on my phone, a Tachyon scarf (particularly good when travelling on airplanes), a Tachyon device on my laptop, and I sleep with a Tachyon eye mask. Orgonite is also very popular: I would recommend Etsy for some beautiful pieces that you can place around your home.

I believe EMFs are a real danger, that in the future, we will look back on like we look back on the marketing of tobacco in the 50s now. We will wonder how people so blithely ignored the well-established dangers, and made it look like something cool and trendy, when actually it was killing us.

Sleep

Nowadays, most people go to the gym, or at least practice some form of physical training, and if they don't, then at least they are aware that they should be! Same with nutrition: the importance of eating organic wholefoods and following a healthy diet is widely accepted. But although we've got to grips with the importance of diet and exercise, unfortunately, sleep hasn't been given the same "cool" status just yet. It's still fashionable to be busy, running round, spinning many plates, taking endless calls and texts, posting it all on social media, all while chronically sleep-deprived. Like the problem with prolonged EMF exposure, I worry what prolonged sleep deprivation is doing to our health as a generation.

I'm not about to lecture you on the amount of sleep you need, because I believe that that's an individual thing, and I'm not in the 8-hours-for-everyone-every-night camp (another thing that would lead to the collapse of Western civilization, I think!). Nor am I in the go-to-bed-at-10pm camp (I personally am a night owl for whom 1am is an early night). What I do believe is key is the *quality* of sleep you get, and making sure you get to sleep *at regular hours*. The more your body can predict a routine, the stronger and healthier you will be. If you go to bed and rise at approximately the same time every day, and eat your meals around the same time, the body can relax and get on with its tasks without being on high alert all the time. So more important than how long you sleep for, is making sure you go to bed and rise at the same time every day, and keep that rhythm as consistent as possible.

To ensure a good night's sleep, most important is to remove all electrical devices from the bedroom. Crystals and plants are calming. Consider an eye-mask to make sure you are able to fully switch off; light pollution is a hindrance to the production of melatonin. Get an ionizer, or use salt crystal lamps as natural ionizers. Sleep on a grounding mat or sheet. Turn the phone and the WiFi router off. All these things will make a huge difference to the quality of your sleep; I think many of us nowadays have forgotten how it feels to wake fully rested and ready for the day. We have got used to interrupted and disturbed sleep, and to always be a little bit tired has been normalised. Next time you're feeling run down or out of sorts, before you go popping pills, or booking expensive therapies, just see what a difference a few weeks of proper sleep can make; I literally feel like a different person when I'm managing to keep to a sleep routine that works for me.

Reflect

We live in an era of over-saturation, receiving an endless stream of images and messages through print media, TV, computers and phones. We can travel round the world in relatively short times and cover more miles in a year than our ancestors would have travelled in a lifetime. All this stimulation puts us out of balance if we don't create time to reflect and process the information we have received.

Furthermore, so much of the information we allow into our consciousness contains messages that are detrimental to our health. Advertising that encourages us to feel inadequate and buy more products to bolster up self-esteem. News items that encourage us to feel fearful and believe that the world is a hostile and dangerous place. Media that encourages us to judge and mock celebrities, rather than being sympathetic and compassionate to whatever our fellow humans are going through. If we are not careful, we start running a programme of feeling not good enough, being scared and highly competitive; a reptilian mindset. Definitely not a healthy state to be in! The antidote to all this is meditation. Take up some kind of practice, where you daily seek to connect to the wisdom within. You don't have to sit cross-legged in front of a Buddha! It could be walking the dog, swimming in the local pool, or simply going to bed an hour early and allowing yourself to stare at the ceiling. But make it a point to daily tune out the noise of the external world, and listen to what your inner world is telling you. We have all the answers we need inside of ourselves, all the rest is merely distraction. A solid connection to your inner wisdom will prove invaluable in times of stress and crisis. A sense of inner peace will carry you through the dramas that life throws at you. It's just another easy and free habit that, if you can take it up daily, for as little as twenty minutes (although I would say an hour is ideal), can be life-changing and have a profoundly positive impact on your well-being.

I love this Krishnamurti quote, "It is very important to go out alone, to sit under a tree—not with a book, not with a companion, but by yourself—and observe the falling of a leaf, hear the lapping of the water, the fishermen's song, watch the flight of a bird, and of your own thoughts as they chase each other across the space of your mind. If you are able to be alone and watch these things, then you will discover extraordinary riches which no government can tax, no human agency can corrupt, and which can never be destroyed."

Movement

Remember, we are water? Around 80% water. Water has to be continuously moving, that is its nature. If it becomes still for too long, it becomes stagnant. We are the same. We are designed to be constantly moving. Sitting down all day goes against all our natural instincts, but they train us into it from an early age at school. The sedentary lifestyle is one of the biggest killers today - just as damaging as smoking cigarettes! I always choose walking over the bus, the stairs over the lift, and standing over sitting. I am not rigid about it, but I try and avoid sitting down all day, for at least 12 hours. The less I sit, the happier and more alive I feel. Plus I have great thigh muscles…. Get some exercise into your life daily, even if it's just walking. One thing I have learned over time, is that it's better to do a little every day, than do a lot one day and then none the next. It never ceases to amaze me how quickly I can shift my energy in just ten minutes on a yoga mat.

Like all the principles in this section, it's a base requirement for our bodies. I shouldn't need to even be saying this, just as I wouldn't need to recommend that you clean your teeth or feed your pets every day. If your lifestyle doesn't allow for that kind of time, then make it a priority to adjust your lifestyle so that you can work in enough sleep, meditation, and movement to ensure health, before your lifestyle starts to make those demands of you! You may be surprised at how the universe works to support us in taking up good habits. Even if it feels impossible in your current situation that you could create that kind of time, set the intention, make steps towards it, and see your goals for a happier healthier you realised. A you that is naturally happy, without a dependency on prescription drugs, caffeine, nicotine, sugar, alcohol, social media, weed, or any of the other toxic substances so widely accepted in our world.

Dips & Dressings

No offence to lettuce, but a salad is nothing without a dressing. Firstly, the fats found in foods such as avocados, olives, nuts, seeds, and their oils help with the digestion of nutrients. The more fats in your salad, the more carotenoids you will absorb (they are a fat-based nutrient). Another example is curcumin, the active ingredient in turmeric, which is also a fat-soluble nutrient. Secondly, if we are practicing a ketogenic diet (see p15), then we are looking to the fats to provide our fuel. Eating a beautifully prepared bowl of raw veggies may be delicious, but they are not going to provide us with the energy we need on their own. Vegetables are high in nutrients, high in fibre, but low in calories, so they might fill us up in terms of literally filling up the gut with fibre, but they leave us unsatisfied, and craving something with more calories to fill that gap. Enjoy your salad with an abundance of dressing and a sprinkling of superfoods, such as the medicinal mushrooms and the micro-algaes, and you have a feast that will leave you fulfilled. Dips and dressings are pretty interchangeable – thin out a dip to turn it into a dressing, or add a spoon of baobab or maca to a dressing to thicken it into a dip for crudités, or a spread for crackers and nori rolls.

Mystic Mayo

I always say a good mayonnaise is a bedrock of raw cuisine. And this one is very good. I am having an asafoetida phase right now. They come every once in a while. It's an Indian spice, also called hing, which is used as a garlic replacement. A lot of yogis choose not to use garlic and onion because it is said to be too stimulating, so asafoetida is a great substitute.

Ingredients

1 cup (100g) sunflower seeds, soaked 2-4 hours
1 tomato, quartered
1 sprig parsley
2 tbsp extra virgin olive oil
juice 1 lemon
½ tsp asafoetida
2 tsp oregano
1 tsp liquid aminos
¼ cup (60ml) water

**Makes 8 servings
Takes five minutes to make with 2-4 hours pre-soaking
You need a blender**

Put everything in the blender together and whizz it up well for a minute or so until it's creamy and there's no bits of parsley or tomato left. Brilliant on chia crackers.

Chlorella Pesto

When I was at the Raw Life festival in Sweden one summer, they wanted a demo of a detox recipe. So I whizzed up this chlorella pesto and marinated some kelp noodles in it. I used it again when we did the very first Raw Magic dinner party in London in 2012. When I served it on the plate I was worried about how very green it was – especially alongside a kale salad. I knew I liked it but I was concerned it was maybe a little too "raw" for our guests. However, I'm delighted to say, every single plate came back empty. I've been making a lot and having it as a salad dressing, or spread on my current favourite, Chia Toast.

Ingredients

1 cup (125g) shelled hemp seeds
¼ cup (30g) whole hemp seeds
1 tsp honey
½ cup (125ml) olive oil
¼ tsp salt
1 clove garlic
1 tbsp apple cider vinegar
2 tsp chlorella powder
1 bunch (100g) basil

Serves 4
You need a high-power blender
Takes 10 mins

Put both kinds of hemp seeds in the blender and whizz up for a few seconds to get them broken down. Next, add the honey, oil, salt, garlic, apple cider vinegar, and chlorella and blend again to make a cream. Finally, add in the basil and blend until smooth. Store in an airtight jar in the fridge, it keeps pretty well, for at least a week.

Wasabi & Broccoli Pesto Dressing

At the moment, I'm really into making these kind of green creamy dressings to liven up my dinner. I'll pour them over green leaves or a bowl of fermented veggies, or perhaps spread them on crackers. I've tried lots of different combos, like spinach instead of broccoli, or adding a teaspoon of chlorella powder in, but what follows is my favourite so far.

Ingredients

100g broccoli
2 tbsp tahini
1 tbsp pesto (I favour Seggiano)
1 tbsp wasabi paste (I use Biona)
½ lemon, juiced
½ tsp honey
pinch salt
4 tbsp extra virgin olive oil

Serves 4
Takes 10 mins
You need a blender

Chop the broccoli into pieces small enough for your blender. Put everything in the blender together and blend to a purée. Keeps well in an airtight container in the fridge for up to a week.

Bayonnaise

As baobab is an incredible natural flavour enhancer, it is a wonderful addition to raw vegan mayonnaise, bringing out hidden riches of flavour and adding depth to whatever dishes the mayonnaise is used to complement.

Ingredients

1 cup (125g) brazils, pre-soaked 4-8 hours
¼ cup (60ml) extra virgin olive oil
1 lemon, juiced
¼ tsp rock salt
¼ tsp cayenne pepper
1 tbsp baobab powder
¾ cup (180ml) water

Serves 4
Takes ten minutes to make, with 4-8 hours pre-soaking
You need a blender

Soak your brazils in pure water for 4-8 hours. When you're ready to make the mayonnaise, drain your nuts, and add them to the blender with the olive oil, lemon juice, salt, cayenne pepper, and baobab. Turn your blender on, and as it's running, add the water gradually to make a smooth cream. Once all the water is added, it's turning over nicely, and your mixture is smooth, your mayonnaise is ready. Serve as a dip with crudités or spread it on crackers. Store leftovers in the fridge for up to five days.

Divine Sauce of Big Love

I was going back through my notes and saw that years ago someone had asked for a Divine Sauce of Big Love recipe. Not being particularly sure what that might be, it lay at the bottom of the pile, gathering dust (if emails could do such a thing). Just recently I was struck with inspiration, and so here you have it. I love mixing things up right now and pairing previously unimaginable flavours to create something new and exciting. Here we have Japanese umeboshi, South African baobab, and Turkish sumac all combined to create a zesty sauce that manages to pull off sweet, spicy, salty and sour with flair. Pour it over kelp noodles, or use as a salad dressing with a kick. It's Divine, it's Big, and you're going to Love it.

Ingredients

2 red peppers
2 tbsp tahini
4 tbsp extra virgin olive oil
1 tbsp baobab
1 tsp umeboshi paste
1 tsp sumac
1 clove garlic
¼ tsp salt

Serves 4
Takes 10 mins
You need a blender

Chop the peppers for your blender and remove the stalks and seeds. Put everything in the blender together and whizz for a minute until there are no chunks of pepper left. If you're not using it all at once it will keep well in the fridge in an airtight container for up to a week.

Krautamolé

Sometimes, you wonder why it took you so long to put two of your favourite foods together in a certain way. This is one of those instances. When I made my first visit to Helsinki in 2013, I had the pleasure of meeting Marianne Linqvist. It is her cakes that grab your attention, but as well as having an outstanding eye for artful presentation, and an exceptionally imaginative approach to cake-making, she makes a mean savoury pie as well, or what in the UK we would call quiche. Her secret is to blend avocados and sauerkraut together to make something that is light and creamy, and gently tart in flavour. She then pours this into a pie crust and decorates it with thin slices of veggies like tomatoes and mushrooms. Maybe I will progress onto such wonders, but for now I'm content adding a healthy dose of kraut to my molé.

Ingredients

2 avocados
1 tomato
1 cup sauerkraut
1 lemon, juiced
pinch salt

Scoop out the flesh from the avocados and put it in the blender. Chop the tomato and add that in, along with the sauerkraut, lemon juice, and salt. Give it a whizz for a minute until it's smooth. Store in the fridge in a glass airtight container; it will keep pretty well due to the kraut and the lemon, up to a week. Try it with red kraut for a beautiful pinkamolé. Serve as a dip for crudités, in nori rolls, on crackers, or use as a rich piquant salad dressing.

Zucchini Hummus

Ok, so let's start by clearing up the whole zucchini/courgette thing. I've taught raw foods in over 20 different countries. And I think the only one they call it courgette in is the UK. Plus, zucchini just sounds nicer. It rolls off the tongue, it sounds exotic, enticing. Whereas courgette sounds decidedly pedestrian, like spuds or cabbage. So, sorry British people, as the rest of the world (as well as me personally) has a preference for zucchini, that's what we are sticking with for now.

Ingredients

1 cup (125g) sesame seeds, pre-soaked
1 ½ courgettes (preferably peeled)
1 tbsp tahini
1 lemon, juiced
¼ cup (60ml) extra virgin olive oil
1 tbsp baobab powder
1 clove garlic
1 tsp cayenne powder
pinch salt

Serves 4
Takes 10 mins to make, with 2 hours pre-soaking
You need a blender

You get a better colour and flavour if you peel your zucchini first, but obviously you're losing a lot of the good nutrition that way, so it's your choice. Soak your sesame seeds in advance for at least an hour. When they are ready, grind them a little first, and then add the rest of your ingredients: the zucchini, tahini, olive oil, lemon juice, baobab, garlic, cayenne powder and salt. Blend until you have a thick purée. Keep in the fridge in an airtight container, keeps for up to four days.

Dream Chease

If you've followed my work for any time, you'll know that I rate a good raw mayo as one of most essential components of a happy raw kitchen. With this recipe I have taken it to a whole new level. I was playing around, trying to make a hard cheese using Irish moss. I still need to pursue that idea because I think it might work, but on the way, I got sidetracked by this amazing cream cheese. The addition of Irish moss makes it lighter, fluffier, and way more nutritious.

Ingredients

1 cup (125g) sesame seeds, soaked
15g Irish moss
2 tbsp extra virgin olive oil
2 tsp paprika
¼ tsp salt
2 limes, juiced
1 cup (250ml) water

Makes 8 servings
3-5 days to prepare your Irish moss, 2-4 hours pre-soaking seeds, 10 mins to make
You need a blender

Prepare your Irish moss according to the instructions (see glossary p285). Soak your sesame seeds 2-4 hours in advance. When you're ready, drain your sesame seeds. Put the Irish moss in the blender with 1 cup water and blend to a paste. Then add in all the other ingredients: the drained sesame seeds, olive oil, paprika, salt, and lime juice. Blend for a good minute until it goes good and creamy. Store in the fridge in an airtight container, it will keep for 5-7 days. I love it spread on Chia Toast (p130).

Black Velvet

I have to admit to a slight obsession with black tahini since I discovered it. I've had black tahinis in the past that have been very bitter and not very palatable. However, the one we carry from Sun & Seed has all the creamy richness of white tahini, but with this epic black hue. I find it very grounding to eat, and also fun to make black dressings for my salads, kale chips, kelp noodles, or as a spread on crackers. This dressing contains a whole bunch of earthy ingredients. If you're feeling a little spaced out, this is the thing that could put your boots back planted firmly on the earth. Shilajit, in case you're not familiar with it, is an Ayurvedic mineral that's rich in fulvic acid, so it's a great detoxifier. If you haven't got shilajit, activated charcoal works just as well. Kelp is the most mineral rich sea vegetable. And umeboshi, another favourite ingredient of mine, is a Japanese pickled plum paste which is very alkalising.

Ingredients

1 tbsp black tahini
1 tbsp hemp oil
1 tsp umeboshi purée
½ tsp shilajit powder or activated charcoal powder
1 tsp kelp powder

Serves 1
Takes 5 mins
You don't need any special equipment

Put all the ingredients in a bowl and mix together by hand with a spoon. Keeps well in the fridge for at least a week.

Muhammara

Muhammara is a traditional Lebanese dip. The raw version doesn't differ much at all from the traditional version, which chooses to cook the peppers and also include breadcrumbs. A nice easy tasty combo. I marinated some kelp noodles and sauerkraut in it for 12 hours and it was amazing!

Ingredients

1 cup (100g) walnuts, soaked
2 red peppers
2 tsp honey
1 tsp cayenne pepper
2 tsp smoked paprika
¼ tsp salt
1 lemon, juiced
4 tbsp extra virgin olive oil

Serves 4
Takes 10 mins with 4-8 hours pre-soaking
You need a blender

Pre-soak the walnuts for at least four hours. Don't over-soak them or your dip will go off too quickly. When they are ready, drain them, and put them in the blender with all the other ingredients. You don't need to add water because the peppers are so liquid in themselves. Blend until smooth, then store in the fridge for up to five days.

Middle Eastern Guacamole

I just learnt how to make preserved lemons and I'm all over them. Blend them into dips and dressings for that umami flavour – a little sweet, a bit salty, and a definite hit of sour. This is my current favourite spread that I keep in the fridge for its versatility. I put it on kelp noodles and it was incredible (I used about half the below recipe). But mostly, I am spreading it on my crackers, and in my nori rolls and coconut wraps. Sumac is one of my favourite spices, and it complements the lemons perfectly. You can also find it in Divine Sauce of Big Love (p32) and Muddy Crackers (p117).

Ingredients

2 or 3 avocados
4 pieces preserved lemon (½ lemon)
1 tomato
1 tbsp white tahini or hemp butter
4 tbsp hemp oil
1 tsp apple cider vinegar
1 tsp kelp powder
1 tbsp sumac
1 tbsp Seagreens

Serves 4
You need a blender
Takes 15 mins

Scoop the flesh out of the avocados, and put it in the blender. Quarter the tomato, and add that in. When I make my preserved lemons, I cut each lemon into 8 pieces, so we are using half a lemon here. If you are using shop-bought ones, you may need to alter the quantities, depending how salty they are. You need to remove the flesh of the lemon, and just use the peel. The flesh is too salty to use. Add the tahini, hemp oil, vinegar, and kelp, and blend to a cream. Once it's smooth and all the lemon is blended nicely, stir the sumac and the Seagreens in by hand, so that it's got some texture. Stored in the fridge, it keeps well, up to a week.

Umamayo

In the beginning of the book (p19), we mentioned the four main flavour profiles we use in raw cuisine: salt, sour, sweet and spicy. If you have been to my classes, we have probably touched on the fifth, which is umami. Umami is hard to define, it's pungent, tangy, and addictive. It's sweet, sour, and salty all at the same time. It's MSG: think Pringles, McDonalds, and smoky bacon crisps. Foods that naturally have a lot of umami flavour are sun-dried tomatoes and capers. In my cuisine, I often use baobab, balsamic vinegar, or liquid aminos for their umami flavour as well. This recipe combines them all! It's about as umami as raw food gets, and warning, very addictive. Amazing over kelp noodles.

Ingredients

1 cup (125g) sesame seeds
1 cup (60g) sun-dried tomatoes
1 tsp baobab
1 tsp liquid aminos
1 tbsp balsamic vinegar
¼ cup (60ml) extra virgin olive oil
1 cup (250ml) water

Serves 4
Takes 10 mins, with a few hours pre-soaking
You need a blender

Soak the sesame seeds and sun-dried tomatoes in advance, for at least an hour. You can soak them in the same water. When you're ready, drain, and put in the blender with all your other ingredients: baobab, liquid aminos, balsamic vinegar, olive oil and water. Blend for a minute until you have a thick purée. Store in an airtight container in the fridge; should keep for up to a week.

Hey Pesto

When I was speaking at the Boom festival in Portugal in 2010, I had a lovely raw meal which included some hemp pesto dressing. Now you probably know what a big fan of hemp I am, so this is something I had to recreate for myself. With some extra added superfoods, of course.

Ingredients

½ cup (50g) whole hemp seeds, soaked 2-4 hours
100g (1 large) bunch basil
1 tsp Klamath Lake blue-green algae
2 tbsp apple cider vinegar
¼ tsp rock salt
1 tsp raw honey
½ cup (125ml) olive oil

Serves 8
You need a blender
Please pre-soak your seeds for 2-4 hours first

Soak the hemp seeds in pure water for 2-4 hours. Drain them and put them in the blender or grinder, whatever you use to break them down as much as possible, into a paste. Remove excess stems from the basil, and snip it into pieces so it will go in your blender easily. Put the hemp, basil, blue-green algae, vinegar, salt and honey in the blender, and give it a whizz until you have a paste without any big bits of basil remaining. Finally, drizzle in the oil slowly as the blender is turning. Keep the blender going until all the ingredients are amalgamated. When it's ready, scoop it out and store it in the fridge. It will keep well for up to a week. Goes best spread thinly on crackers or as a dressing for kelp noodles.

What is Raw?

When I first saw a product label marked "raw food" (in about 2000), I actually shed a tear of joy. Having been raw since the early 90s, I had spent a long time calling up companies, trying to ascertain which products were raw and which weren't. Foods like olives, tahini, dried fruits; companies like Sunita, Biona, and Infinity; I would pester them with questions they didn't understand, let alone know the answer to. When Raw started being a label that companies thought was worth mentioning, it was a huge relief to me. Gradually, since then, more and more raw products have appeared on the market. Where there was nothing, health food stores now have entire sections: chocolate, crackers, crisps, granolas, superfoods, even the smallest and most out of the way health food store now has some concession to the raw foods market.

This is clearly a positive thing: good that customers are demanding healthier choices, and wonderful that companies are providing them. But more and more, I wonder, what exactly is raw? And how many of the products currently being sold as raw, actually technically are? In the UK, at the time of writing, I would estimate less than half. If a food is labelled as organic, it has to go through a rigorous (and expensive) inspection process to carry that label. But anyone can stick "raw" on their product and most consumers won't be any the wiser as to how raw it actually is. This upsets me! I'm sure the vast majority of producers aren't setting out to intentionally deceive their customers, and I know that what they are offering is still a vast improvement in terms of health and nutrition than their baked or fried counterparts. But I think a lot of companies are jumping on the bandwagon without fully researching their ingredients, and I don't like to see people mislead in this way.

In our company, we seek to get guarantees from our suppliers of the temperature that the foods have been heated to. Sometimes, we have to ask many times to get that information; people can be strangely reluctant to give it. Even once we have it, we are just taking their word for it, we do not have a way of actually checking up on anyone.

The situation is further complicated by the fact that there is not one single agreed temperature at which a food stops being raw. The consensus is around 42°C. I personally believe that there is a spectrum, and some foods will be more sensitive to heat than others. I would put it somewhere between 41-49°. Some producers heat foods to 46° and still claim they are raw, whereas other people would say at that temperature they are not considered raw anymore. Furthermore, the whole point of raw is to eat foods which are alive, and in which the enzymes are still intact. So I wonder, if flax crackers have been dehydrated for days, packaged in plastic, and sat on a shop shelf for 6 months, really how many enzymes are left? And what about fermented foods, such as miso and tempeh, which may not be raw, but still contain enzymes, would you include those in the raw category? (I would).

When you start looking into it, you start raising more questions than you answer. I hope in the not too distant future, someone will start a certification board, akin to organic, that will become the recognised standard. For now, it's important to bear in mind that even if these raw products are incorrectly named as such, they are still great food choices, and whether they are technically raw or not only really matters to someone who is trying to be strictly,

100% raw. What I want to do here is identify some of the common grey areas so that you can do your research and decide for yourself if you are happy to consume foods that contain these ingredients.

Dates - most dried-fruit is heat-treated to stop it going moldy, and keep it longer on the shelf. If you have a fresh date, like a Medjool date, it's soft and juicy. The harder and drier the date, the more likely it's been heated at high temperatures. At home in recipes, I always use fresh dates. I have been told sun-dried fruits aren't heat-treated, so look out for those.

Nuts – it's the same with nuts, virtually all nuts have been heat-treated to inhibit mold growth. Safer to assume they are not raw than that they are. If you buy from the raw companies online, then you should be able to trust that they are, but if you're buying from a health food store or a supermarket it's unlikely. In the UK, almonds and hazelnuts are usually raw. Cashew nuts never are, unless you can afford to buy the hand-cracked ones. Pine nuts, macadamias, pecans - unlikely. Seeds tend to be raw though, with the exception of pumpkin seeds. All Chinese pumpkin seeds are heat-treated, and it's the Austrian Styrian seeds that you need to look out for, which are a much darker green in colour.

Oats – virtually all oats are steamed to stabilise them. We carry raw oats, and there are a few more brands popping up now, but unless they are specifically labelled as such, they won't be. Raw oats don't keep well, so if you're buying a health food bar that claims to be raw and it contains oats, I would be very dubious.

Agave was first introduced to the health food market in 2005, and back then it was definitely raw. As it became more popular, more companies started producing it, and most of them aren't. Raw agave costs over twice the price of normal agave, so there's your first clue! Understandably, when a company makes a product it wants to keep costs as low as possible to make it affordable to the consumer, so the temptation would be to use non-raw agave in order to make the product accessible.

Coconut Sugar isn't raw at all, although it perplexes me why so many raw companies use it and overlook that fact! Some coconut sugars, such as Big Tree Farms and Coconut Secret, are heated at low temperatures.

Cacao is another highly debatable area. If you're buying beans or nibs, you're safe. Powder and butter are more dubious. It all depends on who you're talking to and which way the wind is blowing that day! There are a lot of South American producers now who claim to make raw products, and may well use less heat than in conventional cacao production methods, but still include heat-treatment stages in the production. I prefer to work with nibs and paste, and rarely use butter and powder, personally.

Fermented foods like yoghurts, cheeses, miso, tamari, tempeh, sauerkraut, kombucha and kefir will all be living foods if they are unpasteurised (this will be labelled, and they will need to be refrigerated).

Superfoods - ironically, most superfoods aren't raw. Most come in powder form, and have been heated in the drying process. As all superfoods should be consumed in small amounts (from 1-10g a day), this shouldn't affect your overall raw intake too much.

If I was creating an accreditation system, I would want to see certificates of inspection for every ingredient used, and I would allow up to 10% non-raw ingredients (e.g. superfoods, seasonings), otherwise they wouldn't be allowed to put the word raw on the label. Until that's in place, you have to be your own certification board! If you have a favourite product that you've started having doubts about, contact them, establish that information, and then share it with everyone. But for now, if you want to be on the safe side, I would assume that that chocolate brownie made with dates, cashews, oats and agave, isn't as raw as it might appear....

Soups, Sides & Sushi

They may be named "sides," but these dishes have enough character to form a meal in their own right, if you're only looking for a light lunch or supper. Or pair two together for a beautiful main course. I think sushi has to be my favourite food of all time. I discovered nori sheets when I got into macrobiotic foods in the 80s, and I've never looked back: there's probably not a week gone by since then that I haven't enjoyed them, usually as a lunch, but very often I make a big batch like the recipes here, and enjoy them for dinner with friends, or keep them in the fridge to last a few days.

Reuben's Garlick Soup

Here we have a guest chef! My son Reuben is a whizz with the blender, and this was his favourite recipe when he was 14. I've called it Garlick cos you'll be licking the bowl clean when you've finished.

Ingredients

2 cloves garlic
2 large carrots
20 cherry tomatoes
10g parsley
1 tsp tamari
2 tbsp extra virgin olive oil
1 cup (250ml) freshly boiled water
2 tbsp coconut oil
1 tsp curry paste
100g (4oz) broccoli, finely sliced
2 pickled beetroot, finely sliced (or one raw beetroot, grated)

Serves 2
Takes 15 mins
You need a blender

Peel the garlic, and chop the carrot into chunks small enough for your blender to handle them easily. Put the garlic, carrots, tomatoes, parsley, tamari and olive oil in the blender, and whizz for a minute until you have a purée. Next, add the freshly boiled water, coconut oil and curry paste and blend again. Once it's nice and smooth, finely slice the broccoli and beetroot and stir them in with a spoon. If you want to warm the soup, the best way is to stand it in a heatproof bowl, inside a saucepan of boiling water. Heat it gently enough to warm it, but don't bring it to boiling or you will destroy precious nutrients. Or use a Thermomix if you are lucky enough to have one.

Ecstatic Soup

Down in the dumps? Eat this for dinner every day and see how long that lasts...

Ingredients

1 tbsp cacao nibs
2 tbsp goji berries
2 tbsp shelled hemp seeds
3 tomatoes
1 red pepper
4 sticks celery
1 tbsp hemp oil
pinch salt
½ -1 tsp curry powder or paste
¼ tsp Klamath Lake algae powder
⅛ tsp Aulterra (optional)
2 cups (100g) spinach

Serves 1
Takes 15 minutes
You need a blender

If you have a high-power blender, put the cacao nibs, goji berries, and hemp seeds in and grind them up to a powder. If you don't have a blender, you'll have to do this separately first in a grinder. Either way, remove them from the blender, and prepare your veg for the blender, chopping the tomatoes, pepper, and celery, so they are going to fit in comfortably. Blend them up, and when you have a nice purée, add in the hemp oil, salt, and curry powder. Introduce the ground nibs, gojis and hemp into the mix and blend again. Next add the algae and Aulterra, and give it a quick whiz. Finally, stir in the spinach, blending it for just a few seconds so there's still plenty of contrast left in the texture. Serve immediately. If it's too ecstatic for you to eat all in one go, it should keep in the fridge for a couple of days.

Green Goddess Soup with Kelp Noodles

This was one of the recipes on my raw chef course for many years. We served it on the last day, as a starter before the burgers for main, and Quantum cake for dessert. If I made too much, sometimes I would be eating it for days afterwards. It's deeply alkalising and refreshing, and very easy on the digestion.

Ingredients

1 packet kelp noodles (340g)
¼ cup (60ml) olive oil
1 tsp tamari
1 tbsp apple cider vinegar
1 tsp barleygrass powder

1 cucumber
2 sticks celery
1 large or 2 small heads fennel (about 500g)
1 cup or 75g spinach
½ cup or 60g hulled hemp seeds
juice 2 lemons
2 tbsp pumpkin oil
1 tbsp lecithin granules
1 tbsp barleygrass powder
1 tsp liquid aminos
sprinkle of black pepper
½ tsp cayenne
2 tsp oregano
¼ red onion

Serves 2
You need a blender
Takes 10 minutes, plus 4 hours marinating time

To prepare the kelp noodles, rinse them well in warm water, then chop with them with scissors to make them more manageable. Pop them in a bowl with the marinade – the olive oil, tamari, apple cider vinegar and barleygrass, and ideally leave them for 4 hours so they get nice and soft.

Prepare the cucumber, celery, fennel and spinach for your blender, chopping it into pieces small enough that your blender can cope. Put the cucumber in the blender with the hemp seeds, lemon juice and pumpkin oil. Blend to a soup. Add in the celery, fennel, and spinach, and blend again. Once you've got a cream, add in the remaining ingredients – lecithin, barleygrass, liquid aminos, black pepper, cayenne, oregano and red onion. Blend for another minute until its good and smooth.

Stir in the kelp noodles – they should have absorbed all the marinade, but if not, save the remainder for a salad dressing.

Heat gently, serve gracefully, and eat greedily.

Soup of the Woods

In my early days of raw, I ate a lot of soups like this. I lived in South London, where creamed coconut was in plentiful supply in the Caribbean stores; I remember you could get 4 boxes for £1! So I would make a stock base with creamed coconut, miso and rice flour, add water, and then stir in chopped veg which would be raw or near-raw.

"Creamed coconut" is a little confusing here because around the world, we have different names for it. You might see it called coconut butter or coconut cream, or there is a brand called coconut manna. Whereas coconut oil is simply the fat of the coconut, coconut cream/butter includes the flesh to make something more like a nut butter. Hope that hasn't confused you too much!

Anyway, all that is a way of explaining that this recipe uses creamed coconut (or coconut butter), to make a rich smooth soup which is great on chilly Winter (and Spring?!) days.

Ingredients

50g (½ cup) coconut butter
2 carrots
4 sticks celery
1 tomato
1 litre (4 cups) water
1 tsp miso
1 tsp balsamic vinegar
1 tbsp Out of the Woods or your favourite green powder blend

Serves 2
Takes 15 mins
You need a blender

Heat the water, either by boiling it, or preferably by heating it to 80°C. Melt the coconut butter (creamed coconut) in a heatproof bowl stood in a pan of hot water, or a porringer. In a blender, blend the tomatoes, carrot, celery and hot water. Once it's smooth, add the miso, vinegar and Out of the Woods, and blend again. Serve immediately, while warm. If you want to make more of a meal of it, serve with bread (such as Chia Toast) to dip into it.

Hot Tub Soup

It's snowing as I type. Is cold food appetising? No. Does the thought of a salad fill me with excitement? No. How about a bowl of warm soup? Mmmmm. 118°F (46°C) is still considered raw, and as my friend Alex pointed out, a hot tub is 104°F (40°C) and that's pretty warm. So here we go, hot tub soup, my favourite dinner this week.

Ingredients

3 tomatoes
½ cucumber
large handful (25g) parsley
large handful (5g) dulse
1 red chilli pepper
½ tsp curry powder
2 tbsp coconut oil
1 tsp apple cider vinegar
pinch salt
½ cup (125ml) water, heated
2 tbsp sauerkraut

Serves 1
Takes 10-15 mins
You need a blender

Put all the ingredients apart from the water and sauerkraut in a blender. Make sure you've chopped the tomatoes and cucumber small enough so your blender can cope with them easily. Remove the seeds from the chilli pepper because this is where the heat is.

Blend it up for a minute until it's as smooth as you can get it. Warm your water, either by boiling it in a kettle, or if you prefer not to heat it so much, warm it in a saucepan. Add it to the blender and blend again.

By hand, stir in the sauerkraut. If you want to warm your soup more, either stand it in a heatproof bowl in a pan of simmering water, use a porringer, or invest in a Thermomix. The Thermomix has a temperature control feature, which you can use to heat your soup to 45°. If you don't have a Thermomix and you want to be exact, invest in a cook's thermometer. You will soon get to be able to tell the right temperature by taste once you've done it a few times. Apparently, the rule is to put your finger in and if you can hold it in for three seconds, it's still raw. I call it the Mummy Bear temperature – it's the temperature that tastes just right – not too hot and not too cold.

Thai Soup

I love that this is a hot, spicy, well-combined soup that isn't based around tomatoes. You could also do it as a Mexican or Indian by switching up the spices.

Ingredients

1 large courgette
½ red pepper
1 cup (250ml) water
½ red chilli pepper or ½ tsp chilli powder
juice 1 lemon
1 clove garlic
pinch salt
1 tsp Thai curry paste
4 sun dried toms (pre-soaked)
½ avocado
1 cup (25g) spinach

Makes 2 Mummy Bear sized portions, or 1 Daddy Bear portion.
Takes 10 minutes
You need a blender

Make sure you've pre-soaked your sun-dried tomatoes. Prepare your vegetables for the blender: chop your courgette and pepper so they are in small enough pieces to comfortably fit in. Put the courgette and the pepper in with water and blend to a purée, so there are no lumps left. Then add the next set of ingredients to the blender: the chilli, lemon juice, garlic, salt, curry paste and sun-dried tomatoes. Blend it all up once more, again until it is lump-free. Next add the avocado and blend briefly, just enough to make sure they are amalgamated. If you blend these for too long, the avocado goes gloopy, that's why we add them at the end. Finally, add the spinach in, and again blend briefly, so you do have pieces of spinach left in the soup. Warm gently if desired: you can heat your soup up to around 40°C and still preserve vital nutrients. I heat mine in the Thermomix, or you can use a Bain Marie.

Hold On to the Light

We are seasonal beings, just as much as the trees and the flowers. As we pass the Autumn Equinox, our bodies' needs start to change drastically. The more in tune we are with our own nature, the more we notice how the different climate puts new pressures on us that we need to respond to if we want to stay healthy. It's no coincidence that California, with its extra-long and beautiful summers, was the original raw food capital of the world, and currently the tropical paradise of Bali holds that title. Raw food is much easier to do in a warm climate. Everything is much easier to do in a warm climate!

As facetious as it may sound, I honestly believe the best way to give our bodies what they need is to take a winter vacation in the sun. While I appreciate that this isn't always possible for a lot of us, real sun is the best way to make our bodies happy and healthy. Spending a week in a bikini (or shorts, guys) under perfect blue skies, is essential at least every three months in order to naturally meet our vitamin D needs.

While I am on the subject, I should mention my own experience of tanning and burning. It seems kind of crazy to me that everyone is now scared of the sun, and believes the sun can give you cancer. It's not the sun that causes cancer, it's the chemicals and toxins that are in your skin that react with the sun. I never use sun cream, and I never burn. People often comment on my golden tan, and I know this is because I use natural skincare products, I drink plenty of water, and most importantly, I eat an abundance of healthy fats and I never eat cooked fats. Think about it, it's basic chemistry. If you are consuming hydrogenated fats and oils that have been fried, when the sun reaches the fat in your body it's going to have a very different chemical reaction than it does when it reaches whole, unadulterated fats. Fats are the building blocks of the cells, healthy fats build healthy cells, and healthy cells love the sunlight, it's the source of all energy!

Failing that mythical winter sun holiday, there are many tips and tricks we can employ to keep our engines purring.

Warm your food as much as possible. Soups and sauces can be heated up to 42°C before the enzymes are destroyed; this is actually warmer than you may imagine. Think hot tubs! Hot tubs are warm, right? And they are usually heated to 40-42° (Check out the Hot Tub soup recipe on page 49). You can stand a heatproof bowl of food in a saucepan of simmering water, or I use my Thermomix which has a temperature control I can set to ensure the food doesn't go over 45°C.

Drink warm teas. The optimum temperature for brewing herbal teas is 80°C. This will activate the herbs but not destroy the goodness or the flavours. Try it, you will be surprised at how much better your tea tastes! I have a Cuisinart temperature control kettle, and there are many others on the market. I drink 1-2 litres of herbal teas daily.

Eat thermogenic foods. These are foods that help your body create heat from within. Ginger is one of the most effective thermogenic spices. Also, turmeric, garlic, onion, cayenne, schizandra, maca; all these foods and many more assist the body in generating heat.

Make sure you get your vitamin D somehow. If you're not averse to eating animal products, consider including raw dairy products in your diet. Raw dairy is less acidic and mucus forming than pasteurized dairy products. Find cultured dairy products such as cheese and yoghurt, as the bacteria in them makes them more digestible. Look for sheep's and goats' products that come from organic and cruelty-free farms. I would recommend that dairy products form no more than 10% of your dietary intake. If you prefer not to include animal products in your diet, as I do, then find a good quality vitamin D supplement; it's D3 you need, not D2. D3 is hard to find in vegan form – my preferred brands are Garden of Life and Better You.

Daily use of adaptogens and tonifying herbs builds your core body strength. Reishi, ashwagandha, schizandra, chaga and maca will all help improve your body's resistance to adverse conditions.

Take cold showers and cold baths. The issue for many of us in the West is that our body thermostats no longer know how to work correctly. In the same way many of us have lost touch with our natural thirst mechanism, and are unable to correctly identify thirst signals, the thermostat "muscle" has become weak as well. People are used to turning the heating up all winter and travelling around in heated cars, so aren't exposing themselves to real cold like previous generations did, and our bodies forget how to deal with it when it comes. Think of kids who can go out in the snow without a jacket: that's because their ability to regulate their body temperature is still strong (if you're curious about this concept, check out the work of Wim Hof). Additionally, when we eat hot food all the time, our bodies are constantly having to work to cool down. When we are putting food in that is already at body temperature, we are conserving energy, so our inner thermostat becomes stronger, and we can deal with external changes in temperature more efficiently when they occur. Taking a cold shower in the morning helps improve the body's ability to regulate the internal temperature, whatever the external fluctuations. Have your normal shower, then finish by letting the cold run all over your body. Run the hot once again, and then finish on the cold. Once you get used to it, it's not as bad as it first seems. I've been taking cold showers for over 20 years and find them invigorating and refreshing. I take a cold bath once a week, and love the endorphin hit I get from that. After a hot bath, get out, and run a cold bath in its place. Get in and lie there as long as you can. Be sure to dip your head right under! I usually only manage a minute or two, but it really gives my system a boost. Whereas after a hot bath, I feel all cosy, warm and sleepy, after a cold bath I feel very awake and alive.

Have the heating on as low as is comfortable. Central heating dries out the body. When you do have to have it on, put small dishes of water on top of the radiators so they will evaporate and release moisture back into the air. Put essential oils in them too, and make the room smell nice at the same time! Keep windows open, even if it's just a crack, to keep fresh air circulating. Real fires or under floor heating are better options than central heating. But before you do anything, add an extra layer, as this encourages the body to do the work itself, rather than encouraging it into laziness by putting the heating on.

Slow down – protect your spleen. In Chinese medicine, the spleen is the organ of nurturing and feeling supported. Issues around feeling unsupported usually reflect a week spleen. The spleen hates cold and damp, so is challenged in a winter climate. The winter is the time for hibernation, so take time out to nurture yourself. If you are the kind of person who is always doing too much, and giving a lot of your energy away, make sure during the winter months you put in some time to conserve energy, nourish your body, and support your system.

Sweat at least once a week, preferably more. Saunas use dry heat, so are dehydrating, steam rooms are preferable. It's really beneficial to the body to get heated right through to the core like this, and warm your cold bones. Plus you're sweating out toxins at the same time. I used to love hot yoga, and felt it was deeply beneficial for my raw body.

Find an Infrared sauna. Infrared rays do not damage the body like UV sunbeds, but they do provide the body with the healing rays we need. Infrared saunas have been used to treat a wide variety of complaints, including cancer and autism. As infrared technology becomes more widely recognised as a safer alternative to UV tanning beds, salons are popping up all over the place, so look out for one in your local area. Sometimes health practitioners will have them in their homes and you can book sessions with them (Like me! If you are in London you can book a session through Raw Living). They are also available to purchase for home installation. I personally don't rate the sleeping bag or dome tent kind of version, but if it's a question of budget it might be the best option for you.

Take regular exercise. Nothing like a workout to raise the body temperature! A good run or session at the gym will raise your core body temperature for a good few hours after. If you have a rebounder, have it out in the living room or somewhere accessible, and promise yourself to have a go on it for at least five minutes a day. It's amazing how much difference a short session on a rebounder can make.

Castor oil holds light. External use of castor oil can be very soothing. Castor oil packs are a traditional naturopathic technique, and are essentially very simple, involving little more than lying down with a hot water bottle! Consult a trained naturopath for detailed instructions. Do one once a week while you watch a movie, or take time to do one three nights in a row for optimum benefits. Whenever I do a pack in the evening, I always wake up the next day feeling lighter and sunnier.

Flaxseeds also hold light. I find flax crackers to be one of the best winter foods for making me feel whole and grounded. Include generous helpings of flax oil in your dressings – flax embodies the energies of gold, sunshine, abundance and light

At a talk I did recently, someone questioned me over the phrase "hold light." I had to agree, it is a bit of a nebulous phrase. But as I mention so often, it's very hard to put what we are doing here into words; we just don't have the right concepts and reference points within our culture. When it's grey and grim outside, the world can seem a depressing place, especially when we are in cities and cut off from nature. The more work we can do on our bodies to transform on a cellular level, to eliminate toxicity and operate from a place of deep alignment, then the more we feel light, bright and sunny inside even on the gloomiest of days. Practising all these techniques listed above, helps us build a solid foundation of inner radiance that dispels the darkest storm clouds.

Simple Kale Salad

Kale salad is one of those things that seems so obvious, you don't think to write it down. Like Green Juice. Took me years to work out what that actually was. So, in case you are wondering how to turn those fearsome green leaves into something you would joyfully consume, here's the kale salad lowdown.

Ingredients

300g kale
3 tbsp extra virgin olive oil
½ tsp rock salt
1 avocado
1 tbsp balsamic vinegar
1 tsp smoked paprika
25g goji berries
½ cucumber

Serves 4
Takes 15 mins
All you need is a strong pair of hands

I would apportion 100g kale per person if the salad is the main part of the meal, and 50g if you're serving it as a side salad. I would recommend looking to add something else green to make the salad less full-on - in this case we are using cucumber, but you could use rocket, alfalfa, or any other favourite green vegetable. I would also recommend including something slightly sweet and fruity, to lift the denseness of the kale. I've included goji berries here, and I also love longan fruit, but you might want to use something more humble like tomatoes or red peppers.

The number one thing to remember is to massage the kale. Tear your leaves into bite-sized pieces and remove unwanted stems. Pour the olive oil on, and sprinkle the salt over. Then, with your clean hands, rub the salt and oil into the kale. If you've ever made sauerkraut, it's the same process; you're seeking to break down the fibres. This will probably take the best part of five minutes to do properly. You're really kneading the kale, squeezing it between your hands. It should end up about 50% in volume. When you're happy you've had your way with it, you can add the rest of the ingredients: pour the balsamic vinegar on and add the paprika and gojis. Cube the avocado flesh and add that in. Cube the cucumber and add that in, and then mix everything together well.

Kale salad is one of those dishes that keeps well in the fridge for at least a few days. I generally make more than I need in a single sitting, then eat it on its own, stir it into curry sauces, mix it with zucchini noodles or kelp noodles, and turn any leftovers into kale chips.

Sauer Slaw

I first created this for an Asparagasm pop-up dinner I did in October 2013. The sauerkraut makes it extra tangy, and it has much more zing than a normal coleslaw. You could use any mayo that you have to hand, but the avo mayo here is super quick and easy. Now, I often serve it as a starter at my dinners, as I think it's important to get the digestion going by including the fermented foods at the start of the meal.

Ingredients

2 carrots
1 beetroot
½ red onion
2 avocados
½ lemon
1 tsp cayenne
2 tsp tamari
500g sauerkraut

Serves 4
Takes 10 mins
You need a blender and a grater

Grate your carrot, beetroot and onion. Stir them together with the sauerkraut. Blend the avocados, lemon juice, cayenne and tamari together to make a cream. Stir the cream into the vegetable mixture. Store in the fridge, will keep for up to four days.

Hemp Tabbouleh

Tabbouleh is traditionally made with bulgar wheat, which we wouldn't use because it contains gluten, and needs to be cooked. You may have tried it with cauliflower or quinoa, but my favourite way to do it is with hemp. Really, it's all about the parsley and the mint, so get abundant amounts of fresh leaves, and don't forget to be generous with the lemon juice as well. At dinner parties, I serve this with Falafel and Hummus (p34), and it goes down a treat.

Ingredients

2 cups (250g) shelled hemp seeds
4 tomatoes
½ cucumber
100g fresh parsley (curly or flat leaf, the preference is yours)
25g fresh mint leaves
2 lemons, juiced
½ cup (125ml) extra virgin olive oil
pinch salt

Serves 4
Takes 15 mins
You don't need any equipment

Remove the stems from the mint and parsley, and chop them as fine as you can. You can cheat and use a food processor with the S-blade if you want, to get them super fine. Add them to a large mixing bowl with the shelled hemp. Dice the tomatoes and cucumber and throw those in. Dress with the lemon juice, salt and oil, and give it a good mix. It keeps well because of all the lemon juice – up to 5 days in the fridge.

Cali Rolls

I saw a post of Chef Ito's Cali Rolls on Instagram, and instantly I was smitten. Seaweed, avo, some fermented veggies, and coconut, all in one dish, what's not to love? On a trip to LA in 2015, I was blessed to try them for real, and they were just as incredible as I had anticipated. I also got to enjoy Annie Jubb's Sea Wrap, which is a very similar concept, but she uses wakame rather than dulse. I love wraps; I have a nori roll or a coconut wrap for lunch very often, and sometimes I may even have them for dinner as well! This is my favourite way to do them, and I think it could actually even be my favourite thing ever to eat; something about this combination is entirely satisfying, both in terms of flavour profile and nutrition. Try them and let me know!

Ingredients

2 nori sheets
1 cup cauliflower rice (p58)
½ young Thai coconut
½ avocado
2 handfuls (10g) dulse
4-5 slices pickled cucumber (p172)

Serves 2 as a light snack, or 1 as a main meal
Takes 15 mins (again, if you have the rice pre-prepped)
You don't need any equipment (if you've already made the cauli rice)

Place your nori sheet on a flat surface, ready to fill. Prepare your cauliflower rice, if you haven't done so already. Take two heaping spoons of rice and arrange the rice across the middle of the nori, in a strip. Take a few pieces of pickled cucumber, maybe 4 or 5, and spread those across as well. Rinse a handful of dulse, and add that to the wrap. Take half an avocado, remove the pit, and score it into thin slices. Arrange the slices in the nori sheet, next to the rice. Lastly, take your coconut meat. If you haven't prepared it already, now's the time to cut it into strips around ½cm wide. If you can't get fresh coconut, of course you can omit it, but it's what makes these really special. Now you're ready to roll your wrap up. Press it down tightly, and use a little water to seal the edge.

Then move onto your second sheet. You may find it easier to prepare them both at the same time, but I prefer to complete one and then do the next. Finally, you're going to cut them up. Unless you have a professional sushi knife, I recommend you use scissors. Each nori roll will cut into five pieces. You can eat all 10 pieces yourself! Or maybe you would like to share them with a friend. Or you could put half aside and have them for lunch tomorrow. They don't keep so well, maybe up to 24 hours in the fridge.

Cauliflower Rice with Baobab & Turmeric

I'm sure if you are reading this book, you have stumbled across "alt-carbs." It's the concept of using veggies to replace the traditional carbohydrate elements of a meal. In raw food cuisine, we make bread and crackers with flaxseeds rather than grain flours, we use courgettes and squash to make noodles, and my personal favourite is to use cauliflower as a rice substitute. I'll often make a big batch of rice like this and keep it in my fridge for the week. Some will go in a salad, say with wild rice and olives. Some will go in sushi, and some will get smothered in a warm (not cooked! just warmed) curry.

Every time I make this recipe for people, someone says, "I don't usually like raw cauliflower, but this is wonderful!" Try it and let me know if it doesn't work its magic on you.

Ingredients

1 cup (90g) almonds (activated if possible)
1 cauliflower (approx. 500g or 1lb)
1 tbsp baobab powder
1 tsp turmeric powder
¼ tsp black salt
4 tbsp hemp oil

Serves 8
Takes 15 mins
You need a food processor and some kind of food grinder, ideally

Grind the almonds to a powder in a high-power blender, coffee grinder or spice mill. Transfer to a large mixing bowl. Prep the cauliflower by chopping it into florets. We need to break it down into pieces the size of rice grains: the best thing for the job is a food processor with the S-blade in, but if you don't have one I would do it by hand. A high-power blender makes it too fine, and you want to leave some texture in, so I don't recommend those. It needs to have a bit of bite to it! Once you're happy with the consistency, transfer it to the mixing bowl, and add in your other ingredients.

We are including hemp oil for those all-important healthy fats, black salt for its wonderful sulphurous flavour (you can use any kind of rock salt if you don't have black salt), turmeric to add a little colour and because of its anti-inflammatory properties, and lastly, baobab, a South African super-fruit that's one of my personal favourite ingredients. I love baobab for many reasons, but chiefly because it's a natural flavour enhancer. Basically, it works with everything, equally at home when highlighting sweet notes as savoury. Try adding it to smoothies, desserts, cakes, chocolates, dressings, dips, sauces, even kale crisps. Here in the rice, it adds a subtle, but vitally uplifting note that prevents the cauliflower being bland.

Mix everything together, and store in a covered container in the fridge (I use glass or ceramic rather than plastic). Will keep for up to five days, and you'll even find that the flavours improve after a day or two.

Sublime Sushi

This is another dish that was inspired by my beautiful Icelandic friend Solla, and the sushi she used to serve at her chain of restaurants, Glo. She puts extras like cucumber, carrots, celery, and even mango into hers. I like it plain, so that once it's been in the fridge for a day or two it softens and all the flavours intertwine. Then when you eat them, they almost melt in the mouth, they are so soft and succulent. They keep for about five days, and when I've made a batch I like to nibble on them as snacks during the day. This is also a fantastic and easy dish to multiply up and serve at parties when you're catering for a lot of people.

Ingredients

For the Hazelnut Mayo:
125g (1 cup) hazelnuts (pre-soaked 4-8 hours)
60ml (¼ cup) olive oil
1 lemon, juiced
25g wasabi paste (I use Biona)
¼ tsp rock salt
1 date
½ cup (125ml) water

For the Cauliflower Rice:
1 cauliflower (500g or ½ lb each)
½ cup (50g) sesame seeds
1 cup (50g) coconut chips
1 tbsp tamari
4 tbsp sesame oil
1 tbsp rice vinegar
1 tbsp coconut nectar

8 nori sheets

Makes 8 sushi rolls or 40 pieces
Takes about 45 mins, with pre-soaking for at least 4 hours
You need a blender and a food processor

First, it's time to make the Mayo. Drain your pre-soaked hazelnuts and put them in the high-power blender with the oil, lemon, wasabi, salt, dates and water. Blend well until it's really smooth and creamy.

Next, grind up your sesame and coconut in a grinder or high-power blender. In a food processor, pulse chop the cauliflower into small pieces, around the size of a grain of rice. Transfer the ground sesame and coconut, plus the cauliflower, to a mixing bowl, and then add the remaining ingredients: the tamari, olive oil, vinegar and coconut nectar.

Finally, you're going to assemble your sushi. You can watch my video on YouTube for tips on assembling sushi. Basically, you need to put a line of Mayo down the middle, and a line of rice on top. Not too much or your roll will be too fat and squidge apart! Not too little or it will come out cigar-shaped. Look at how much you've put down the centre line and imagine if that's the kind of size you want your roll to be. Don't forget to make sure your strip reaches right to the outside edges.

Take the edge furthest away from you and wet it thoroughly. Take the edge nearest you and roll it over tightly, pressing down firmly on the wet edge. Hold it for a few seconds and it should stick. Out of the mixture you have, you should be able to make around eight nori sheets.

Once they are all assembled like this, the final step is to chop them into small pieces. You need a good sharp knife, or kitchen scissors also work. A single nori sheet should cut into about five sushi pieces, leaving you with forty altogether. Stand them end up on the plate. Leftovers will keep in the fridge for up to about five days, stored in an airtight container.

Rainbow Sushi

I love sushi, in case I hadn't already mentioned that! This isn't the most straight-forward recipe, but there is something very elevating about eating rainbows, so I recommend the extra effort.

For Your Rainbow:

Red = 1 Red pepper, in very thin strips

Orange = Garlic Goji Relish (below – original recipe in my Raw Magic book) ½ portion or 4 tbsp

Yellow = Turmeric kraut. I made this myself using the recipe on p170 (check the variation at the bottom). If you don't have any, you can just buy some plain white kraut & stir turmeric powder in (1 cup kraut + 1 tsp turmeric powder). Or use a ready-made brand from your health food store.

Green = Kale, massaged in salt & olive oil. I recommend always having kale salad (p54) in the fridge. I do a whole bag at once and then use it as I need it for sandwiches, nori etc. For this recipe, you need 100g kale, a pinch of salt and 1 tbsp olive oil.

Blue = Blue Guac, see below

Purple = Dulse 25g

Pink = Cauliflower Rice. Try this really simple recipe across.

5 Nori Sheets

Makes 5 rolls or 40 pieces
Takes 1 hr
You don't need any special equipment

Goji Relish
Ingredients:

200g or 1 red pepper
100g or 1 cup goji berries
2 tbsp apple cider vinegar
2 cloves garlic
½ tsp salt

Chop and deseed the pepper. Blend everything together! Leftovers will store in a jar and keep well for a couple of weeks.

Blue Guac
Ingredients:

2 avocados
1 tbsp tahini
2 tsp preserved lemon paste from Eaten Alive, or 2 tbsp preserved lemon juice . If you don't have either of these, you can use the juice of 1 lemon and a pinch salt.

½ teaspoon E3 Live Blue Majik. This turns it a beautiful cyan blue. If you don't have this, you can use Klamath Lake algae, but it's not quite as vibrant.

Scoop the flesh from the avocados. Blend everything up together. This is wonderful as it is! Make extra and use on crackers and as a dip.

Pink Rice

Ingredients:

½ cauliflower (approx 250g)
1 tsp honey
2 tsp umeboshi purée (for flavour & to make it pink)
2 tbsp hemp oil

Chop the cauliflower into pieces the size of rice grains in a food processor with an S-blade or by hand. Don't use a high-power blender, that will destroy it, and if you've got a Thermomix it's easily done on a speed 5 setting. Stir in your honey, umeboshi and hemp oil.

To assemble your rolls, lay out your nori sheet, with the guidelines going horizontally. You're going to need a very small amount of each ingredient if you want to make nice tight rolls. This is key to the success of the recipe! Think fairy-sized bites, not big hunks you will need to tear into.

Start with the cauliflower rice – just 2 tablespoons, spread in the middle of the sheet as thinly as you can. Then spread a strip of guac over the rice – 2 teaspoons will do it. Then a thin lick of relish. Lay down your red pepper strips - 3 is probably enough. Then a couple of teaspoons of turmeric kraut. Then less kale than you think – it's very voluminous! Next comes a few strands of dulse – Icelandic is my fave.

Moisten the far edge of the nori sheet with a little water, and carefully roll it up and seal it. Transfer to a plate while you make the next one. Once you've made all 5 rolls, using a good sharp knife, cut each roll into 5 or 6 pieces. The smaller you can get them, the more delicate and melt-in-the-mouth they are.

Serve as a starter, a lunch for four, or as canapés at a buffet. Leftovers will keep for a few days in the fridge, and taste even better when they are a day or two old and the flavours have marinated together.

Stuffed Avocado 2.0

Stuffed avocado is one of those recipes from my first book, Eat Smart Eat Raw, that I still make. It's hard to believe that that book is over twenty years old now, and yet there's plenty of recipes in it that I still refer to.

What follows is my updated version of stuffed avo; the original is made with pumpkin seeds and sunflower seeds that have been marinated in tamari and dehydrated, making a full-bodied and meaty stuffing. This version is much lighter and fresher, and, it goes without saying, equally wonderful.

Basically, I love avocados and any excuse to eat a whole one is good with me. Serve half as an accompaniment to salad, or both halves as a quick but filling snack lunch.

Ingredients

¼ cup (25g) goji berries
¼ cup (10g) coconut flakes
1 stick celery
½" (1cm) ginger root
½ tsp seaweed salt
½ cup cauliflower
1 tbsp tahini
2 avocados
25g alfalfa sprouts

Serves 4 as a side dish or 2 as a main
Takes 10 minutes
You need a food processor

Start by grinding up the gojis and coconut together, either in a grinder or high-power blender. Then transfer them to your food processor, or continue in your high-power blender. Add in the celery, ginger, seaweed salt, and cauliflower, and process until it's as smooth as it will go. Finally, add the tahini, and process one last time.

Take your avocados, slice them in half lengthways, and remove the stones. Take big spoonfuls of your mixture, and use it to fill the holes where the stones were. You should have enough to spread a thin layer of stuffing over the top of the avocado. Sprinkle some alfalfa sprouts over the top, and you're done. Eat immediately. How long they keep is dependent entirely on the quality of your avocados, but most avocados don't do so well once they have been cut open.

Transition Town

It's never wise to go 100% raw overnight. Oftentimes, people discover raw foods and naturally get a little over-excited at the prospect of long sought-after life-changes the diet can bring about. Many people have the kind of personalities where they love to jump headlong into things and explore them fully. This is great, but just be aware, that I don't believe anyone has ever gone totally raw successfully overnight and never gone back to cooked foods again.

The willpower may be there to quit the junk, but buried emotional and physical issues are bound to surface that can slow you down. Don't be frustrated with these lapses: they always serve to deepen your relationship to your body and strengthen your connection to your intuitive voice.

I would advise always lowering your sights, always underestimating what you and your body are capable of achieving. If you feel super-confident about going raw, aim for 80 or 90 %. If you feel it's the right thing but don't know if you can quite manage it, try 50% to start off. However much raw you decide to include, it's got to be better than what you were doing already, and so you are guaranteed to see an improvement in your health and energy levels.

What's vitally important is that you nurture yourself through the process: that you learn to love, honour and obey your heart's true desires. The kinder you are on yourself when you have those inevitable slip-ups, the quicker they will pass and you can get back into your groove. If you've set your sights on 75% raw and you find yourself accomplishing that easily, you'll feel so good about yourself. You'll feel positive, excited, and full of confidence. If you've got to that level and stayed there for a while, you'll feel much happier about upping your raw percentage and knowing it's going to work for you. It's a much more useful and enjoyable process than aiming for 100% raw and then beating yourself up every time you don't make it.

While you're transitioning, there are two approaches that people tend to find helpful. The first is to include some raw foods at every meal. No matter what else you are eating, make sure you have raw foods with it, and that you have more raw than cooked. Still want toast for breakfast? Have it with a raw spread on and wash it down with a fresh juice. Craving a baked potato? Smother it in raw mayo and serve it with a large side salad. Insatiable desire for ice-cream? Serve it with heaps of fresh fruit. This way, you're never denying your cravings and desires, but always making sure your body's getting that raw loving at the same time.

The other approach that works for a lot of people is to gradually convert your meals from raw to cooked. Many people find that they can eat raw all day and then just have a cooked meal in the evening. The best place to start is with a raw breakfast. Then make all your between-meals snacks raw. If you're just doing that, and still having cooked lunch and dinner you're going to be feeling better. Next start having a raw lunch, and finally, only when you're ready, move over to a raw dinner.

It took me ten years before I really stopped craving any cooked foods at all. It's much easier now because we have access to so many more amazing foods, there are so many incredible raw recipes around, and there is so much fantastic support available. But I still think it needs a long-term approach to exploring this path, in order to truly say to yourself that you know you will never eat anything cooked again. It's a lot of work on the cellular level and a huge leap to make out of the consensus reality, one that takes time and patience. It's a cliche, but being a raw-fooder is very much a journey, not a destination. Paradoxically, like everything in life, the more you slow down and appreciate the journey, the quicker you will get to where you want to be.

Mains

Let's be real, not all of these recipes are quick and simple. Many require up to an hour of pre-prep, and maybe some time in the dehydrator. But I can assure you, they are all worth the effort. I think if you're used to eating conventional food, you get spoilt by the incredible variety of menus and the complexity of dishes available to you. When you go on any kind of elimination diet, such as gluten-free or dairy-free, suddenly your pool of choices shrinks dramatically. Once you feel the benefits of cutting out these foods, then the sacrifice doesn't seem too great. But however healthy all that kale and kraut makes you feel, most people are going to crave the depth of flavours and textures you find in a really well put-together cooked meal. If you have been raw for any length of time, you are going to appreciate these recipes so much! To be able to eat such appetising dishes and still feel wonderful at the end of the meal, is an all too unique feeling for most of us. Usually we end up sacrificing taste for health benefits, or eat something wonderfully tasty that we know isn't so good for us; it's very rare that we can combine the two and feel satisfied on all levels. Try it and see how these recipes really can revolutionise your mealtimes.

Tart's Spaghetti

This is a traditional Italian dish called Spaghetti alla Puttanesca – the story goes that it was so cheap, quick and easy to make, the prostitutes could make it between clients. Well, I don't know if any of you reading this are actually selling your bodies, but I'm sure many of you, like me, do your fair share of hustling in a day. So in the spirit of easy, here's my raw puttanesca.

Ingredients

3 tomatoes
2 tbsp extra virgin olive oil
1 tsp honey
1 tsp chilli powder
¼ tsp rock salt
1 tsp balsamic vinegar
2 courgettes
2 tbsp capers
100g pitted black olives

Serves 2
Takes 10 mins
You need a blender and a spiralizer

Prepare the tomatoes for the blender. Put them in, along with the olive oil, honey, chilli, salt and vinegar. Whizz for a minute until you have a thick purée.

Spiralize your courgettes, and stir them into the sauce, along with your capers and olives. Done!

Shepherd's Pie

I make it a point of honour to try out a recipe at least four or five times, usually more, before I publish it. Very rarely does something come out perfect the first time; usually I feel it needs more of this and less of that, and I keep making it until I'm happy I've got the balance of flavours and textures just right. Plus, very often a recipe is not replicable; I'm sure you've done it, where you've made something wonderful, and when you've come back to try it again it's not turned out the same at all. So I make things over and over to ensure that the recipe I'm writing down and passing onto you is going to turn out the same for you as it does for me. I take this bit of my job very seriously!

However, today I'm about to make an exception. When I was a kid, Shepherd's Pie was my favourite dinner. I don't know why I never thought of trying to do a raw version before. I think I always stumbled at the mashed potato and never tried to get past that. I don't remember why or how I got the idea of making mash using Irish moss to get some lightness and fluffiness in it. Anyway, inspiration struck, I made this, and it came out perfect first time. I made it again, and it came out just as right. Maybe it was all those years of enjoying Shepherd's Pie when I was younger, so the Shepherd's Pie formula is just encoded in my DNA, and it has taken me a while to unlock it. Hence, I am proud to unveil here, the world's first raw vegan Shepherd's Pie, for your delight and delectation.

Note: I have a feeling Shepherd's Pie might be an British thing? It's a layer of minced beef in a tomato sauce, topped with a layer of mashed potato. Also known as Cottage Pie.

Ingredients

3 cups (about 6) tomatoes
1 cup sun-dried tomatoes (pre-soaked 2-4 hours)
½ cup (125ml) olive oil
2 tbsp balsamic vinegar
1 tbsp tamari
½ red onion
2 tsp honey
3 carrots
2 red peppers
1 cup (100g) sunflower seeds (pre-soaked 2-4 hours)
1 cup (100g) walnuts (pre-soaked 2-4 hours)
1 cup (25g) dulse flakes
2 tsp paprika
1 tsp cayenne
½ tsp Raw Living 14 mushroom blend

½ cup cashews (pre-soaked 4 hours)
1 (about 500g) cauliflower
½ oz (15g) Irish moss (pre-soaked 3-5 days)
2 cups (500ml) water
2 tbsp coconut oil
2 tbsp olive oil
1 tbsp liquid aminos
sprinkling of black pepper
2 tbsp lecithin
1 date
1 tbsp apple cider vinegar
2 tbsp nutritional yeast flakes

Serves 8

Takes 45 mins, with 4 hours pre-soaking and 4 hours dehydrating, as well as 3-5 days for pre-soaking the Irish moss. You need a blender and a food processor. A dehydrator is not essential but it does improve the flavours.

We are going to start by making the tomato sauce. In your blender, put the tomatoes (ready chopped, so your blender can handle them easily), sun-dried tomatoes, olive oil, tamari, balsamic vinegar, red onion, and honey. Blend to a purée. Next, roughly chop your carrots and peppers in preparation for your machine. There's a few ways to do this next stage, depending on what equipment you have. We need the carrots, peppers, sunflower seeds and walnuts chopped into pieces about the size of rice grains or minced beef pieces. I put it in the Thermomix with the sauce and process it on a 5 setting for about 10 seconds. If you have a Vitamix, you could probably do the same; process it on a low setting until it's finely chopped but not puréed. If you don't have either of these machines, I would chop these four ingredients together, (but separately from the sauce) in a food processor using the S-blade, and then stir it back into the sauce by hand. Once you've mixed everything together, and it's looking like mince, all that remains is to add the spices and superfoods. Either by hand, or using your machine on a low setting, stir in the dulse flakes, paprika, cayenne, and 14 mushroom blend. The 14 mushroom adds to the flavour as well as the nutritional content so I would recommend sourcing some if you don't have it already. You could always replace it with similar mushroom powders such as cordyceps or Lion's mane if that's what you have (although I wouldn't recommend reishi as it is very bitter).

Now you need a big casserole dish just like the one your mum used to use. Spoon the "mince" into it so you have one even layer, and put it to one side while we make the "mash."

You should have some Irish moss ready to go. If you're using red Irish moss like I do, follow the instructions here (p285). First, we are going to grind the cashews to a powder. Then you need to blend the Irish moss up with one cup (250ml) water. It won't purée completely down, but do the best you can with your machine. When you think it's broken down as much as it will go, add all the other ingredients apart from the cauliflower to the blender: the ground cashews, coconut oil, olive oil, liquid aminos, black pepper, lecithin, date, and apple cider vinegar. Blend for a minute, and the Irish moss should break down some more so what you have is as close as it will get to a purée. (It's also very delicious at this stage, have a taste!). Finally, we are going to add the cauliflower. Cauliflower is very sulphurous and if you over-blend it, it releases chemicals that make it very bitter to the palate. So we have to be careful not to blend it too much or it will ruin our Shepherd's Pie! Chop it up into small pieces and add it to your blender. Blend it just enough to get it smooth, adding the last cup (250ml) of water gradually as you do. I would say that if you're not confident that your blender is strong enough to make it smooth without totally blitzing it, it would be better to have slightly lumpy "mash," than overdo it and risk it tasting weird.

Once it's ready, spoon it over the "mince." It will still be quite liquid; it will thicken once the Irish moss sets. Sprinkle some more black pepper and salt over the top, even some nutritional yeast flakes if you favour them. You can eat it like this, but it is even better warmed in the dehydrator. You'll need to remove a shelf or two to fit your dish in, and be careful it's not too heavy for the trays; if it is, just remove the bottom trays and stand it on the floor of the dehydrator. I think it's best warmed for about 4 hours, though you could leave it longer if you are going to be out, I wouldn't suggest more than 8 hours. You'll get a nice crust on top of your "mash," and it will help to bring out the flavours. Plus, it's way more convincing as the genuine article when it's warm straight out of the dehydrator than when it's cold.

It keeps well in the fridge, and in fact the flavours improve after two or three days.

Renegade Chia

There just seems something really extra about mixing chia AND kelp noodles AND wakame. Surely it's breaking all the rules? Are you really allowed to mix so many of your favourite foods in one dish? Can you really pack so many nutritious foods into one meal? Well, let me tell you the answers are yes, yes, and yes again, and it is totally wonderful.

Ingredients

1 packet (340g) kelp noodles
1 cup (100g) sundried tomatoes
¼ red onion
2 cloves garlic
1 fresh date
1 cup (250ml) water
½ cup (125ml) olive oil
2 tbsp tamari
1 cup (125g) chia
1 cup (150g) tomatoes
6 mushrooms, finely sliced
1 cup (25g) soaked wakame
1 tsp Raw Living 14 mushroom blend
1 tsp paprika
1 tsp cayenne
3 cups (750ml) water

Serves 4

Takes ages! First you need to prepare the marinade (which takes about 5 mins) and leave it for an hour. Then you need to make the marinade (which takes about 10 mins) and marinate the noodles for 3 hours (and don't forget to soak the wakame for an hour). Then you need to prepare the chia (which takes another 10 mins), and leave that marinading for at least another 3 hours. It's worth all the effort though, and you can easily get four meals out of it, so if you're just making it for yourself, it will last you most of the week.

You need a blender to make the marinade.

First, we are going to prepare the marinade for the kelp noodles. Take your sun-dried tomatoes, your onion, garlic, and date, and in a small bowl marinate them in your water, olive oil and tamari. You need to marinate them for at least an hour, maybe two, until the tomatoes are soft. When you're ready, blend everything up, oil, water, and all, to make a tomato purée. This will taste very oniony at this stage, don't worry.

Open your kelp noodles, and rinse them well under the tap. Chop them up with kitchen scissors so they are a more manageable length. Put them in a medium-sized bowl, and pour all your marinade over the noodles; it will more than cover them. Leave your kelp noodles to marinate for at least three hours, so they soften nicely and absorb all the flavours. Don't leave them longer than a day.

At some point while you're waiting for the kelp noodles, you also need to soak the wakame for an hour.

When you're ready for the next stage, blend your fresh tomatoes to a purée. It doesn't matter if there's a few small lumps of tomato left, this can be quite nice to add more texture to the dish. Slice your mushrooms finely. Then we're going to take a large bowl, and mix everything together.

Start with the chia, tomato purée and water, and give that all a stir. Then add in the mushroom powders and spices: 14 mushroom, paprika and cayenne, and stir again. Then put in your sliced mushrooms and chopped wakame. If the wakame isn't already in small pieces, you want to cut it with scissors into pieces about 1cm in length, so they don't dominate the dish. Finally, stir in the kelp noodles along with all the marinade, every last drop.

Leave it for a couple of hours minimum to allow all the flavours to mingle. I'd say it's optimum after 12-24 hours. It will keep in the fridge easily for 4-5 days. Warm it gently in the porringer if you choose, or eat cold from the fridge in summer.

LasanYea

Dish of the day! I lived on this over the winter. Doesn't quite match my Shepherd's Pie (p69), but second best I'd say. I teach it in my level two chef courses, so maybe we'll get to make it together someday.

Ingredients

"Tomato" layer:
3 red peppers
2 carrots
1 cup (15g) dulse
½ cup (60g) goji berries or sun-dried tomatoes
2 tsp umeboshi purée
2 tsp sumac
2 tbsp baobab
8 tbsp extra virgin olive oil

"Cheese layer":
1 cup (100g) sunflower seeds
1 lemon, juiced
1 tbsp baobab
1 tbsp za'atar
1 tsp miso
1 clove garlic
¼ cup (60ml) olive oil
¾ cup (180ml) water

"Pasta layer":
2 cups (60g) spinach
1 zucchini
1 tbsp extra virgin olive oil
1 tsp balsamic vinegar
¼ tsp rock salt
2 tbsp nutritional yeast flakes
2 tbsp nori flakes
½ tsp seaweed salt

Serves 12
Pre-soaking/marinating time at least 2 hours. Prep time 1 hour. Dehydrating time 4 hours (optional).
You need a blender. A mandolin and dehydrator are helpful but not essential.

Start, as always, with your marinating and pre-soaking. You need to soak the gojis or sun-dried tomatoes, whichever you are using, in pure water, for at least an hour. You also need to soak the sunflower seeds for at least two hours. And you need to fine slice the zucchini, with as thin a blade as possible, preferably a mandolin. Once you've sliced the zucchini, marinate it in the olive oil, balsamic vinegar, and salt. This will help remove some of the liquid from the zucchini – if you don't do this, the zucchini water content will escape into your lasagna and make it watery. It needs marinating for at least an hour.

The first layer we're going to make when you're ready is the "tomato" layer (although if you're using gojis this layer actually has no tomato in it!). Put all your ingredients in your blender together. Deseed and remove the stalks of the pepper, and top and tail the carrots. Prepare them so they fit in your blender happily. Rinse the dulse. Drain the goji berries or tomatoes. You don't need to use the soak-water; discard it if you're using tomatoes or drink it if you're using gojis. Add in the umeboshi, sumac and baobab (these three ingredients are not essential but give it a unique and interesting flavour). Add in the olive oil and dulse, and blend for a minute until creamy and there's no lumps left.

Put to one side and make the next layer. Drain your sunflower seeds, and blend with the lemon juice, baobab, za'atar, miso, garlic, olive oil and water. If you haven't got za'atar, you can just use dried thyme. Blend for a minute until creamy. Now you're ready to start assembling. Use a ceramic or Pyrex baking dish for best results. First is half the red sauce. Next pour over half the white sauce. Then take your spinach leaves and layer those over the top of the white sauce. Now it's a second layer of red sauce, covered with a second layer of white sauce. Your last layer is the zucchini. Discard the marinade – you can save it for a salad dressing later. Layer the zucchini over the top of the dish. Sprinkle with the seaweed salt, nori flakes and nutritional yeast flakes.

You can add extra layers in after you've put the spinach layer in, if you choose. Solla puts kale chips in hers. I've done it with a layer of sauerkraut. If you're a fan of sea veg you could use wakame, or perhaps you want to make a mushroom lasagna.

You can eat it like this just as it is, but I like to put it in the dehydrator for a few hours. It's so much nicer eaten warm, straight out the dehydrator, especially on a cold winter's day when a salad just isn't going to cut it. To warm through, I would suggest somewhere between 4-8 hours. It also helps firm it up so it's denser and easier to slice.

It makes 12 generous slices, and keeps in the fridge for up to a week. Like most raw dishes, the flavours improve over time, and are optimum on about day two or three. I cover it in foil and if I know I'm going to want a slice, I try to warm it up in advance first.

Kraut & Kelp Noodles

I eat this all the time! This is one of my default staples, if there's no appetising veg in the fridge. It's a really obvious recipe, but sometimes the obvious is easily overlooked, so I thought I'd post it for you here to make sure you don't overlook it. It's also a great illustration of the virtue of having lots of mayo in the fridge, as I always preach.

Ingredients

1 packet kelp noodles (340g)
1½ cups your favourite mayo (e.g. sour cream p85, umamayo p39)
2 cups sauerkraut

Serves 2
Takes no time at all if you have the mayo ready-made
You don't need any equipment if you have the mayo ready-made

Rinse the noodles well in warm water. Put them in a large bowl and chop them up with scissors, so they are a manageable size. Add the kraut, pour over the mayo, and stir it all together. Kelp noodles always suit marinating for a while, so if you can leave this at least four hours it will taste better, but you can eat it straight away if you need to. Sometimes, I just can't wait!

Wise Investments

During this time of great change, many people are looking for answers; many people are feeling helpless. It's not unusual for me to have a conversation with a friend, where we discuss something awful that is going on, politically or environmentally; there are so many devastating occurrences these days. And as we go over the facts, filling each other in on the gaps in our knowledge, sharing elucidating viewpoints, very often the conversation ends with my friend wailing, "But what can we do?" Bureaucracy creates structures that are so far from democracy it's ludicrous, and even if we are moved enough to take action on a particular issue, to reach who is responsible for making the decisions can be a fruitless task.

But what can we do? Because to me, it seems there is a very simple answer staring us straight in the face, that gets constantly overlooked. What we have witnessed in the last few generations is the demise of democracy. Like all good ideas, it has been corrupted, and now the majority of the leaders that we have elected are there to represent the interests of big business, not the people who voted for them. We are being ruled by the money men, who merely put on a puppet show for us to make us believe that we have some influence, but more and more it's becoming clear that politicians are not actors on the main stage, they are puppets at a sideshow, and the corporations are pulling the strings and commanding the real action.

These corporations, in the main, are big Pharma, big Agra, and big Chem. Companies like Coca-Cola, Nestlé, and Monsanto operate with a lack of respect for the health of humanity and the earth. Their tactics are greed, bullying and deception, and a blatant disregard for our collective future. These are the people we are fighting against, not the politicians, and the way to reach them is glaringly obvious. If we are being ruled by money, how do we change that? We stop giving them our money.

This process is two-fold. Firstly, corporations set an agenda that encourages us to think that we are not worthwhile unless we have "things." That material possession is the highest good available to us, and the most worthy investment of our time and energy. We need to move away from that mind-set, and know that kindness and compassion is what makes us human; looking out for each other and supporting each other. Material goods cannot make us happy if we don't take care of ourselves and the people around us. The pursuit of the material as the purpose of human existence should be replaced by the pursuit of a stable and nurturing community. These are the kind of decisions we make on a micro-level every day. When we wake up in the morning, we decide what we are going to prioritise, and where our value system lies. For most of us, it's a very subtle shift, to move away from prioritising work over family, and business over ethics, but it's an essential one.

Secondly, and even more straight-forwardly, we need to stop giving them our money! If money is what gives them power, it's an easy thing to strip them of it. Examine a list of the big corporations active in your city. Do you invest in any of them regularly? If so, can you seek alternatives? One of the main reasons I don't have a car is because it would break my heart to give that much money to the oil companies consistently. I think really carefully about where I spend my money. I don't give to charities, but I give in micro-ways constantly.

I will pay more at the local store rather than go to Tesco. I will pay more for fair-trade and organic. Where possible, I give my money to small independent businesses with human faces, rather than dehumanising corporations.

And don't get me started on Amazon! Amazon also breaks my heart. I have long been aware of their unfair practices, because ever since they started, they have treated authors and publishers terribly. They know that the first place a person goes to look for a book is on Amazon, so they know you have to be listed on there, and they can set the terms. They ask for massive discounts off of the publisher's price, so neither the publisher nor the author can make any money. Whenever someone tells me they bought my book off Amazon, my heart sinks; I make literally pennies from that sale. As well as the fact that they are putting publishers out of business and denying authors an income, then you have the well-publicised fact that they do not pay taxes. In case you didn't know, that's 20% of the end price! That's so unfair to UK businesses that are paying their tax. You may think you are saving 20% by buying from them, but on a larger scale the losses are much greater. And then also you have the issue of the way they treat their staff, which is the closest thing to slave labour that I have heard of in the UK. They set up factories in impoverished areas where people are desperate for jobs, and then pay them appallingly and make them work like robots. How do you think they stock so many items and get them to you so quickly? To me, Amazon sums up our desire to put money before people. In the pursuit of saving a few pounds, we overlook our artists, our community, our workers. The fact that Amazon is not an ethical company may roll through the back of our minds, but the fact that we will get a bargain overrides that.

The greed and selfishness of the corporations just reflects our unthinking greed and selfishness as people. Companies like Amazon only exist to serve a need, and if we relinquish that need, they will stop damaging our earth and our communities. And I know there will be people reading this who will say, what about people on a budget, what about people who can't afford to make those choices. Well of course, for some people it is harder than others, but there are always possibilities. Shopping at the market at the end of the day can be cheaper than Tesco. Making gifts and cards is cheaper than buying more mass-produced tat. I love to barter, swapping superfoods for clothes or a massage. And for those of us that do have more options, this makes it even more important that we engage with them. For I believe that when we invest wisely, we call in the laws of abundance, and the universe conspires with us to enable us to keep investing wisely. Like everything, it just involves small baby steps: if Amazon notices the tide of public opinion turning against them, if they notice their profits dipping, maybe they will start announcing support programmes for workers. Even when it starts out as just "greenwashing," it's small incremental steps towards change.

We actually have all the power. The corporations only control us if we let them. They thrive only when we let our own greed and short-sightedness thrive. Take back your power now. Make all your choices ethical. Make all your purchases investments in companies you would like to see flourish. Buy as much as possible from companies that care about people and our planet. And watch the rest lumber off into the sunset like the dinosaurs that they truly are.

The Glorious LasanYea

The weaknesses of my first were firstly, serving: it had a predilection for slopping all over the plate, even after a few hours in the dehydrator. Secondly, the cheese had a tendency to dominate the flavours. With this version, I've addressed both those issues, and taken it to a whole new level with the addition of two of the finest foods on the planet, cacao and kale. Some recipes develop over months, evolving to a perfected state after many tryouts and tastings. This was one of those rare beings that came out fully formed: divine inspiration one Saturday delivered this baby with no pre-planning or extended gestation period. Here she is, my new favourite thing I ever made.

Ingredients

Mole Sauce:
5 tomatoes
2 large purple carrots
15g (1 cup) dulse
2 tbsp extra virgin olive oil
pinch black salt
1 tbsp balsamic vinegar
½ cup (50g) cacao nibs
1 red chilli pepper

Cheese:
1 cup (100g) sunflower seeds
1 tbsp baobab
2 tsp turmeric powder
2 tbsp extra virgin olive oil
pinch salt
2 tbsp apple cider vinegar
1 ¼ cup (300ml) water

Mushrooms:
250g (½ lb) Portobello mushrooms
60ml (¼ cup) olive oil
1 tbsp tamari
1 tbsp balsamic vinegar
1 tsp chipotle powder

Layers:
4 coconut wraps
100g (4oz) curly kale
1 tbsp Rawmesan

Order of proceedings:
Mole
Cheese
Wraps
Mole
Mushrooms
Wraps
Kale
Rawmesan

Serves 6
Takes 1 hour, with 2 hours pre-soaking and 4 hours dehydrating
You need a high-power blender, and a dehydrator is helpful

First of all, you need to soak the sunflower seeds for the "cheese". You need to do this a couple of hours before you start. You also want to marinade your mushrooms in advance, although that's not so essential. Slice the mushrooms into fat pieces, about 1cm thick, so you're slicing each mushroom into about 4-6 slices (depending on the size of your mushrooms). Put them in a bowl with a large base, and cover them with the olive oil, tamari, vinegar and chipotle. Mix together well, and leave to one side.

To make the mole sauce, prepare the tomatoes and carrots for the blender. Grind the cacao nibs in advance. Deseed the chilli pepper. Rinse the dulse. Put the tomatoes in the blender first to make a sauce. Then add the carrots and blend again. Then add all the remaining ingredients – the dulse, olive oil, salt, vinegar, nibs and chilli. Blend until you have a thick purée. Spoon half of it over the base of your dish, and reserve the other half for the next layer.

To make the cheese, drain your sunflower seeds, and add them to the blender along with the other ingredients: the baobab, turmeric, olive oil, salt, vinegar and water. You should have quite a runny cream when you're done. Pour about half of this over your tomato sauce. You don't want it too thick or it will dominate: spread it as thin as you can, while making sure it's still covering the tomato nicely.

Next comes the coconut wraps. Obviously, if you don't have these, you will have to improvise with zucchini instead, but they are part of what makes this really special. Take two sheets, and cut each sheet into about 10 pieces: cut them in half horizontally, and then cut each piece into five. Layer them over your "cheese": you should find they cover it perfectly.

Fourth layer is more mole. Use it up!

Fifth layer is the mushrooms. Layer them on. If there's any spare oil in the bottom of the bowl, drizzle it over.

Next is another layer of coconut wraps. Repeat as before, with two more sheets.

Lastly, we have our kale topping. Take your kale leaves and tear them into small pieces. Pour the remaining "cheese" over the kale and massage it in. When I say massage, I am talking sports massage, not aromatherapy. Really get in there! Break that kale down, baby. Scatter it on the top of your . If there's any sauce left, you can drizzle it over the top. Finally, take the Rawmesan and shake it over the whole thing. If you don't have Rawmesan, you could just use nutritional yeast flakes.

Now ideally, it would go in the dehydrator for four hours, although if you don't have a dehydrator you can eat as is. I slide the bottom trays out of my Excalibur, and put the dish in on a high temperature – about 147°F or 9.0pm on the dial. I have it high like this because the is very dense, and in a heavy dish, and so it won't get anywhere near that hot in four hours. I eat it warm, straight out the dehydrator. Store leftovers in the fridge. If I'm eating it later, I will warm it up in the dehydrator just for an hour.

Spaghetti Supernese

When I was in junior school, Spaghetti Bolognese was one of my favourite dinners. Once I went to Caroline Robertson's house and her mum put peanuts in it. I thought that was the height of sophistication. Now I'm even more sophisticated, I put cashews, cacao and acai in it.

Ingredients

1 cup (60g) sun-dried tomatoes
1 packet kelp noodles or 1 spiralized courgette
3 tomatoes
1 tbsp tamari
1 tsp agave or raw honey
¼ cup (60ml) extra virgin olive oil
large handful/small bunch basil
1 clove garlic
4 sticks celery
¼ cup (25g) cashews
1 cup (25g) dulse flakes
1 tbsp acai powder
1 tbsp cacao nibs

Serves 2
2 hours marinating, 10 mins to make
No equipment needed

Pre-soak your dried tomatoes for at least an hour, until they are soft (if you're using ones already in oil, you don't need to soak them).

Rinse the kelp noodles well in warm water. They are preserved in a seaweed water which has a strong taste, so you need to make sure you've washed it off properly. If you haven't got kelp noodles, and you have got a spiralizer, you can make your noodles out of courgettes instead – one large courgette should be ample.

In your blender, put the fresh tomatoes, tamari, agave and olive oil, and blend to a liquid. Then put in your harder ingredients – basil, garlic, celery – and drain your dried tomatoes and put those in as well. Blend again until you have a sauce with as few lumps as possible.

Pour this over your noodles, and mix well so it coats them evenly. Your noodles won't be swimming in sauce; the sauce should just cover them nicely. Stir in the cashews, acai, dulse flakes and cacao nibs and give it another mix so it's even.

Leave to marinate for at least two hours. The noodles will absorb the marinade and soften considerably. If you're using courgetti, you may find they create excess liquid, which you should drain off – use it for a soup or a sauce.

Will keep in the fridge for a couple of days, and is at its best when its 1-2 days old.

Thai Coconut Noodles

This is so unbelievably good, and so easy. It goes without saying, these noodles tick every single dietary box you could dream of – gluten-free, dairy-free, raw and paleo. Coconut meat makes the softest, most succulent noodles, and although technically this makes two portions, I wouldn't blame you if you ate it all in one sitting. If you're vegan, coconut and cacao are the only two sources of saturated fat, so it's important you consume them regularly. (Yea, I said it! Eating chocolate is an essential part of a healthy diet).

Ingredients

2 coconuts (200g meat)
2 purple heirloom carrots (of course, orange will do if you can't find these)
1 lime
2 tbsp white tahini
small bunch (25g) coriander
1 tomato
2 tbsp water
pinch salt
1 tsp honey or agave
1 cm ginger root

Serves 2
Takes 15 mins
You need a blender, and a spiralizer is helpful

First of all, make sure you've got your coconut meat ready. If you have frozen meat, make sure it's been defrosting for at least 12 hours. If you're using fresh meat out of the coconut, scoop the flesh out with a spoon. We want long pieces if possible, so try and spoon out big chunks with long sweeps of the spoon, rather than lots of little stabs.

Take your coconut meat, and slice it thinly into strips. To make strips with the carrot, you can choose between a spiralizer, a mandolin, or failing that a good old potato peeler. If you don't have purple carrots you can of course use orange ones, or courgettes also work well. Mix your carrot and coconut noodles together in a bowl. To make the sauce, juice the lime, quarter the tomato, and roughly chop the coriander. Put them in the blender with the tahini, water, salt, honey, and knob of ginger. Blend to a smooth cream. Pour over the noodles. Eat instantly, or leave until the next day when the flavours will have merged more, and the carrots will have softened in the sauce. Should keep for up to three days in the fridge.

Nachos Nachos

So good I named it twice.

One of my favourite raw places in the world was Rockin Raw in NYC, and as well as her outstanding desserts, Tere's signature dish was her Fully Loaded Nachos. A gargantuan pyramid of tacos, chilli, guacamole, sour cream and cheese sauce would arrive at your table if you ordered this, either as a starter or an entrée. Best of all, for me at least, was virtually all Tere's food was nut-free, so you could enjoy this feast without any heaviness or digestive difficulties. It was truly one of the best raw meals I've ever had.

In the early 2010s, it turned into a bit of a tradition that I become obsessed with making quite a complicated savoury dish over the winter, and made it repeatedly until I perfected it. This worked for me because firstly, this was the only time of year when I was at home enough to spend that much time working on a single recipe, and secondly, because although I eat fairly simply on the whole, December/January time was when I craved something a little more complex and substantial to nourish me in the cold dark days. First, it was The Shepherd's Pie, and another year it was the LasanYea. 2014 was the year of the Nachos, and in tribute to Tere and NYC, we are naming it twice: Nachos Nachos.

The beauty of this dish is, although it is time-consuming to be making all these separate components, they can all be used individually for other meals. I ended up just having the tacos with the guacamole quite often as a snack. Leftover chilli got mixed up with sauerkraut and wilted kale for a dinner one night. There's a lot of extra cheese which I used as a dressing on some kelp noodles. So although the dish makes four portions, if you're just making it for yourself, you could eat two portions and make the rest into different dishes.

Ingredients

Tortilla Chips:
2 cups (150g) flaxseeds
3 cups (750ml) water
1 tsp purple corn
¼ tsp chipotle
¼ tsp salt

Chilli:
¼ cup (25g) cacao nibs
4 tomatoes
1 carrot
1/4 cup (approx 6) sun-dried tomatoes
1 cup (90g) almonds (pre-soaked 4 hours)
4 tbsp olive oil
1 tsp tamari
1 tsp balsamic vinegar
1 tbsp acai powder
1 red chilli pepper

Guac:
Take your favourite Guacamole recipe (such as this one p38) and use 4 avos – 1 per person

Sour Cream:
1 cup (100g) shelled hemp seeds
1 tbsp baobab powder
½ lemon, juiced
¼ tsp black salt
1 tbsp olive oil
½ cup (250ml) water

Cheese:
1 cup (100g) sunflower seeds
2 tbsp extra virgin olive oil
1 tbsp turmeric powder
2 tbsp apple cider vinegar
1 cup (250ml) water

Serves 4
Takes 1 hour to make, with 4 hours pre-soaking, and you need to make the chips at least 24 hours in advance
You need a dehydrator (unless you buy pre-made chips) and a blender

First of all, we need to make the corn chips. As corn has such a short season in the UK (and that season is not December!), I didn't use any fresh corn in this recipe. If you have access to fresh (frozen corn is pre-cooked), you may want to look up a recipe online that is a little more authentic than mine. But if you're sticking with good old flax, we need to start by soaking the flaxseeds in the water for at least 4 hours, and up to 12. Once you're ready, stir in the purple corn extract, chipotle and salt, and then spread onto dehydrator trays - not too thin because then they will be too crispy. It should cover one and a half trays. Dehydrate for 8 hours, and then flip. At this point, they should be pliable enough to cut into triangles. If you leave it too long they get too hard to cut and then you get some over-sized and very misshapen tacos. You need to make at least 24 tacos. You can cut a sheet into 9 squares, and then cut each square diagonally into triangles; it's easier to cut with scissors than a knife. The second smaller tray you might get as many as 6 squares, or 12 tacos out of. Dry for a couple of hours longer, until they are fully crispy.

To make the chilli, we need to pre-soak the almonds for at least 4 hours. You also want to soak your sun-dried tomatoes for an hour. This would also be a good time to soak your sunflower seeds for your "cheese" - they need at least 2 hours. When you're ready to make your sauce, start by grinding up the cacao nibs in a high-power blender or grinder. De-seed your chilli pepper, and wash your hands carefully. Then add it to the blender with the tomato, carrot, sun-dried tomatoes, balsamic vinegar, tamari, olive oil, and cacao nibs together. Basically, everything but the almonds and acai. Blend until smooth. Take the almonds separately, and chop them into small pieces, ideally about the size of rice grains. You can do this in a food processor or a high-power blender. Transfer your sauce into a bowl and stir the almonds and acai in. The almonds kind of absorb into the sauce so they are not immediately discernible, but give it some kind of texture.

Set the chilli to one side, and next let's make the sour cream. Put all the ingredients into the blender together. Blend until smooth, and then transfer to a bowl. For the guacamole, you can make whatever your favourite recipe is – I've been making the Middle Eastern guacamole here (p38). You need one avocado per serving, so if you're following that recipe, I would double it.

Last component is the cheese. Drain the pre-soaked sunflower seeds and put them in the blender along with all the other ingredients. You want quite a runny cream.

Now, we are going to assemble it. On each plate, take 6 tacos, and arrange them in petal formation on the plate. Next take your chilli - you want a little under a cup of chilli per serving. Put it in the middle of the plate, so the tacos are still peeping out around the edges. Next up is the guacamole - take large teaspoon size scoops of the guac and arrange it on top of the chilli, North South East West. Then take smaller teaspoon scoops of the sour cream - you want about half as much sour cream as guac. Arrange the blobs of sour cream between the guac. Lastly it's the "cheese." For this, you need a squeeze bottle. I use one bought from a cookware store: they are handy to have around for sweets as well as savouries, and they only cost a couple of pounds. If you don't have one, maybe you have something else with the same kind of lid. Or you could use a piping bag. Fill your bottle with the cheese, and pipe it over your plate in a criss-cross fashion.

Serve immediately, or everything keeps in the fridge well for at least a few days.

Magic Bubble & Squeak

I really love the sushi rice and make it quite often just to have by itself or with a curry. Recently, eating some old rice that had gone very soft, it reminded me of mashed potato, and I remembered how I had loved Bubble and Squeak as a child. I added mushroom powder and liquid aminos which somehow gave it that fried, slightly burnt flavour (I don't know if that's how your mum used to make it, but ours was always a little charred!).

For cultures not lucky enough to experience this culinary delight, Bubble and Squeak was a way of using up leftovers after a roast dinner. Leftover potatoes would be mashed, and the leftover cabbage mixed in. This gourmet creation was then fried in a pan and served as a snack lunch or supper.

Ingredients

1 cauliflower
1 cup (50g) coconut chips
¼ cup (60ml) extra virgin olive oil
4 tbsp tahini
1 tbsp liquid aminos
1 tbsp rice vinegar
1 tbsp nutritional yeast flakes
2 tsp Raw Living 14 mushroom blend
pinch salt
1 cup sauerkraut

Serves 4
Takes 15 mins
You need a food processor

Grind the coconut flakes to a powder. Mash the cauliflower in a food processor or high-power blender. Don't over-blend, because if you do the cauliflower releases a sulphurous compound that doesn't taste so good. Just process it to the size of rice grains, don't blitz it. Now, still in the machine, add the coconut flakes back in. Also add the tahini, olive oil, liquid aminos, nutritional yeast, rice vinegar, and mushroom powder and process again. Once it's smooth, stir in the sauerkraut by hand, and it's ready to eat. If you want, you can dehydrate it for around 4 hours, and serve it warm. Keeps well in the fridge, and in fact improves with age on day two or three as the cauliflower softens.

Vanilla Marinara

In Costa Rica in 2015, we visited a spice farm called Villa Vanilla, where they grew their own vanilla and cacao, among other things. We were lucky enough to have a conversation with the owner, who, without knowing who I was or what I did, went into a long speech on cacao, fermentation and alchemy – just the same topics I had been talking on all the past few days! He talked about uses for vanilla and mentioned that it goes well in tomato sauces. In this recipe I combine it with dates to accentuate the sweetness of the vanilla, and also throw in a little cacao in tribute to the magic of Villa Vanilla.

Ingredients

3 tomatoes
2 carrots
1 habañero pepper
4 dates
1 vanilla pod
1 tbsp cacao nibs
2 tbsp extra virgin olive oil
1 tsp apple cider vinegar
¼ tsp salt

Serves 4
Takes 10 mins
You need a blender

Prepare your tomatoes and carrots for the blender. De-seed your habañero pepper (I use dried ones, but you can also use fresh, or use a normal chilli pepper if you can't source habañero). Wash your hands straight after handling the seeds, as this is where the heat is. Don't rub your eyes or scratch your nose before you've washed your hands! Chop your vanilla pod up with scissors, discard the very hard ends and put it in your high-speed blender with the cacao nibs. Give them a quick whizz to break them down. If you haven't got a high-speed blender then you want to grind them up quickly in a spice-grinder or coffee-mill, or they won't blend into your sauce. Put the tomatoes, carrots, habañero, vanilla, salt, oil, vinegar and dates (I always use fresh dates for maximum flavour and nutrition, like Iranian or Medjool) in the blender together and blend for a brief minute until smooth. It's nice warmed gently and served with chopped up veg like cauliflower, spinach or mushroom.

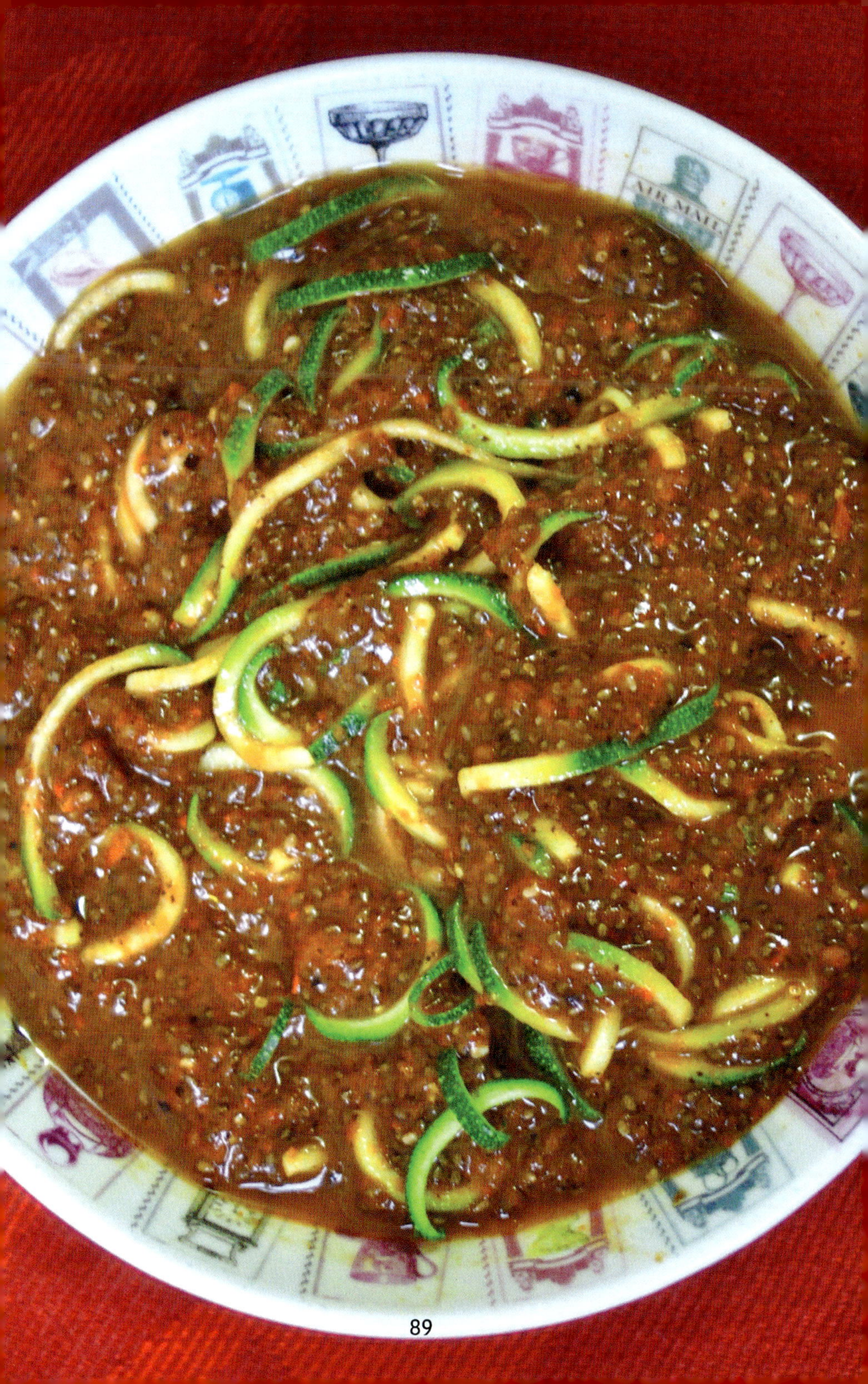
AIR MAIL

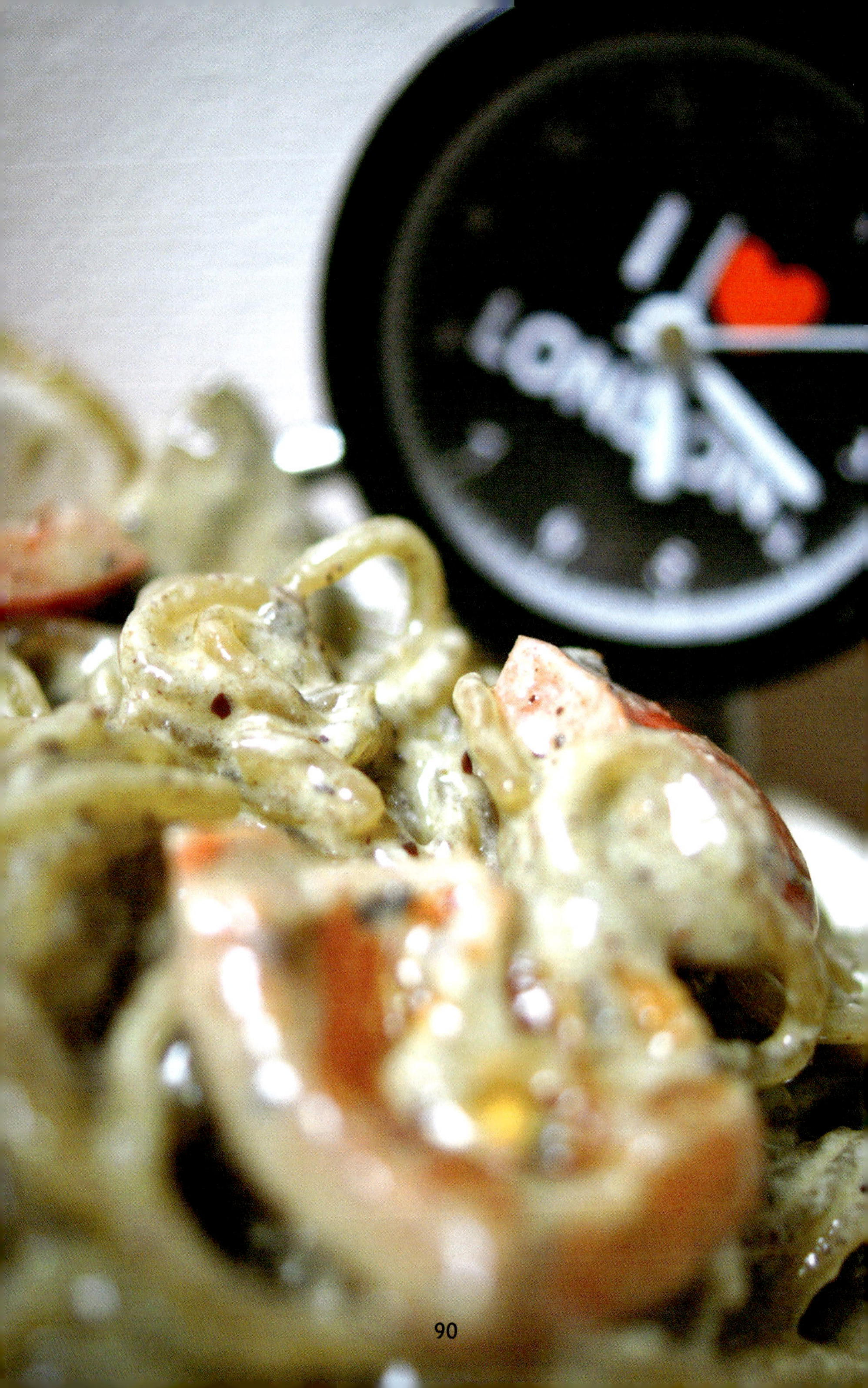

Ten Minute Kelp Noodles

Only got 10 mins? I promise you can make a gourmet raw meal worthy of a 5 star restaurant. You will have to leave them to marinate of course – you could eat them straight away but they are much better after a few hours. If time is really of the essence, just skip the marinating stage and blend the tahini in with the other dressing ingredients from the off.

Ingredients

100g mushrooms
1 red pepper
340g (1 packet) kelp noodles
2 tbsp tahini
¼ cup (60ml) extra virgin olive oil
1 tbsp Tamari
2 tbsp Apple cider vinegar
1 tsp Raw Living 14 mushroom blend
1 tsp garlic powder
1 tsp sumac or other warming spice e.g. paprika, cumin

Serves 2 (or one very hungry kelp noodle lover)
Takes 10 mins, obviously, though marinading time of 2 hours is recommended
No special equipment needed

Fine slice the mushroom and pepper. Put them in a large bowl. Open the kelp noodles, rinse them well in warm water, and cut them up with scissors. Put them in the bowl with the vegetables. Pour the olive oil, tamari, and vinegar over the noodles and vegetables. Stir in the 14 mushroom blend, garlic and sumac. Mix it all together, cover, and leave for at least 2 hours. When you're ready to eat it, put the tahini in a small bowl. Pour out the dressing from the noodles into the bowl and stir it together to make a pouring cream. Pour it over the noodles and mix it all together one last time. Devour!

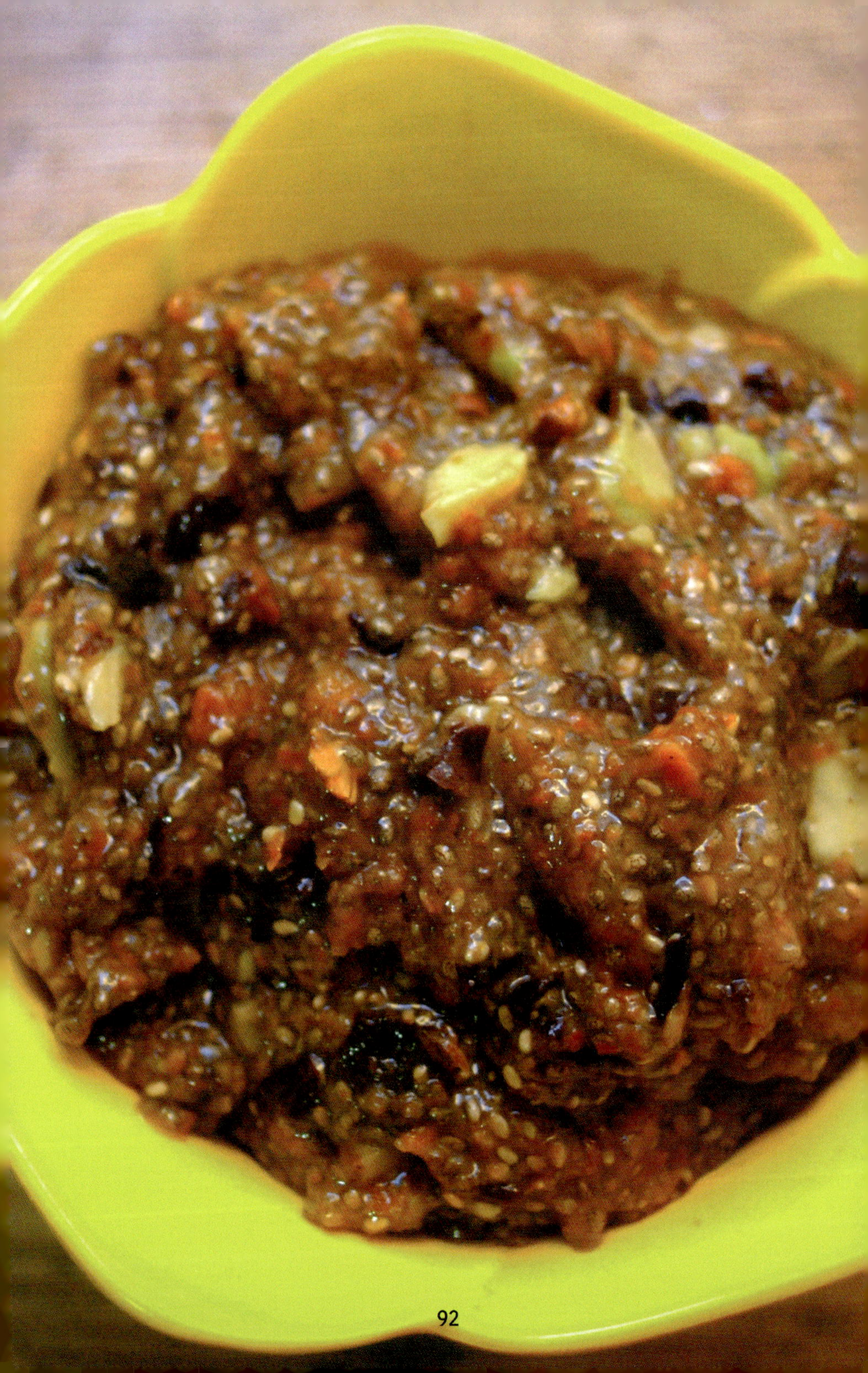

Mexican Mushroom Chia Chilli

Did the Mexicans actually make chia like this? If they didn't, then they should have done. The mushroom extract cordyceps isn't essential if you don't have it. But as well as being an incredible medicinal plant, it adds a deep, rich mushroom flavour to the dish, so I recommend you chuck some in if you can.

Ingredients

6 sun-dried tomatoes
2 tomatoes
¼ red onion
1 cup (150g) chia
1 tbsp tamari
1 tbsp apple cider vinegar
1 avocado, peeled and cubed
1 cup (100g) sauerkraut
1 cup (25g) dulse flakes
1 tsp chilli powder
1 tsp smoked paprika
1 tsp cordyceps
6 brown mushrooms, finely sliced
3 cups (750ml) water

Serves 4
Takes 10 mins to make; needs a couple of hours pre-soaking, plus a couple more for the sun-dried tomatoes.
You need a blender

Soak the sun-dried tomatoes in pure water, in advance, for at least two hours. Once they are soft, you can put them in the blender with the tomatoes and onion and make a purée.

Put your chia in a large mixing bowl with all the other ingredients: tamari, vinegar, sauerkraut, dulse flakes, chilli powder, paprika, and cordyceps. I like to fine slice the mushrooms, that way they marinade better in the sauce. I prefer to leave the avocado in big fat chunks. Mix all these ingredients together before you add the water and the tomato purée to ensure even distribution.

When you are satisfied that it's evenly mixed, pour over the water and the tomato purée and stir it all together well. Cover and leave to stand for at least two hours, stirring intermittently when you can. This dish keeps well in the fridge for up to five days: indeed, after a day the flavours start to improve.

Golden Burritos

Raw food cuisine around the world is influenced by California, and California is very influenced by Mexico. As I visited California more and became exposed to the Mexican dishes, I started to wonder about doing my own versions, as I had done early on with Indian and Thai dishes. I was excited to be opened up to a whole new world of cuisine, and started reading up on Enchiladas, Quesadillas, Nachos, Tacos, Burritos, but found it difficult to get my head around the differences between these exotic sounding dishes.

What I realised after a while is that the Mexicans employ the same kind of simplicity that I advise you to do when preparing your foods. They take the same few basic items - chilli, guac, salsa, cheese, sour cream, and bread, in a nutshell – and throw them together in different ways to create different dishes.

My Burritos then, aren't that dissimilar from my Nachos. You can use the same sour cream and cheese (although I have given you a new recipe here), sub the chilli for salsa, and the key I feel in making a Burrito fun is lashings of lettuce. It's the dense greenery you can stuff into the bready wrap that stops it being too heavy and makes it into something vibrant.

Ingredients

2 Wrawps*
sour cream (p85)
cheese (p162)
6 large leaves lettuce

Salsa:

3 tomatoes
¼ cup golden berries
1 tbsp olive oil
¼ tsp black salt
1 tsp paprika
1 tsp vinegar
10g coriander

Serves 4 as a snack or 2 as lunch
Takes 30 mins (you can eat straight away but they are better 24 hours later)
You need a blender

You need to start by soaking your seeds for the cheese, if you're making it. Follow the recipe here (p162). You can also follow the recipe for sour cream here (p85).

I find salsa is best made by hand. If you use a machine it turns into soup too readily. Finely dice your tomatoes and fresh golden berries, and mix with all the other ingredients.

To assemble each Burrito, use 1 tbsp sour cream, 1 tbsp cheese, and 3 tbsp salsa. Put it all in the middle of your Wrawp in a horizontal strip. Then add at least 3 leaves of lettuce, torn, into each Burrito, and roll tightly. Cut the Wrawps in half.

You can eat them straight away, but I would recommend wrapping each Burrito individually in foil, so you have 4 Burritos. Store them in the fridge for 24 hours, and the flavours will have melded and the Wrawp will have softened and become more bready.

*Wrawps are made in California, and are a bready mix of zucchini and flax. You can use any other raw wraps that you can lay your hands on, but the spirulina Wrawps are the ones I favour.

Kale Pizza

This is the easiest pizza ever! I have been thinking about Kale Pizza for ages. Ever since I made the with the kale topping, I've been dreaming about how good a pizza would be with heaps of kale on the top. I literally got in about 7.30pm one day, really hungry, and was eating this feast within 30 minutes. It's so easy and so simple, I had it again for dinner the next day as well. Now, it's become one of my favourite dinners, and if you follow me on Instagram, you'll have already seen me post it a bazillion times.

Ingredients

Base:
1 packet Wrawp Pizza bases

Tomato Purée:
3 tomatoes
1 carrot
2 tsp fermented hot sauce e.g. Eaten Alive

Toppings:
50g Botija olives
8 mushrooms
2 tbsp sweetcorn
150g kale
2 tbsp olive oil
pinch salt

Tahini Turmeric Cheese:
1 tbsp tahini
1 tsp white miso
½ tsp mustard
1 tsp turmeric powder
60ml water

Makes 2 pizzas
Takes 15 mins to make and a little time to dehydrate – an hour is good
You need a dehydrator, although it would still work if you don't have one

First, you need to marinate your topping. Take the kale and massage it well in the olive oil and salt. When it's broken down nicely, stir it in a bowl with the olives, mushrooms and sweetcorn, and leave to marinade while you prepare the rest of the layers. Add a little extra oil if you need to. You don't need to use Botija olives of course, but they are amazing and will take the pizza to another level. Fresh sweetcorn is only in season for a couple of months in the summer, so if you can't get it you can use jarred or frozen, although it won't be raw. I confess I just helped myself to a jar in the fridge for convenience!

For the base, I am in love with the Wrawp Pizza bases. They are so easy and taste so good! Of course, the spirulina flavour is my preference. I like a bready base for my pizza, rather than a cracker, but you can use crackers at a push.

To make the tomato purée, just blend the three ingredients. I use Eaten Alive Sriracha which is really concentrated and adds tons of flavour, as well as all that fermented goodness. If you don't have it you can omit it, but then I would add a little salt and vinegar for flavour, and maybe a few sun-dried tomatoes. Spread it thinly over your bases – it should cover two Wrawp bases.

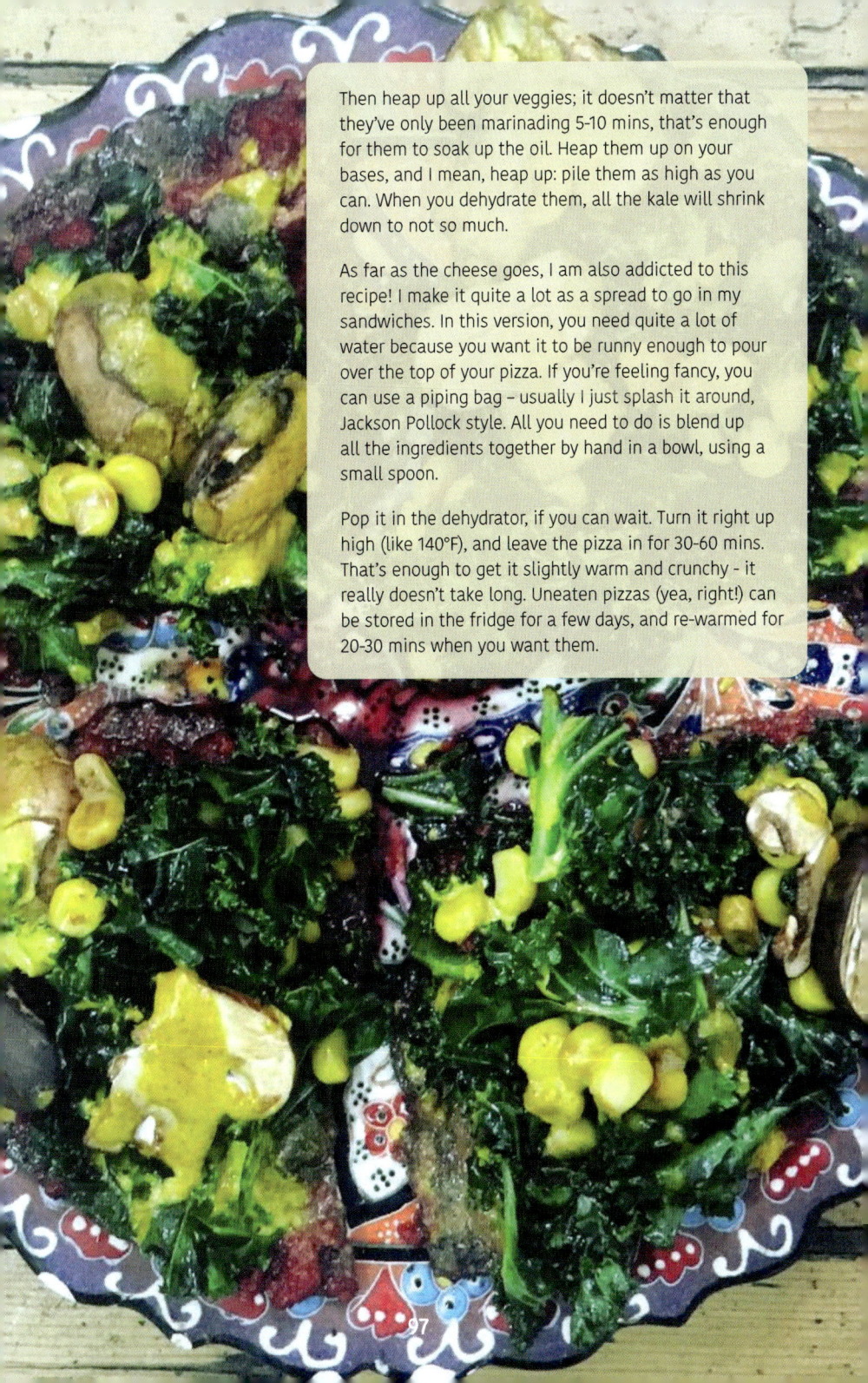

Then heap up all your veggies; it doesn't matter that they've only been marinading 5-10 mins, that's enough for them to soak up the oil. Heap them up on your bases, and I mean, heap up: pile them as high as you can. When you dehydrate them, all the kale will shrink down to not so much.

As far as the cheese goes, I am also addicted to this recipe! I make it quite a lot as a spread to go in my sandwiches. In this version, you need quite a lot of water because you want it to be runny enough to pour over the top of your pizza. If you're feeling fancy, you can use a piping bag – usually I just splash it around, Jackson Pollock style. All you need to do is blend up all the ingredients together by hand in a bowl, using a small spoon.

Pop it in the dehydrator, if you can wait. Turn it right up high (like 140°F), and leave the pizza in for 30-60 mins. That's enough to get it slightly warm and crunchy - it really doesn't take long. Uneaten pizzas (yea, right!) can be stored in the fridge for a few days, and re-warmed for 20-30 mins when you want them.

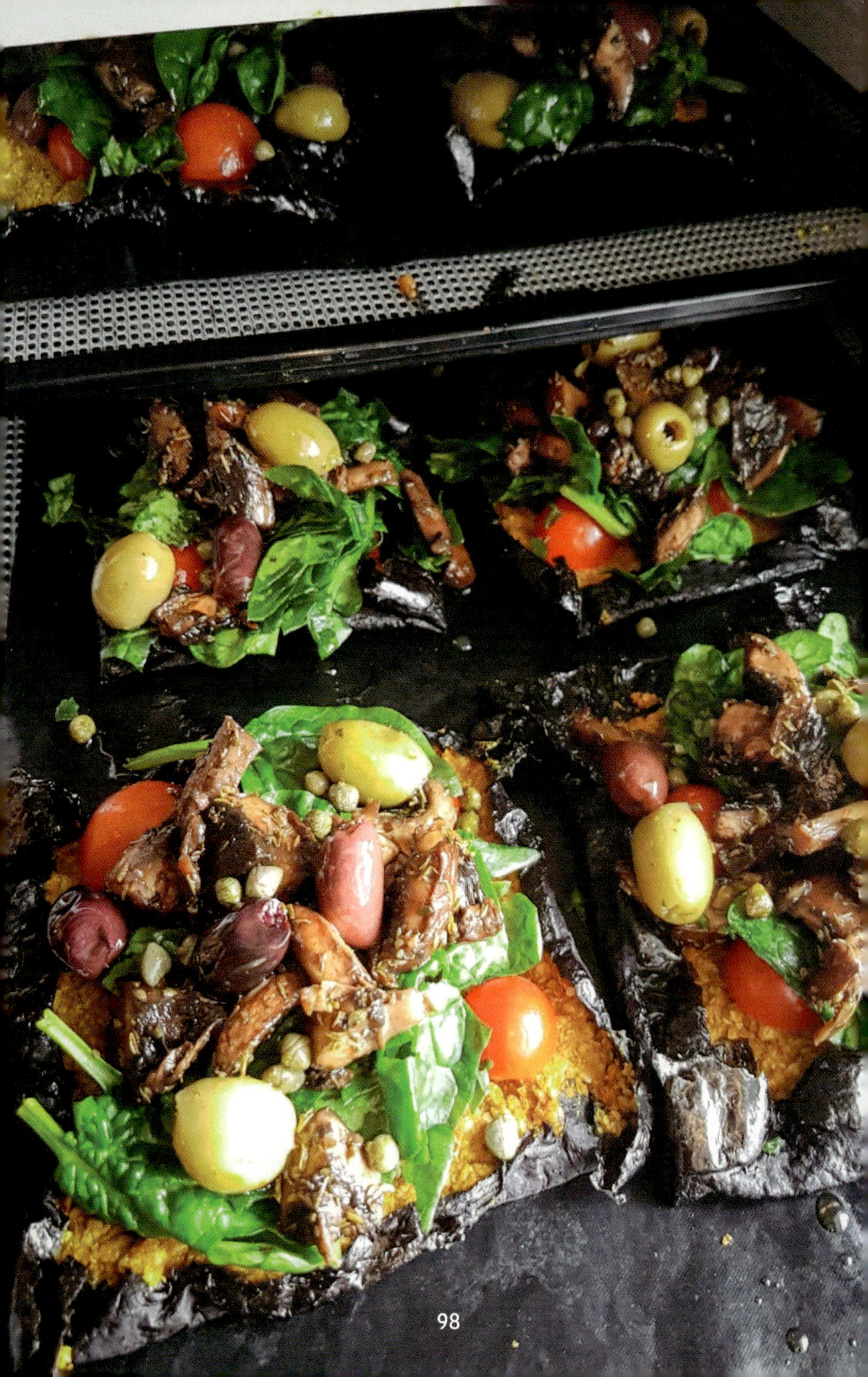

Nori Pizzas

Unless you're a nori freak like me, these won't sound that appetising. But they are one of those, "you won't believe it until you try it" dishes. Close your eyes, and you wouldn't know you were eating seaweed, you would think it was a standard thin crust pizza. These will definitely be on the menu of my restaurant when it opens.

Ingredients

Bases:
4 sheets nori
1 cup (125g) sesame seeds, soaked 1-2 hours
1 tbsp tahini
1 tbsp turmeric powder
2 tbsp extra virgin olive oil
1 tbsp liquid aminos
1 tsp cane juice crystals
1 lemon, juiced
1 cup (250ml) water

4 tomatoes
8 mushrooms (200g)
1 yellow pepper
2 tbsp extra virgin olive oil
1 tbsp tamari
20 olives (250g)
30g capers
1 tbsp herbs de Provence

Serves 4
Takes 12 hours for first dehydration, and 1 hour for second
You need a blender and a dehydrator

Firstly, pre-soak your sesame seeds for 1-2 hours. Then drain them, and blend them up with the tahini, turmeric, olive oil, liquid aminos, cane juice crystals, lemon juice and water. This actually makes enough to do 8 pizzas, but it's hard to blend up a smaller amount than this. You can reserve the leftovers, and make a second batch of pizza, or just use it as a salad dressing. Lay your nori sheets out on the dehydrator, and spread the sesame cheese out on each sheet. Leave around 1cm edge all the way around without cheese on, and then fold it up to create the crust. It won't stay up very well at first, but after they've been in the dehydrator for a little while, if you have a little fiddle, they are crispier and will stand up more easily. Dehydrate for 12 hours. Then you can store the bases (in an airtight container in the fridge or a cool spot), until you are ready to use them.

When it's time for Pizza Night, fine slice your tomatoes, and arrange one tomato on each pizza. You can also use halved cherry tomatoes, 4 tomatoes to each pizza. Then fine slice your mushrooms and pepper, and pour the olive oil and tamari over them. Evenly distribute this mix over the tomatoes. Sprinkle some olives over the top (around 5 to each pizza), and a few capers. You can also add baby spinach leaves, wilted kale, sweetcorn, or whatever your favourite toppings are. Finally finish the lot off with a scattering of dried herbs. Put them back in your dehydrator – an hour is enough to soften the veggies and crisp up the bases. Eat warm, straight from the dehydrator.

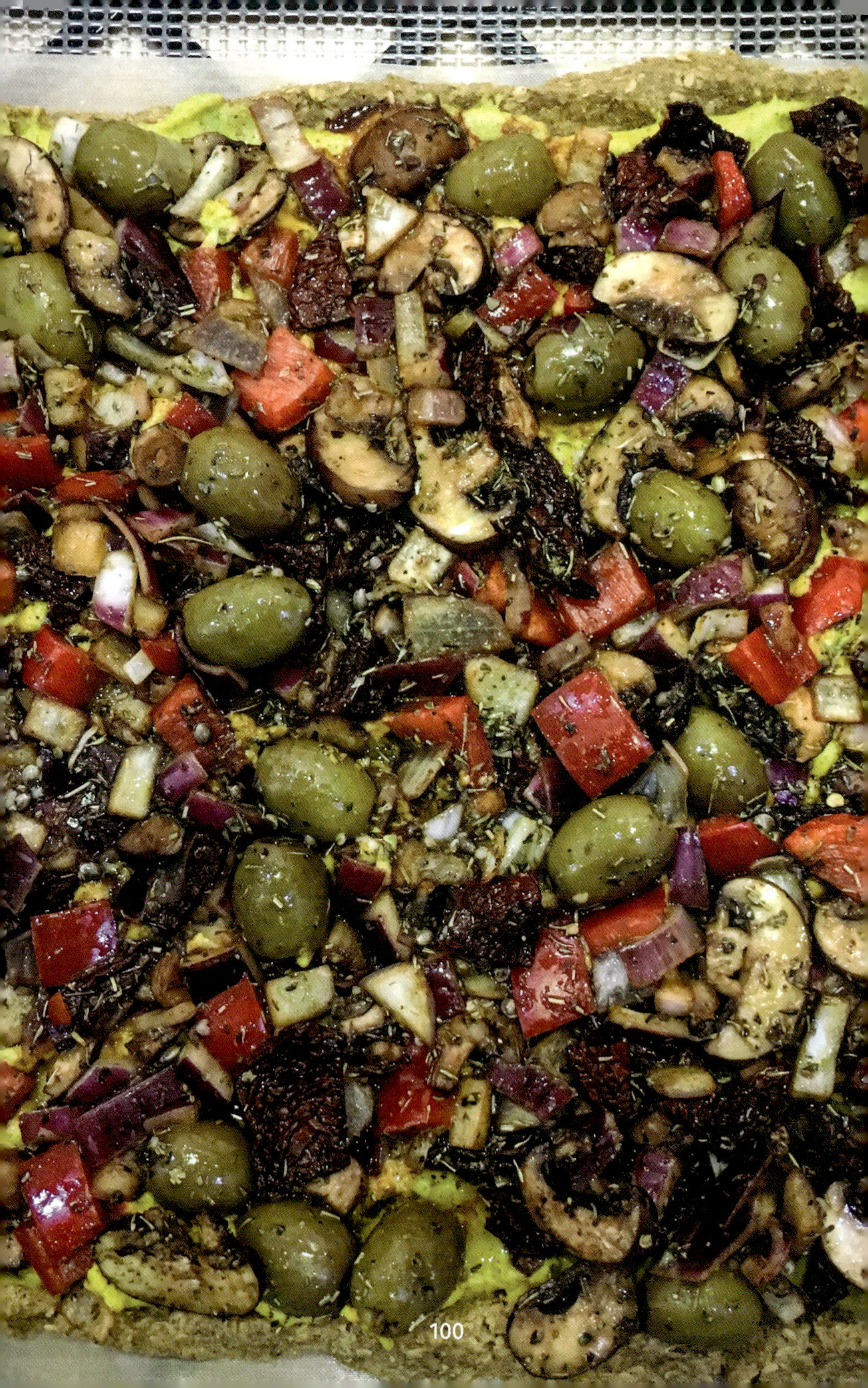

Perfect Pizza

My first ever job was working in the Perfect Pizza on Twickenham High Street when I was 16. I would venture to say that this pizza is a little more perfect than the ones I used to assist in creating back then. It's so delicious, you may be tempted to eat two slices; I would advise against it. It's not great for your gut to eat too much dense and overly-combined foods. One slice you can get away with, but two, your tummy might not forgive you for.

Ingredients

Pizza Base:
(This is basically GarLac Bread p134)
500g (4 cups) golden flaxseeds
2 tsp psyllium
4 cloves garlic
¼ tsp salt
500ml (2 cups) water

Cheese Topping:
125g (1 cup) brazils, soaked 4-8 hours
1 lemon, juiced
60ml (¼ cup) olive oil
1 clove garlic
pinch salt
2 tbsp nutritional yeast flakes
splash agave
125ml (½ cup) water

Serves 8
You need to start making it around 24 hours before you want to eat it
You need a blender and a dehydrator

Grind the flaxseeds together in a grinder or high-speed blender. Leave them in the blender and add all the other ingredients, and blend to a dough, making sure all the garlic's broken down. Spoon onto a dehydrator tray and shape into a pizza base that's about 1-2 cm high. Dry for around 4 hours, then flip it, and dry for another 4-6 hours. Once it's in the dehydrator, this would be a good point to start soaking your brazils.

If your timing's not good, the base will keep like this for at least a week, but it's better to eat it fresh.

Drain your brazils, and put all the ingredients in the blender, adding the water gradually to blend. Once it's nice and smooth, spoon it out and put a thick coating over your pizza base, reaching close to the edges. Then put your pizza back in the dehydrator for around 4 hours, to allow the cheese to thicken.

At this point, you want to marinate your vegetables.

Pizza Topping:
100g (1 cup) mushrooms
½ red pepper
½ red onion
100g (1 cup) pitted olives
12 sun-dried tomatoes (pre-soaked in water for at least an hour)
½ cup (125ml) olive oil
1 tbsp tamari
1 tbsp apple cider vinegar

Make sure you've pre-soaked your dried tomatoes. Slice your mushrooms and peppers into small, bite-sized pieces. Chop your onion as thinly as you can. Snip the tomatoes into pieces with scissors. Then in a large, shallow serving dish, place all your chopped veg, your olives, and your sun-dried tomatoes. Pour over your oil, tamari and vinegar and give it all a good mix together. Leave it to marinate for 2-4 hours.

After this time, take your pizza base out of the dehydrator, and heap your toppings on. When I say heap, I mean heap. Your meals should always be about the vegetables and not the nuts and seeds. Pile them on until you can't fit any more on. Then put in the dehydrator one more time, for another 2-3 hours.

Slice your pizza into eight, and as I said at the beginning, try and only eat one slice at a time!!

Schedule:

Make pizza base
Dry pizza base for about 8 hours
Soak nuts
Make cheese
Dry base with cheese on for about 4 hours
While cheesy base is in dehydrator, marinate veg for about 4 hours
Put marinated veg on cheesy base, and dehydrate for about 2 hours.
Ping! Your pizza is ready!

Timings can be tricky. It works best for me if I do the pizza base overnight, then put the cheese on in the following morning or afternoon, and the pizza will be ready for lunch or tea accordingly.

Laurie's Kale & Kelp Noodles

In NYC in 2012, I stayed with Laurie, who was a newbie to raw foods, but she wanted to have a play while I was there, so I bought her some kelp noodles. She didn't think she had any raw ingredients in the house, but we managed to rustle up this delicious dressing. It's very simple, and similar to a few things I've made before. But so good, and so easy, and so definitely worth sharing.

Ingredients

250g kale
4 tbsp extra virgin olive oil
½ tsp rock salt
1 packet (340g) kelp noodles
2 carrots
2 tbsp tahini
2 dates
1 tsp hot chilli sauce
2 limes, juiced
handful (10g) coriander
¼ cup (60ml) water

Serves 3-4
Takes 15 mins with 4 hours marinating time
You need a blender

Tear the kale into bite-size pieces. Put it in a bowl with 2 tbsp olive oil and the salt. Wilt the kale by massaging the oil and salt in. It should shrink down to half its size. As I've mentioned, I always prepare my kale like this to make it more digestible.

Rinse the kelp noodles thoroughly, and cut them up with scissors. Put them in the bowl with the kale. Chop the carrots and put them in the blender with the tahini, dates, chilli sauce, olive oil, lime juice and coriander. Blend, adding the water gradually. You may need to add more, depending on the size of your carrots. Pour the sauce over the kale and the kelp and mix it all together. Leave to marinate for at least four hours.

Spring Rolls

There's a version of Spring Rolls in the Raw Living book, but it employs a lettuce wrap and doesn't invoke the mighty kelp noodle. This is on a whole other level.

The timing of this recipe is really crucial. If you dehydrate the wraps for too long, they go crispy and then they won't wrap – they turn into crackers! Once they are the right consistency, pliable without being soggy, you have to turn them into rolls straight away. So you need to make sure you're in about four to six hours after you put them in the dehydrator so you're there and ready to make them into rolls. Then they need heating again in the dehydrator. They really are best served warm, so if your timings don't work out then and there, roll them and wait to dry them when you're going to want to eat them in a few hours. You can reheat them if you need to.

Ingredients

For the Wraps:
150g (1 ½ cups) flaxseeds, soaked in 500ml (2 cups) water for 4-8 hours
½ red onion
small bunch coriander
1 tsp cayenne pepper

For the Filling:
1 cup sauerkraut
1 red pepper
2 cups mixed vegetables e.g. carrots, mushrooms, cauliflower, courgette, celery
1 packet kelp noodles
¼ cup (60ml) sesame oil (toasted sesame oil is obviously not raw but has more flavour)
¼ cup (60ml) olive oil
2 tbsp tamari
2 tbsp apple cider vinegar
1 tsp yacon syrup or honey
1 cm ginger root
1 clove garlic
a few sprigs of coriander

Makes 6
Takes ages! 15 mins to get started, 4-8 hours pre-soaking and marinating, 5 mins to get them in the dehydrator, 4-6 hours dehydrating, and then 15 mins to assemble them, and another 2-4 hours dehydrating.
You need a blender and a dehydrator

First, we need to make the wraps. I use the recipe in the Raw Living book for coriander wraps. Soak your flaxseeds for 4-8 hours in advance. They will absorb all the water in this time. Then put them in the blender with the onion, coriander, and cayenne. Blend them up as much as you can, until the flaxseeds are indiscernible in the mixture. Once it's as smooth as you can get it, spread them onto dehydrator trays. The mixture should fill one and a half trays. Make your edges as straight as possible, so you can get nice, even spring rolls. Your half tray is best done as a rectangle that covers one side of the tray.

Dry them for 4-6 hours. Flip after about 4 hours. It's imperative you do not let them go crispy or they will not wrap! You're going to dry them again later, so it's better they are slightly on the soggy side than too crispy.

At the same time that you begin soaking your flaxseeds, you need to start marinating your filling. If you forget or you haven't got time, you can do this stage at the same time that you put your wraps in the dehydrator, but the longer the better as far as the marinating process is concerned.

Grate or finely process your red pepper and your vegetables. Personal favourites are mushrooms and carrots, but you can use absolutely any vegetable that you favour and have to hand. If you're using a food processor at this stage, a good idea is to add your ginger and garlic to your vegetables and make sure they get processed down together. If not, you need to mince the ginger and garlic by hand. Rinse your kelp noodles, and cut them up with scissors, so they are not so unmanageably long. In a large bowl, put your kelp noodles, your chopped or grated vegetables, ginger and garlic, and your sauerkraut. Snip the coriander with scissors into tiny pieces and add that to the bowl. Then pour the marinade over: the sesame oil (I prefer cold-pressed, but you can use toasted if you're not 100% raw), olive oil, tamari, apple cider vinegar and yacon syrup. Give it all a good stir, cover it and leave it to marinade for at least four hours. If you're around in the kitchen, it doesn't hurt to stir it every now and then while it's marinating to help mix the flavours.

Once your wraps and your filling are both ready, you can begin assembling your spring rolls. Using scissors, cut your wraps into six pieces: your full sheet will go into quarters, and your half sheet just needs cutting in half. Put a couple of spoons of the filling onto the wrap as if you were making a nori roll: along the middle and right to the ends. Roll it up and press it down to seal. It won't seal properly, but it should hold together pretty well. You will probably have some marinade left over; don't throw it away, you can use it in a soup or sauce.

Once you've assembled all six put them back in the dehydrator for a couple of hours. This part isn't essential, but firstly, it helps them hold together better, and secondly, the oils in the filling drip into the wrap a little, which makes them have that greasy texture reminiscent of fried spring rolls.

These will keep in the fridge for a few days, but they are best eaten warm straight from the dehydrator.

Easier cheat: use pre-made coconut wraps instead of making your own.

Enchiladas

Enchiladas are a Mexican dish involving, like all good Mexican dishes, chilli and cheese. There's a multitude of variations, but we are sticking with the obvious here, and not going too fancy. This is comfort food at its best, and is wonderful served warm - if you don't have a dehydrator, or you don't have the time to dehydrate, you can just warm the chilli before you wrap it.

Ingredients

Chilli
4 tomatoes
2 carrots
2 beetroot
1 date
pinch salt
1 red fresh chilli
1 tsp chipotle
1 tbsp vinegar
¼ cup (60ml) extra virgin olive oil

1 veggie Wrawp

Cheese
1 cup (125g) shelled hemp seeds
1 tbsp tahini
1 tsp turmeric powder
1 tbsp baobab powder
2 tbsp extra virgin olive oil
1 cup (250ml) water

Serves 1 as a very substantial main, or 2 with an accompanying side dish
Takes 45 mins and dehydrating time if you want to warm it up
You need a high-power blender

To make the chilli, grate the carrot and beetroot. Blend together the tomatoes, date, salt, chilli, chipotle, vinegar and olive oil, then stir the grated veggies in.

To make the cheese, blend all that set of ingredients together in the blender until smooth.

To assemble, get a Wrawp and cut it in half. You can use another flavour of Wrawp if you prefer (or make your own wrap), but I find the veggie ones are a bit thinner and easier to work with for this recipe. Put one third of your chilli in each half wrap, and roll up neatly. Squeeze them in next to each other, in an appropriate serving dish or plate. Reserve one third chilli, and pour that over the top of the two rolls. If you're not dehydrating the dish, you could warm your chilli in a bain-marie before you wrap it - I've done this a few times (I use the Thermomix) and it's just as good.

To complete, drizzle your cheese over the top. If you have a piping bag, use that, and pipe the cheese in zig-zags across the rolls. If not, you can just drizzle with a spoon. Be as generous as you like. You won't need it all, reserve the remainder for a later use.

If you have the time and inclination, you can put it in the dehydrator at 145°F for a few hours so it gets nice and warm and gets a little bit of a crust. Keeps in the fridge for up to five days.

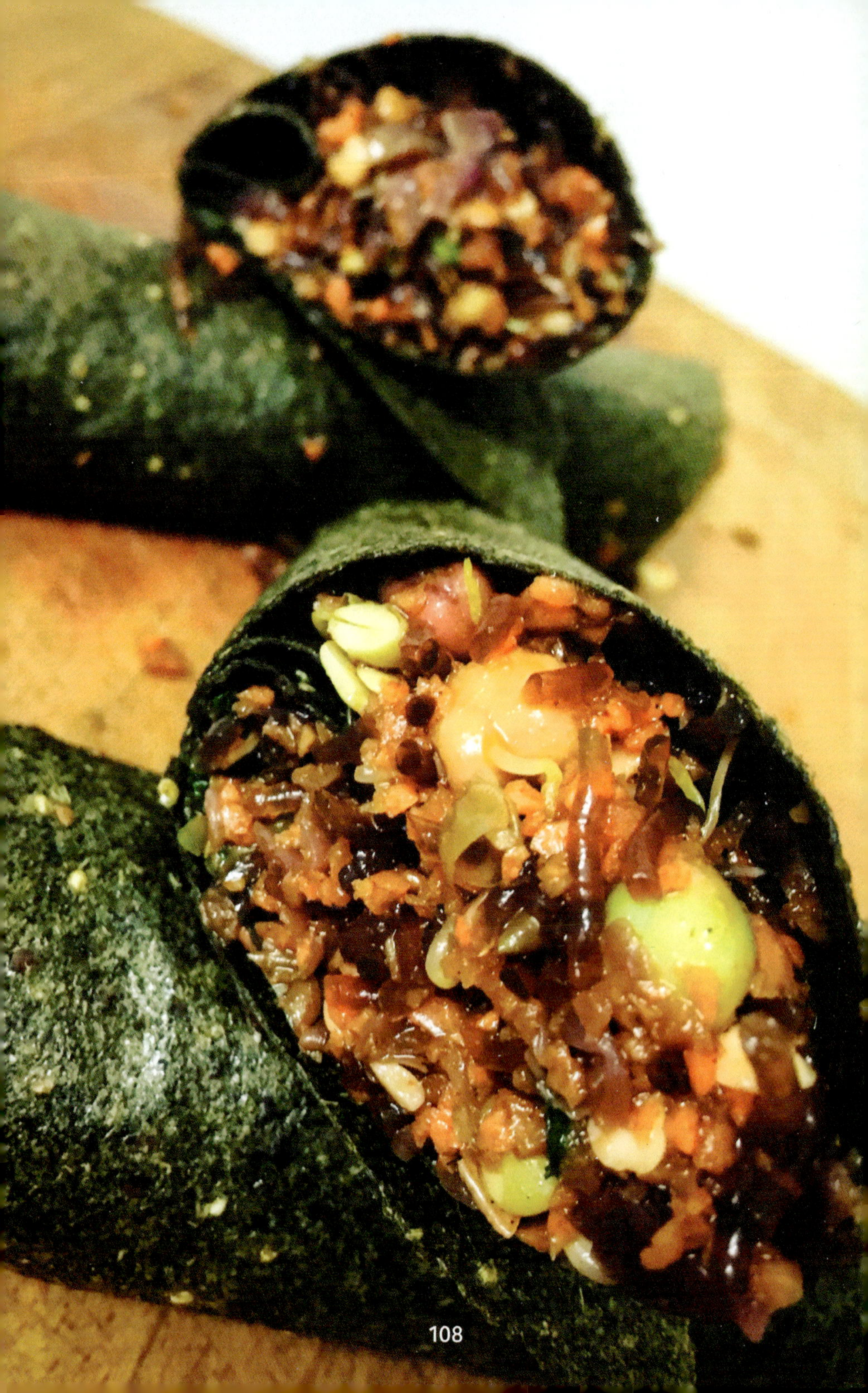

Wrawps

Wraps are a staple item in my house. There are lots of things I love about travelling, and also plenty of things I don't. One of the things I don't love is always needing to think carefully about which ingredients I need to use up before I leave for a trip, and what I can take with me. I hate waste! I try and use everything up, or at least rehome it. But this is one of my favourite ways to deal with the random half a pepper, couple of tomatoes, third of a cucumber, and some broccoli florets that always seem to be left in the fridge drawer. I make as many as I need to in order to use the ingredients up, and then feel reassured that I won't go hungry on my journey.

Ingredients

2 Wrawps
300g vegetables e.g. cauliflower, broccoli, cucumber, tomatoes, mushrooms, celery, kale, pepper, anything!
2 avocados
1 tbsp baobab powder
1 tsp smoked paprika
2 tbsp hemp oil
pinch salt
2 tsp apple cider vinegar
1 tsp honey

Makes 2 wraps
Takes 15 mins
You need a food processor

In the food processor, add your leftover veggies that you want to use up. You really can use any combination that excites you, however, I wouldn't use too many watery vegetables like tomatoes and cucumbers, or it will be too soupy. Process them on an S-blade so that they are broken down to somewhere between the size of almonds and rice grains, depending how crunchy you like it. I think it's nice to have texture in it rather than it being puréed. Once you're happy with the consistency, add in the other ingredients – avo, baobab, paprika, hemp oil, salt, vinegar and honey. Process briefly, just enough to have it blend in to the veggie mix.

When it's ready, take your wrap and arrange half the filling in it lengthways. Roll it up, and slice it in half on the diagonal. Do the same with the second wrap. It may feel like it's not going to hold together, but wrap each pair individually in foil and that will give it a chance to settle down. Store them in the fridge until you're ready to eat them. They don't keep that well if you are using leftover veggies that are coming to their end of their lifespan!

Nori Tacos

I have tried doing taco shells all the ways. You can use cabbage leaves, although they are a bit chewy. You can use romaine leaves, although they have a tendency to collapse. Nori is the best though, it holds the meat tidily, without dominating the dish. It's a little tricky to get them to stand up nicely, but with a bit of persistence you will get there. Get a piping bag or a squeezy bottle for that professional touch to pipe the cream on the top; they are also handy for piping cheese over pizzas, as well as making desserts look super fancy.

Ingredients

4 nori sheets
3 tomatoes
2 carrots
1 date
1 cup almonds, soaked 4-8 hours
¼ cup (60ml) extra virgin olive oil
1 tbsp tamari
1 tbsp balsamic vinegar
1 tbsp chipotle powder

Cheese:
1 tbsp tahini
1 tbsp extra virgin olive oil
1 tbsp turmeric powder
1 tbsp apple cider vinegar
⅓ cup (80ml) water
1 tsp miso
½ tsp mustard

Sour Cream:
125g shelled hemp seeds
1 tbsp baobab
1 lemon, juiced
¼ tsp Himalayan black salt
2 tbsp extra virgin olive oil
½ cup (125ml) water

Serves 4
Takes 1 hour, with 4 hours pre-soaking
You need a blender

First soak your almonds. When they are ready, you can prep the taco meat. Blend the tomatoes, carrots, date, olive oil, tamari, vinegar and chipotle to a purée. Drain the almonds, and add them into the mix, semi-blending them so they are the texture of minced meat. Put your meat to one side.

To make the cheese, blend all the ingredients together in a bowl with a spoon. Put to one side. Then make the sour cream by blending all the ingredients together in the blender.

To assemble your tacos, take your nori sheets and cut them to the shape of taco shells using scissors. Fold the sheet in half lengthways, and then trim the square edges into a rainbow shape. Open the sheets out, and stand them on a plate. Take one cup of the almond mixture and spread it in the base of the shell. Then take your cheese, and spread 2 tbsp along the top of the meat. Lastly, garnish with the sour cream – this works best if you have a piping bag, but if you don't have one you can just drizzle it with a spoon. You will have sour cream left over – reserve it for use as a delicious salad dressing or dip.

Tweak the edges of the shells up again, and then they are ready to serve. Don't wait too long, or the nori will go soggy. The individual constituent parts keep well in the fridge by themselves, but once you've assembled your tacos they are not going anywhere but in your belly,

Sociabubble

Perhaps the most ubiquitous challenge for people transitioning into raw foods are the issues surrounding how we navigate the social waters of dinners, lunches and drinks with friends, family and work colleagues, while we are trying to shift into our new ways of eating. There are many different layers of potential difficulties going on here, so it's worth breaking it down and looking at them individually.

Firstly, maintaining social ease is one of the main reasons people don't try to go 100% raw. 70% raw is the level that people generally feel comfortable with when they first commit to the raw diet. At this point, you're going to be feeling an increase in energy and positivity, but still able to leave allowances for social situations where cooked foods are the only option. If you're not "trying" to be 100% raw, it means you can be flexible and adapt to real life situations.

It's integral to you trusting in the process of going raw: once you start introducing more raw foods into your diet, you will gradually, over time, start wanting more and more. It's about having faith in your body's intuition and allowing it to progress at its own rate. It's about not forcing things and pushing yourself beyond your current limits so you end up yo-yoing back and forth. Committing to being 100% raw when your body is not really ready for it to me implies a lack of faith in the body. Instead, a little patience and trust, and allowing the body to recover its intuition at its own pace, is a far more powerful and sustainable practice.

So if you're still at a point where you can tolerate those old foods, enjoy your cooked meals with friends and family. The energy with which we eat our food can have a great influence over how it affects our body. Try and appreciate your meal, and put aside any feelings of guilt or distaste, and it will fare much better in your body. Eventually, there comes a time where you can't stomach these kind of foods altogether – but more on that later.

If you're going out for a cooked meal, there are ways you can lessen the effects in the body. Before you go out, have a large green juice or hemp milk, so you've got some great nutrition into your body in advance. Take some spirulina or maca, or a similar nourishing super food. If you go out starving hungry, you're more likely to overeat on cooked foods. Juices and micro-algaes give your body that raw high so you can make sensible food choices when you're out.

Digestive enzymes can also help. Once you've been raw for a while, cooked foods can give you a hungover feeling. It's the same process in essence; the body trying to dump toxins, fast. Digestive enzymes can help break down foods in the body, so taking them before and after you go out to a cooked meal can lessen the hangover feeling. Take them the next morning as well. Digestive enzymes are really good to take on holiday or over Christmas, when you know you're going to be exposed to a lot of unusual foods and have less choice over what you eat.

When you're eating socially, there's different ways of tackling the actual meal. Being invited out to a friend's home, should be an easy situation to deal with. Offer to bring a large salad with you. Bring enough to put out on the table, for everyone to share. Chances are, people will love it! Most reports I hear are of people's salads being the most exciting thing on the menu. Your fresh, vibrant food will sparkle next to their cooked offerings. If your hosts prefer to prepare food for you, it's quite easy to explain raw foods (although once I was offered a bean salad with croutons!). People are more and more accustomed to the vagaries of gluten-free and dairy-free diets. Catering for different dietary requirements can be a bit confusing, but in contrast, a simple platter of raw fruit and veg can serve as a relief for hosts worrying about how to do a dairy-free lasagne or gluten-free cake.

And while we are on the subject, never underestimate the power of cake! Taking your favourite raw cake with you when you go out to dine is a sure-fire way of introducing people to the magic of raw foods, while at the same time ensuring that whatever else is on the menu, you're going to get something gorgeous to eat.

If you're going to a restaurant, a good chef will welcome the chance to show off his skills. Phone ahead and explain your requirements, and then be delighted with a gourmet salad. Thai restaurants often produce salad extravaganzas if you ask. If it's not the sort of place where they are going to appreciate you asking for something off the menu, like a restaurant chain, then unfortunately you're just going to have to grin and bear it. Maybe have a small salad before you go out. Take some flax crackers with you to have afterwards. If all you get is a few limp leaves of lettuce and half a tomato, if you're green juiced and algaed up beforehand, and then you flax cracker down afterwards, you won't be suffering too much.

If people have prepared foods specially for you, or everyone's enjoying a celebration meal together, sometimes you can get into a situation where you feel socially obliged to eat foods that you know your body won't thank you for. Weigh it all up. If pleasing the people around you is more important than sticking to your principles, then that's what you need to do to feel comfortable. There's no shame in that, it absolutely does not make you a weak person. Humans are social animals and the need to feel accepted is very strong within us.

I know if I ate cooked food, I would feel so awful afterwards, it would take a very extreme situation to push me to that. So now I feel entirely comfortable in refusing cooked foods when they are offered to me. There is not a fibre in my being that wants them. If you don't want to explain yourself to people, you can just say that you "have allergies." That's usually enough to satisfy people. People pick up on the energy behind your words. If you're relaxed about your refusal, they will be as well. If they sense any reluctance, fear or worry, they will be more likely to poke, pry and fuss. I have always been very confident about my dietary choices, and so have been on the receiving end of very little worry and bother.

What most of us find, is that the longer we are raw, the more it's not just a choice, but something that comes naturally. Like being an ex-smoker, revisiting those old, less healthy foods, is simply not an option anymore. Refusing food that is offered to you is a minor discomfort rather than an event that causes a lot of angst and soul-searching. Someone recently told me about eating a bread and cheese vegetarian meal that was provided specially for her, and how she spent the whole of the next day feeling terribly ill. You can bet that next time she is in that situation, she will be more empowered to politely but firmly refuse the meal as something that she isn't willing to put her body through, rather than feeling socially obliged to do something she knows will make her ill. Unfortunately as humans, we learn through pain; we have to put ourselves through these kinds of situations more than once before we are strong enough to stand up for ourselves, but at the same time, they are one of the most effective ways of proving to ourselves that we just cannot eat those kind of foods anymore.

As you stick with raw, you will evolve, and your friends will evolve too. It's a sad but true fact, that you will detox your friends as you detox your diet. But then people who only hang around with you based on certain dietary choices weren't truly your friends anyway, were they? Those kinds of friends are easily replaced. The people who really love you and appreciate you for who you are, will stick by you. The chances are, a lot of them will start including more raw in their diets too, as they see the positive influence it has on you. And as you discover new parts of yourself, so will you attract in new friends who mirror those parts of yourself. People who have a more proactive and empowered approach to life. Never be afraid to let go of people from your past: the act of consciously moving away from someone who is not willing to evolve with you, is guaranteed to draw in far more interesting and rewarding friendships. So before too long, you will find the majority of your friends share your dietary preferences: either because they have grown and shared your journey with you, or because you have been successful at creating new friendships based on common interests.

If there isn't a potluck group in your area already, it's absolutely definitely worth starting one. One woman told me that you only need two people for a potluck! When she started them in her area, she did it with the attitude that even if only one person came, it would still be enjoyable to share food. Now she regularly has more than 20 people attending. Another woman invited me to do a class in her area, because she thought she was the only person who was raw and wanted to inform people of the benefits. From publicising the event, she discovered other people who were already doing it, and now they have regular meet-ups.

We are in a time of great change, and we are all a part of that change. Remind yourself that you are a pioneer, and when the history books are written, you will be remembered as being part of a movement that changed the world. Don't be afraid to stick your neck out for what you believe in. Remember, however resistant people can seem to be on the surface, underneath it all, you are still influencing them for the best. Enjoy and be grateful for all foods that enter your body, raw or cooked, vegetarian or not, and your energies of love and appreciation themselves become fuel for your body.

Trust in your journey, and believe that every single part of it is perfect for you, and an essential component of what you need to experience to create the most wonderful You. On days when you're not feeling good about your food choices, remember everything passes, and miracles are always just around the corner. On days when you're feeling great about your food choices, don't start getting arrogant and judgemental towards others, and instead cultivate a sense of gratitude and wonder at being alive at this incredible time when we have access to such an unprecedented range of amazing foods. These energies of faith and humility can be your greatest allies when dealing with tricky social situations, and aid you in turning potentially uncomfortable scenarios into opportunities for shared growth and insights.

Crackers, Burgers & Other Dehydrated Delights

I hope you have a dehydrator already; if not, I highly recommend investing in one. I consider them the number one piece of raw kitchen equipment, even over a high-power blender or a juicer. If you have a basic blender, a spiralizer, a milk bag, and a dehydrator, you can do practically every raw recipe in existence. And not only do you open up a whole world of recipes, you save big bucks. Crackers and kale chips are expensive to buy in the store, but make them at home and they literally cost pennies. Then there's "bite": we love salad, but it simply just doesn't cut it by itself. Our tastebuds crave different textures, especially something with a proper crunch like a nice cracker or burger. And the final reason to go for it? Dehydration is a method of preservation, so dehydrated foods keep really well, for months at a time if you've dried them properly. The higher water content a food contains, the more likely it is to go moldy, so if food is dried out properly (for around 24 hours), the low water content significantly decreases the risk of spoilage.

Masala Crackers

I always say this, but I think these might be my new favourite ever crackers. I always put chia in my crackers, it makes the texture better, plus I really feel the benefits for my digestion. The addition of sauerkraut also improves the texture – straight flax can be just a bit too dry and crispy. My favourite lunch currently is to take four of these crackers and make them into two sandwiches, filled with avo, seed cheese, spinach, kale, sprouts, fermented cucumbers or turnips, wasabi, pesto, and all sorts of wonderfully amazing things that make my heart sing.

Ingredients

2 cups (250g) flaxseeds
1 cup (125g) chia seeds
7 cups (1.75 litres) water
2 cups sauerkraut
1 tsp turmeric powder
1 tbsp baobab powder
1 tbsp apple cider vinegar
¼ tsp salt
1 tbsp garam masala

Makes around 60 crackers
Takes 10 mins to make, but then you need to soak for at least 4 hours and dehydrate for at least 18 hours.
You need a dehydrator

So simple! Put everything together in a very large bowl. Give it a stir and let it sit for around 4 hours; a little longer doesn't hurt, if you need to leave it all day while you're out, or overnight, that's fine. When you're ready, spread the mixture over 3 dehydrator trays. Dry for 12 hours, score and flip, and dry for another 6-12 hours. Store in an airtight container, these will keep for months.

Secret Garden Burgers

One of my business partner's favourite snacks when he's travelling is dulse and brazil nuts. He simply takes a piece of dulse, wraps it round the nut, and pops it in his mouth. When I was speaking at The Secret Garden Festival in 2010 I was enjoying that very same snack, and thinking how wonderful the combination would be in a little raw burger. Here it is!

Ingredients

1 cup (150g) brazils, pre-soaked 4-8 hours
½ cup (12) sun-dried tomatoes pre-soaked 1-4 hours
¼ cup (30g) flaxseeds
½ red onion, chopped
2 fresh dates
2 cups (30g) dulse, rinsed

Makes 8 burgers
Needs at least 4 hours pre-soaking, then it will take you about 10 minutes to make. Dehydrating time is 12 hours.
You need a food processor or blender

Pre-soak your brazils and sun-dried tomatoes. When they are ready, drain them. Grind your flaxseeds in a food grinder or high-speed blender. Add them into the machine you are going to make them in (I would use a food processor if you have one, but a high-speed blender will do just fine). Also put in all the rest of your ingredients: brazils, tomatoes, chopped onion, dates and the dulse. Process it all for a minute until you have a very thick paté.

Form the mixture into patties an inch or so high, and place on a dehydrator tray. You're only going to get 6-8 patties out of it, so if you know they are going to be popular in your house, you may want to double the amounts. Dry for 6 hours, flip over and dry for another 6 hours. The original mix is quite dry as it is, so it won't need long – 12 hours max.

Serve in a romaine leaf "bun" with lashings of mayo, ketchup and pickles.

Muddy Crackers

I teach these crackers on the Raw Magic Advanced Course and everyone loves them. They go particularly good with a nice creamy mayo, such as Bayonnaise (p31), to offset the piquancy of the crackers themselves.

Ingredients

3 cups (375g) golden flaxseeds
6 cups (1.5 litres) water
1 cup (60g) sun-dried tomatoes
2 cloves garlic
½ red onion
¼ cup (30ml) tamari
½ cup (125ml) olive oil
1 tbsp sumac (or warming spice such as cumin, paprika)
1 tbsp kelp powder
1 tsp Raw Living 14 mushroom blend

Makes about 90 crackers
You need 4-8 hours for pre-soaking, 15 mins to make them, and 18 hours to dehydrate them
You need a blender and a dehydrator

Soak the flaxseeds in a large bowl, in 5 cups (1.25l) water. At the same time, in a separate bowl, soak the sun-dried tomatoes, garlic, and onion in the tamari, olive oil, and remaining 1 cup (250ml) water. The sun-dried tomatoes and garlic can be soaked whole, the onion needs to be cut into chunks.

After at least four hours, blend up everything in the tomato bowl until you have a purée. Stir that purée into the flax mix, which should have by now absorbed all the water. Put your powders – kelp, sumac and 14 mushroom blend – in the bowl as well and give it all a good stir.

Spread it over four and a half dehydrator trays, and dehydrate for 18-24 hours. After about 12 hours, score them into crackers (about 20 on each sheet) and flip them, then dry for a further 6-12 hours.

They will keep for months stored in an airtight container. 90 crackers sounds like a lot, but as they keep, it makes sense to make a big batch. If you really don't think you will get through 90 crackers in 3 months (that's one a day!) then you can always half the recipe.

Caraway Crackers

I first made these for my friend Ysanne, when I was staying in her downtown LA apartment while she was away. She was having trouble with vampires in her life around that time, so I put lots of garlic in.

Ingredients

1 cup (125g) flaxseeds
½ cup (60g) chia
½ cup (50g) sunflower seeds
4 cups (1 litre) water
1 tsp chlorella powder
1 tbsp caraway seeds
4 cloves garlic
1 tsp tamari

Makes about 18 crackers
Takes 10 mins to make, then 4 hours to pre-soak, and 18 hours to dehydrate
You need a dehydrator and a blender

Put the flax, chia, sunflower seeds, chlorella powder, caraway seeds and tamari, together in a large bowl. Peel your garlic cloves and put them in the blender with one cup of water. Blend them up so you have no bits of garlic left. Pour this mixture over the seeds in the bowl, along with the other 3 cups of water. Give it all a good stir, and leave it to stand for 4-8 hours, to allow the flavours to fully absorb into the seeds. Once it's ready, spoon it over your dehydrator sheets; it should cover one and a half trays. Dry for at least 12 hours, then score and flip and dry on the other side for another 6 hours. Stored in an airtight container, this will keep well for months. I like mine served spread with some raw hummus, a heap of green salad, and a sprinkle of Klamath Lake algae.

Chia Onion Bread

Whenever I come home from a trip away, and it feels cold and gloomy in England, I always crave onions. The first things I think about making are usually onion bread (p132), and since I created it, the Shepherd's Pie (p69), or the Spaghetti Supernese (p82). It's warming comfort food, that smells and tastes like home. Just recently, I was craving onion bread, but (oh drama!) I had no sunflower seeds. "I can't make onion bread without sunflower seeds," was my first thought. Then I thought again. "Maybe this is the opportunity for some creative expansion," I told myself. And of course it was. If you dry them to a crisp, they remind me of another youthful favourite of mine, Ryvita. If you leave them soft, they make a flexible but sturdy salad wrap.

Ingredients

1 cup (125g) chia seeds
1 cup (120g) flaxseeds
1 cup (100g) shelled hemp seeds
4 cups (1 litre) water
250g (½ lb) red onions
½ cup (125 ml) olive oil
1 tbsp tamari
2 lemons, juiced
1 tbsp saffron (optional)
1 tbsp oregano
1 tbsp he shou wu
1 tbsp baobab

Makes 40 crackers
Takes 20 mins to make, but you need to soak them for at least a couple of hours first, then dehydrate for 18-24 hours
You need a blender and a dehydrator

To start, you're going to soak the onions and the chia separately. In one large bowl, soak the chia, flax, hemp, saffron, oregano, he shou wu and baobab in all four cups of the water. Stir it all together, cover with a plate or a cloth, and put to one side for at least an hour.

Dice your onions, and in a separate, smaller bowl marinade them in the olive oil, tamari and lemon juice. Again, leave for minimum one hour.

When you're ready, I'd recommend between 1-4 hours later, blend up the onions with all the liquid they've been marinating in. It should blend up to a liquid easily. Stir this mixture into the chia mix, making sure it's all thoroughly mixed, and leave to marinate further. Again, I would recommend between 1-4 hours.

The next stage is to spread the mixture on the dehydrator trays; spread as thin as you can, it should make about three trays, maybe three and a half. Dry for 12 hours then flip. If you want to keep it flexible for wraps, score each tray into quarters, and dry for another six hours. Store in the fridge in an airtight container. If you want crackers, score into five by five, approximately 25 crackers per tray, and dry for another 12 hours until crisp. Store in an airtight container, but they don't need to be refrigerated.

Onion Bhajis

This is one of the best recipes in the book! It's actually pretty easy to do. So easy to eat! I used to love tempura – you can sub mushrooms or peppers for the onion and make tempura the same way.

Ingredients

1 cup (125g) sunflower seeds, soaked 2-4 hours
½ cup (125ml) extra virgin olive oil
½ cup (125ml) water
1 large carrot, chopped
1 tbsp medium curry powder
1 red chilli pepper
1 tbsp apple cider vinegar
1 date
½ tsp rock salt
4 or 5 red onions

Serves 4
Needs 4 hours pre-soaking, takes 15 mins to make, and then 18 hours to dehydrate
You need a blender and a dehydrator

Pre-soak the seeds. When they are ready, drain them, and put them in your blender with the olive oil and water. Blend to a cream. Chop your carrot so it fits happily in the blender jug, pop that in as well, and blend again, until there are no carrot lumps left. Then add in the curry powder, chilli pepper (deseeded), apple cider vinegar, date and salt and blend one more time. Take your onions and fine chop them into slices, as thin as you can. Put them in a bowl, and pour your curry sauce over them. You want to cover the onions in the sauce thickly. Once the onions are coated in the sauce, put them on a dehydrator tray. They should cover two trays. Pour any leftover sauce over the onions, so once they are done the coating will be nice and thick. Dry for 12 hours, then flip. As you pick up pieces of the mix, they should naturally break up and clump into bhajis. Flip and dry for a further six hours. Serve with a big green salad.

Chia Crackers

You can do these two ways. If you dry them out until they are crunchy, they make a cracker with a great snap. But I love them when they are soft and pliable, and then I make salad wraps with them.

Ingredients

1 cup (100g) sunflower seeds
½ cup (50g) pumpkin seeds
1 cup (125g) chia seeds
1 cup (25g) dulse flakes
½ cup (60g) sesame seeds
2 tsp dried oregano
2 tsp sumac (if you don't have sumac, paprika, turmeric or cumin are good substitutes)
1 tsp cayenne powder
½ tsp salt
1 tsp honey
5 cups (1.25 litres) water

Makes about 20 large crackers
Need at least 4 hours soaking and 8 hours dehydrating
You need a dehydrator

Put all your ingredients, every single one, into a large bowl together. Give it a mix round, so all the flavourings are equally distributed. It helps if you can come back to it every hour or so to give it another stir, but it's not essential. When it's finished soaking, and all the water has been absorbed by the seeds, it's ready to put in the dehydrator. You should leave it a minimum of four hours, but there's no harm in leaving it longer, say up to twelve hours.

Spread it over two dehydrator sheets, and leave for around eight hours. Flip, and leave for another four hours if you want wraps; or longer, up to eight hours, if you want crackers. I love to serve them with avocado or nut butter, and a heap of fresh green leaf. Two make a great light snack, and four make a very filling meal.

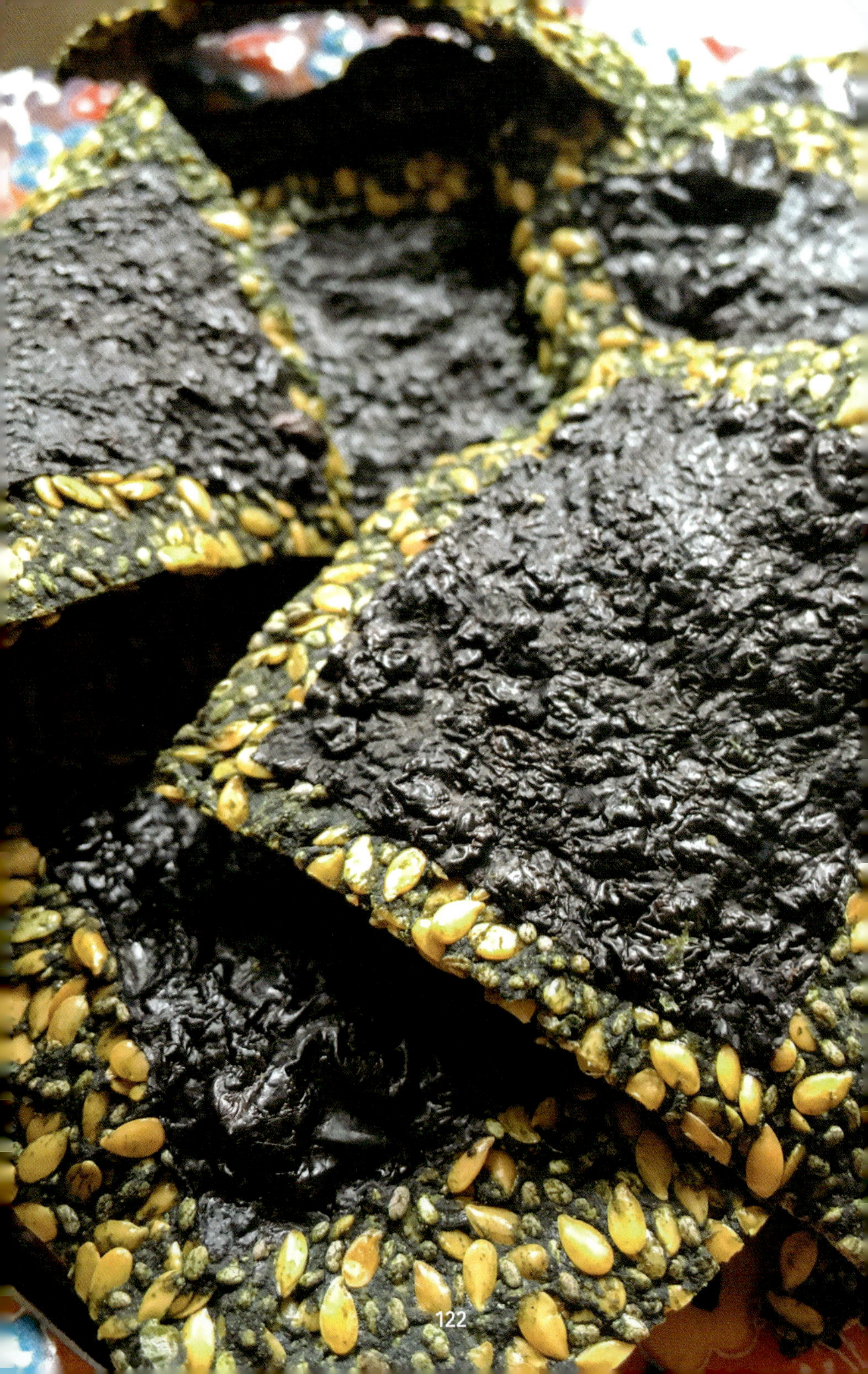

Nori Crackers

These have been my recent cracker obsession. So filling and grounding! I squish avocado on the top, heap up some greens, and I've got a complete meal. I don't know why, but they are particularly good with avocado – I've been cutting thick wedges of avo and then sandwiching them between two crackers for ultimate bliss.

Ingredients

2 cups (250g) flaxseeds
1 cup (125g) chia seeds
8 cups (2 litres) water
1 cup (100g) hemp protein powder
¼ cup (25g) chlorella powder
¼ tsp cayenne
¼ tsp salt
5 nori sheets

Makes 48 crackers
Takes 5 mins with 4 hours pre-soaking and 18 hours drying time
You need a dehydrator

Soak the flax and the chia in a large bowl in the water. You can add all the other ingredients apart from the nori at this point as well – the hemp protein, chlorella, cayenne, and salt. Stir them in well – you may have to revisit it in an hour or so to give it another stir. Leave it for four hours, by which time the seeds should have absorbed all the water.

Spread the mixture out on your dehydrator trays. It's going to cover three trays, maybe a little bit more. Cut each nori sheet into nine squares, and place the squares evenly apart on top of the cracker batter. Press them in lightly. You should then get 16 squares of nori to a sheet of crackers. Dehydrate for 12 hours, then cut (scissors are easier than a knife) round each nori sheet, so you have 16 crackers. Flip and dehydrate for another 6 hours.

It's important with these crackers that they are fully dehydrated or I've found the nori can start to go moldy. Store them in an airtight container and they should keep for a few months.

Buckers

These crackers are the perfect example of how inexhaustible raw cuisine is. When I set out on this path, obviously I hoped it would sustain, but if you'd have told me two decades on I'd still be discovering new foods and new ways of putting them together all the time, I'd have been heartened, but also surprised. Because the common conception of raw foods is that it's lettuce and bananas, and doesn't that get boring?

These were inspired by a trip to LA, where I discovered Mauk Family Farm crackers. These are my favourite crackers in the world, because they are so substantial and rewarding to eat. The trick, I think, is including the sprouted buckwheat, which gives them a greater density than your usual flax cracker. This makes the perfect hybrid vehicle, a combination of buckwheat biscuits and flax crackers, which creates a whole new exciting kind of base for your spreads and nut butters.

Schizandra is one of my favourite Chinese herbs, and it has a great flavour in crackers.

Ingredients

1 cup (150g) buckwheat, sprouted
2 cups (200g) flaxseeds
4 cups (1 litre) water
1 tbsp schizandra powder
½ tsp rock salt
1 tbsp baobab powder

Makes about 60 crackers
Needs 3 days sprouting. They should take you 10 min to actually make. Then another 18 hours to dehydrate.
You will need a dehydrator

Firstly, you need to sprout your buckwheat for two or three days. Buckwheat, if you didn't already know, is a fussy little seed. Soak it for five hours, no more, and give it a really good swishy rinse to remove the slime. If you do both those things it should sprout fine.

Once your buckwheat is looking good (with a tail nearly as long as the seed), get soaking with your flax. You can use golden flax or 1 cup of golden and 1 cup of brown. Add it to the buckwheat along with all the water, and leave it for at least 4 hours. The flax will swell and absorb all the water.

Stir in your remaining ingredients – the schizandra, salt and baobab – and when you're sure it's all evenly mixed, spread it over your dehydrator sheets. It should cover three sheets. Dry for 12 hours then flip and dry for another 6. It's hard to break them into even-sized crackers. I usually just crack them up into randomly sized bits by hand, once they are done. You should get about 20 crackers out of each tray, so 60 in total. Will store in an airtight container for months.

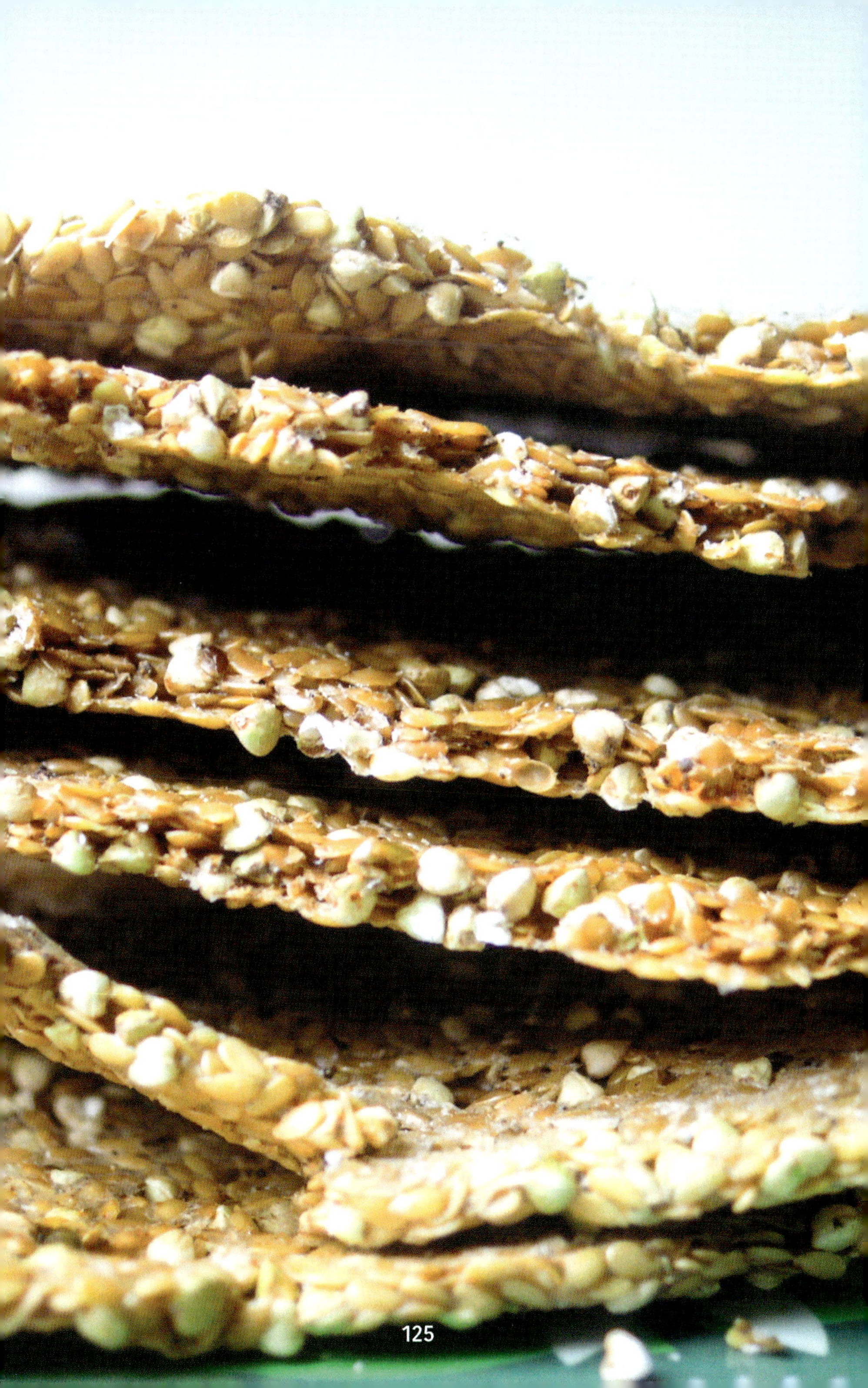

Beautiful Broccoli Burgers

What do you do when you're going away the next day and you have a kilo of broccoli in the fridge needs using up? Invent a delicious new recipe, of course! When I first made these I loved them so much I was having them for lunch AND dinner. So light, but so satisfying. And nearly as addictive as kale chips.

Ingredients

¼ cup (30g) sun-dried tomatoes, pre-soaked 2-4 hours
¼ cup (30g) chia seeds, pre-soaked 2 hours
¼ cup (30g) flaxseeds, pre-soaked 2 hours
500g (1 lb) broccoli (about 1-2 heads)
½ red pepper
½ red onion
1 chilli pepper
½ cup (10g) dulse flakes
¼ cup (25g) shelled hemp seeds
¼ cup (60ml) olive oil
1 tbsp apple cider vinegar
1 tbsp tamari

Makes around 15 burgers
You need to allow time for 2-4 hours pre-soaking, 15 mins to make, and 14 hours dehydrating
You need a food processor and a dehydrator

Soak your sun-dried tomatoes in water for 2-4 hours. Put your chia and flax in a bowl with 1½ cups (375ml) water and soak for at least 2 hours.

Chop your vegetables so they will fit in your food processor. First process the broccoli until you've broken it down as much as you are able. Then add in the pepper, onion, dried tomatoes and chilli pepper. Make sure you've removed the seeds from the chilli pepper (and washed your hands in hot soapy water afterwards!). Process again, so everything is equally broken down.

When you have no large lumps left and you're happy with the consistency, add in olive oil, vinegar and tamari, and process again. You might wonder how it's all going to fit in your food processor, but remember, when you add this stage of liquid ingredients, the mixture will actually start to shrink in the bowl. Next add the flax and chia mix, which by now should be a wonderful sludge. Your mixture should be turning into a batter by this point. If you prefer, you can remove the vegetable mixture and add the flax and chia by hand, in a bowl, stirring it well with a large spoon.

Finally, to your batter, add the hemp seeds and dulse flakes, and stir in well, either using your food processor, if it can still handle the quantity of mixture, or by hand. You don't want to break the dulse and hemp down, just mix them in.

When it's all ready, spoon onto a dehydrator tray. You can lay it out as a sheet, and cut it into squares when it's done, or you can make little patties with it. Either way, they need to be quite thin, about 1-2 cm high. Makes about 15 patties, or two trays worth.

Dry for 10 hours, turn and dry for another 2-4 hours on the other side. If you've made sheets, score them now before you flip them. When they are done they will be slightly crispy outside, and still moist and soft inside.

Stored in an airtight container in the fridge, they will keep up to a month. Eat them on flax crackers with some nut butter and alfalfa. Sandwich one inside two flax crackers for a hearty sandwich. Or choose a large lettuce leaf such as Batavia, and put two burgers inside with pickles, ketchup and mayo.

Kale Burgers

Why did this one take me so long? Maybe because I'm so obsessed with kale chips I never think of doing anything else with this mightiest of vegetables. But these are wonderfully satisfying and a great quick meal on the run, sandwiched between some romaine lettuce or Chinese leaf, with a bit of mayo and pickles.

Ingredients

¼ cup (30g) flaxseeds
½ cup (60g) sesame seeds
300g kale
¼ red onion
1 date
1 tsp apple cider vinegar
2 tsp white miso
1 tbsp extra virgin olive oil

Makes 8 burgers
Takes 15 mins, with 8 hours dehydrating
Dehydrator and food processor needed

Grind up the flax and sesame together. If you're doing this in a high-speed blender, you can leave them in and add the next batch of ingredients. If you're doing it in a food processor, put the seeds to one side. Take your kale and remove any large stems. Put the leaves in whichever machine you are using and process them down, not to a purée, but so there are no large pieces left. Then add in your onion, date, apple cider vinegar, miso and olive oil. If you removed the ground seeds, add them back in as well. Process again, so everything is evenly mixed.

When you're satisfied with the texture (not completely smooth, just without any large lumps remaining), take handfuls of the mixture and form them into patties about 2cm high. Place them on a drying tray; it should make about eight burgers. Dry them for 8-12 hours - not too long or the kale goes too dry and chewy. When they are done, store in an airtight container in the fridge. They keep well, for up to a couple of months.

BBQ Mushroom Breasts

About fifteen years ago, I used to have a marinated mushrooms video up on YouTube that I suspect only got lots of hits because it was called Magic Mushrooms. These mushrooms might not be the kind of magic that those YouTubers were looking for, but they are the kind of magic that we like – as nutritious as they are delicious. It's a long time since I ate any chicken, but these are so what I remember chicken to be – meaty, juicy, satisfying and finger lickin' good.

Ingredients

500g (1 lb) portobello mushrooms
4 tbsp extra virgin olive oil
2 tbsp apple cider vinegar
1 tbsp tamari
1 tsp honey or yacon syrup
1 tsp chipotle

Serves 4
Takes 5 mins, 1 hour to marinate and 4 hours to dehydrate
Dehydrator is optional

Slice your mushrooms into fat strips, cutting each mushroom into four or five pieces. Arrange them evenly in a large dish, so they can soak up the marinade easily. Pour the olive oil, vinegar, tamari, honey and chipotle over the mushrooms and mix well to ensure they are evenly coated. Leave to marinate for around an hour; they soak up the marinade surprisingly quickly, and are ready within about five minutes, but they absorb more flavour if you can leave them marinating longer. Once you're ready, pop them in the dehydrator for 4-6 hours. When they are cooled, transfer them into an airtight container and store in the fridge for up to four days. I like them best as the meat inside a sandwich, or you can add them to salads.

Chia Toast

Another Solla inspired creation, based on something we came up with in her kitchen during my visit in 2012. You may want to double the quantities, because if you think this is as delicious as I do, 8 slices won't last very long.

Ingredients

1 cup (125g) chia
1 cup (120g) flax
15g Irish moss
4 cloves garlic
1 tsp rock salt
1 tsp kelp powder
2 cups (500ml) water
1 tsp honey

Makes 8 slices
3-5 days pre-soaking for the Irish moss, takes 10 mins to make and 24 hours to dehydrate
You need a blender, grinder and dehydrator

Prepare your Irish moss according to the instructions. Grind up the chia and flax in your high-power blender or food grinder. Remove them from the machine. Then blend up your Irish moss with one cup of water, so it's puréed down as much as can be. In a food processor or high-power blender, mix everything together: the ground seeds, Irish moss paste, garlic, salt, honey, and the rest of the water. Mix it until you have a stiff dough.

Transfer the dough to a dehydrator sheet, and form it into a loaf shape. You want an even rectangle because we're going to cut it into slices. It's needs to be about 2" or 5cm high; any taller than that and it won't dry through properly. Dry it for 12 hours, then flip it over and dry for another 4 hours so the bottom gets crusty. Then slice the loaf into eight slices, about 1cm (½") wide. Turn the slices onto their sides, so they can dry out better. After a couple of hours, turn them again, so you have dried them on all four sides. The whole process will take at least 20 hours.

Enjoy served spread with coconut oil, nut butter, avocado, or a raw mayo such as Dream Chease.

Coconut Bacon

Impossibly good, and ridiculously tasty. It's getting easier to buy young coconuts in the UK now. You want the Thai ones, not the older, brown ones you used to find at coconut shies. If you can, buy them with the outer husks removed and then they are relatively easy to hack into. We have a machete! But a really good big kitchen knife will do it. First, you make a hole to get a straw in and suck the juice out (we have a little tap that does this, or you can do it with a screwdriver). Drink the water, then hack the lid off. Once the lid is at least partway off, you can get in there with a spoon and scrape the meat out. With a bit of practice, the whole process won't take more than ten minutes, and it's kind of satisfying to really engage with your food like this.

Ingredients

200-250g fresh young coconut meat (approx. 2 coconuts)
1 tsp olive oil
1 tsp tamari
1 tsp balsamic vinegar
¼ tsp chipotle powder
1 tsp baobab

Makes 2 cups "bacon"
Takes 5 mins, plus marinating and dehydrating times (see below)
You need a dehydrator

Prepare your coconut meat. Cut it into strips approximately 1" (2 cm) wide. This can be very approximate! It's next to impossible to get nice even strips out. Add all the other ingredients together as the marinade. Then put the strips in a bowl and add the marinade, give it a good stir so it's coated evenly, and leave it to marinate. It actually soaks really quickly, so you can skip this step if you're in a hurry, but it's best if you can leave it an hour or two. Then pop it in the dehydrator for at least four hours until it's crispy. The longer you leave it, the crispier it gets.

You will find it hard to not just eat it as it is! But if you do have any willpower, you can put it in sandwiches or add it to salads. I make a mean BLT!

Everyone Loves Onion Bread

As far as I know, Matt Amsden is the originator of raw onion bread. He was the first to mix sunflower and flax and onions, and you can find the recipe in his book Rawvolution (sadly his restaurant in LA has now closed down). When I was in the USA last, I noticed that several other companies are selling their own variations on onion bread, and I have also noticed that EVERYONE LOVES ONION BREAD.

So when it was time to cater for the Brighton Bikram studio Christmas party, I immediately thought of onion bread, as something simple and economical to make, and guaranteed to go down a treat. I have Matt Amsden's original recipe, but I thought I would go online and see if there were any other variations of the recipe to inspire me. Now understand, I don't usually do this. 90% of my recipes are my own inspiration, and if I have adapted a recipe of someone else's, I am always clear about acknowledging them.

I was shocked to find Matt's recipe circulated widely, and rarely had anyone credited him. More than that, the recipe was largely unaltered. Occasionally, someone had lessened the tamari, but in the main it was his exact recipe, posted as "the best onion bread," or "my favourite onion bread." I was surprised on two levels: firstly, the original recipe is very basic and lends itself to tinkering; I was amazed that so few people had thought to liven it up with a sprinkling of herbs or spices. But more than that, it saddened me that no-one had thought to give him credit.

On more than one occasion, I have seen people passing off my recipes, and more than not, they didn't see that they were doing anything wrong. But let's take Matt's recipe as a classic example. That recipe is definitely in the raw food hall of fame! It would be like being a rock musician and singing a Jimi Hendrix song and not telling people you didn't write it. Of course you're allowed to sing it, that's not in dispute. But you can't take credit for it, and not acknowledge the source, that's just not right; it's deceitful and it's unfair towards the artist who first created it.

There's one raw food chef I know who often posts recipes very similar to mine, and I know that he actually tells people in his classes that you can just change one or two ingredients and pass it off as your own. Well, yes, of course you can! But I think it's a sad reflection of our current rip-off, quick buck culture. If we spent more time acknowledging our heritage, and taking time to research the source of good ideas in the world, we would all feel more inspired and motivated to do our own thing, and put more true art into the world. While we see no shame in taking other people's ideas and even profiting from them, we are contributing to the dumbing down of our culture, and doing a disservice to us all. I believe that understanding where we come within a lineage is essential if we want to push the boundaries of where we are at, and that this concept is tragically lost in our instant fix media world.

Anyway, rant over, everyone loves onion bread. Try it for yourself and let me know if it's true.

Ingredients

250g (½ lb) red onions
3 cups (300g) sunflower seeds, pre-soaked
3 cups (400g) flaxseeds
1 cup (250ml) olive oil
2 cups (500ml) water
2 tbsp dried oregano
2 dates
2 tbsp apple cider vinegar
¼ cup (60ml) tamari

Makes 50 pieces
Takes 15 mins, but you need 2-4 hours pre-soaking time and it takes 12 hours to dehydrate
You need a high-power blender or food processor

Pre-soak your sunflower seeds for 2-4 hours. When they are ready, peel the onions, slice them as thin as you can, and put them to one side. Grind the flaxseeds until they are a fine powder, and put them to one side. Now blend the drained sunflower seeds, and half of the onions, along with the remaining ingredients: dates, olive oil, water, tamari, oregano and apple cider vinegar. Process until it's smooth. It should be a very thick batter by this stage. It's probably better to do the next stage by hand, although if you're using a Magimix or a Thermomix you might get away with keeping it all in the machine. But otherwise, I would recommend transferring the batter into a bowl, and stirring in the ground flaxseeds and remaining onions by hand. When you're satisfied that they are evenly mixed, spread the batter over two and a half dehydrator trays. Because of the ground flax, it becomes thick very quickly, and quite hard to spread. Do the best you can; you actually want it quite thick, not thin like a flax cracker, maybe ½cm (1/3") high. Dehydrate it for 12 hours, then score and flip. You should end up with 25 pieces on each tray. Dry for another 6-12 hours on the other side. You want it firm, not soggy, but not crisp either.

When it's done, keep it stored in an airtight container in the fridge; it should keep for up to a month. It's lovely just as it is, as an accompaniment to salads or as a between meals snack. I've used it as a bun for burgers. Or of course you can try the good old avocado and alfalfa sprouts routine with it.

Garlac Bread

This bread was inspired by the magic of Chef Ito in California. Ito makes some of the best raw food I have had in my life, and his restaurant Au Lac is legendary. When I visited, I was slightly concerned about eating more dense and complicated foods than I am used to; I eat so simply and lightly at home. But the food is made with such integrity and love, I felt incredible afterwards.

When I had asked people about Au Lac prior to visiting, without exception, everyone told me to try the garlic bread and the donuts. I did and I wasn't disappointed. So in homage to Ito, I present my own Garlac bread. Not as magnificent as his, but still pretty damn fine.

Ingredients

100g (¾ cup) brown flaxseeds
150g (1 ¼ cups) golden flaxseeds
1 tbsp psyllium powder
4 cloves garlic
¼ tsp salt
250ml (1 cup) water

Makes 6-8 slices
Takes 10 mins to make and then dehydrate 12 hours
You need a dehydrator

Grind the flaxseeds together in a grinder or high-speed blender. If you haven't got brown seeds, you can use all golden seeds, I just prefer the colour and texture with the brown seeds included.

Leave them in the blender and add all the other ingredients, and blend to a dough, making sure all the garlic's broken down. Spoon onto a dehydrator tray and shape into a loaf that's about 3cm high. You can score it now as well if you like, into 6-8 slices. Because there's so little water in it, it will dry quite quickly – turn it over after about 9 hours.

My favourite way to eat it is warm, from the dehydrator, with chocolate spread. Recently, we've been turning it into pizza...but that's another story (p101).

Meal for 6.8 Billion, Sir?

"Food is God. The act of offering is God. The one who offers is God, and he who receives the food is God." Hindu food mantra from the Bhagavad Gita

When the earthquake happened in Haiti in 2010, I read an article about shamanism, and how, if we eat our food with the appropriate intentions, we can transmit some of the nurturing and sustenance it gives us on to others. The article was saying how, it may only be a small thing, but we can help the people of Haiti by remembering them when we eat.

I loved this idea, it totally struck a chord with me, and I have been practising it ever since.

These days, I get a huge amount of pleasure from my food. Virtually everything I eat tastes utterly blissful to me. While I am eating now, I spend some time wishing everyone could get the same amount of pleasure from their food. And I wish for everyone to get the same incredible nutrition that I receive from my food choices. I put this intention out into the world. The intention that all of humanity is as nurtured by their food as I am, and that they experience the same levels of joy when they eat.

As I near the end of my meal and start to feel full, I eat the last few mouthfuls for everyone else, I send the meal out to the world, to those who are hungry and starving and don't have enough to sustain them.

It's only a tiny thing, a drop in the ocean when dealing with the malnutrition and hunger that goes on on our planet. But it's a very fulfilling practice, and one that I believe if more people took up, could actually begin to have an impact.

So next time you're blissing out on kale chips and raw chocolate, spare a thought for the huge majority of humanity who are not as blessed as we are, and a wish that everyone could enjoy these paradise foods. Because, as the Buddha said, "With our thoughts we make the world."

Kale Chips

About 15 years ago, I used to run a Facebook group called Kale Addicts Anonymous, until Facebook changed its rules around public groups and shut us down. We had a few hundred members, and we would mostly post kale recipes. That was at the beginning of the kale craze: consumption of kale has increased by about 1000% in the last decade! I adore kale, so much so, that I have a little kale leaf tattooed on my wrist. I have made literally hundreds of batches of kale chips over the years, and here are some of my very favourite ways to do my very favourite of vegetables.

Brazilliant Kale Chips

Ingredients

1 cup (90g) brazil nuts, soaked 4-8 hours
1 tsp miso
2 red peppers, seeded and chopped
½ cup (125ml) olive oil
1 lemon, juiced
½ red onion, diced
2 tbsp nutritional yeast flakes
400g (1 lb) kale

Serves 4
You need to pre-soak your nuts for 4-8 hours. The kale takes about 15 mins to prepare, and 12-18 hours to dry.
You need a blender and a dehydrator

Pre-soak your brazil nuts in pure water, just enough to cover them. When you are ready, drain them, and put them in the blender with all the other ingredients. De-seed the peppers, chop them into bits small enough for your blender to cope with, and put them in with the nuts. Peel the onion, dice it, and add that in. Pour in the olive oil and lemon juice, and spoon in the miso and nutritional yeast flakes. Blend it all together. You shouldn't need to add any water because peppers are so liquid when blended up, they provide all the liquid you need. Make sure you have a good smooth purée, with no lumps of onion or brazil nut left.

Next, prepare your kale. Remove any extraneous stems. I think when they have a thick creamy sauce on like this, the kale is best left in big leaves rather than torn into small bits. I find green curly kale is the best for chips, then red. Cavalo Nero (black kale or dinosaur kale) doesn't absorb the dressing as well so you need less, but it's still delicious. Don't forget you can use spring greens, spinach or chard if you can't get kale; I've even eaten cabbage chips and lettuce chips before!

When your kale is ready, pour the sauce over, and mix it all together. You don't need to massage the sauce in, just make sure it is coating it evenly. This dressing makes a very thick sauce on the kale. Spread it over three dehydrator trays and dry for 12 hours. Flip the kale pieces and dry for another 4-6 hours until it's all crisp and crunchy.

One day I will make some specially and put them to one side so I can tell you how long they keep for. For now, it's safe to assume that they don't keep well and it's imperative that you eat them all straight away before they lose their crispiness.

Lebanese Kale Chips

Za'atar has long been one of my favourite condiments. It's a Lebanese spice mixture, usually made of thyme, sesame seeds, salt and sumac. Sumac itself is an amazing spice, if you can track it down. Za'atar is available in a lot of wholefood stores or from a Middle Eastern grocer's if you have one near you. I love the Seasoned Pioneers brand, which we stock on our Raw Living website.

I make lots of kale chips, and I like to keep the recipes as simple as possible, so I can make enough to feed the family without too much bother. This recipe is very simple and takes just a few minutes to prepare.

Ingredients

300g (⅔ lb) kale
3 tbsp extra virgin olive oil
juice 1 lemon
2 tbsp za'atar

Serves 2
Takes 5 mins, with 12 hours dehydrating
You need a dehydrator

Prepare the kale by removing the stems and tearing any big leaves. Put it in a large bowl, and pour over the olive oil and lemon juice. Toss the kale, so it's evenly covered. With a spoon, sprinkle the za'atar over the kale, trying to cover as much as possible; if you just throw the spoonful straight in, it will be harder to mix it in evenly. Toss the kale again, trying to make sure the za'atar is evenly distributed.

Spread kale over two or three dehydrator sheets and dry for 12 hours. When it's done and crispy, eat it like it's going out of fashion.

Tahini & Baobab Kale Chips

Tahini makes everything better. When we had the Raw Magic shop in 2006, we had a saying which was, "You can never have too much tahini." However much we got in, it would always fly out the door or get used in our kitchen. These are the boys' new favourite kale chips - Zachary even told me they were as good as Solla's, which is about the biggest compliment he could pay! I've just discovered a new Ethopian spice blend called berbere which I put 1 tsp of on mine – if you like a little heat, add your own favourite spice blend, it complements the coolness of the tahini and the baobab well.

Ingredients

400g (½ lb) kale
¼ cup (25g) tahini
¼ cup (60ml) olive oil
1 tbsp apple cider vinegar
1 tbsp baobab powder
¼ tsp salt
½ tsp berbere chilli
⅓ cup (80ml) water

Serves 4
Takes 15 mins, with 18 hours dehydrating
You need a dehydrator

First, prepare your kale for the dehydrator. Tear it into pieces (not too small, tearing each leaf into two or three should be fine), and remove any large stems which will be indigestible if dehydrated. Put it in a large bowl. Then in a small bowl, stir together all the other ingredients. Put everything together in the bowl – tahini, olive oil, vinegar, baobab, salt and chilli. Mix together well, then gradually add the water, until you have a thick pouring sauce. Pour it over the kale, and stir together so the kale is evenly coated. Spread over two dehydrating trays and dry for 18 hours. They are ready when they are all crispy, with no soggy bits left.

Be Blessed

The first kale chips I ever bought were the Blessings ones from California, back in 2007. It was a complete revelation at the time to buy a commercially produced raw product like that. We used to import them from California, and we had to charge a fortune for them because of all the shipping and customs, but we still sold a ton of them. The reason the Blessings chips taste so good, I am sure, is that the woman who ran the company had Tibetan monks working for her. All the kale chips were hand massaged and blessed by Tibetan monks! How cool is that?

As you may know, I'm not such a big fan of cashews. There's a reason they are inside that poisonous fruit, I believe, and that's 'cos we are not meant to eat too much of them. I know they taste great, and make the most delicious raw creams and mayonnaises, but they don't feel good in my body at all. So I would say, enjoy these, but definitely don't overeat on them.

Ingredients

500g (1 lb) kale
1 cup (100g) cashews
½ cup (125ml) olive oil
1 tsp seaweed salt
1 fresh date
¼ red onion
1 clove garlic
juice 1 lemon
½ cup (125ml) water

Serves 4
You need to pre-soak your cashews for 4-8 hours. The kale chips will take about 15 mins to make. Then they need 18 hours in the dehydrator.
You need a blender and a dehydrator

Pre-soak your cashews for at least four hours. Please use raw ones! Normal cashews that you buy in the whole food store are very acidic and congesting for the body. If you haven't got proper raw cashews, please consider using sunflower seeds or brazil nuts instead of non-raw cashews.

When your cashews are ready, tear your kale into pieces ready for the dehydrator. Remove any excess stalks as these go woody and indigestible when they are dried. There is no need to worry about breaking your kale leaves into tiny pieces. I like them as big leaves, plus if you want to break them down, it's much easier to do it once they are dried and crispy.

To make your sauce, drain the cashews and put them in the blender with all the other ingredients: olive oil, salt, a date, red onion, garlic, lemon juice and water. Blend for a minute until creamy. Don't worry if it tastes too oniony at this stage; the onions will change flavour in the dehydrator and, along with the cashews, imbue the kale chips with their irresistible flavour. Pour the cashew mixture over the kale, and mix thoroughly, so the kale is evenly coated. Spread over three or four dehydrator trays and dry for eighteen hours. After about twelve hours it's good to turn them and check that some aren't still a bit soggy; it tends to be that while most are drying, some get clumped together or have more dressing on, so you want to separate these ones out so they dry properly.

I have been making kale (or spinach or chard or greens) chips more or less every week for over a decade now, and I still have to tell you, I have no idea how long they keep because they have never been known to last more than a couple of hours in our house.

Dragon's Spines

The purple sauce over the deep green spines is a very magical combination, befitting of a dragon. I don't like to eat a lot of nuts, so this sauce made with pumpkin seeds sits much better in my belly than the cashew ones more commonly made. Cavalo nero (or black kale), is a particular variety of kale which has long thin stems. It is particularly suited to this recipe because of its shape, but if you can't find it, curly kale will work just fine, it just won't be so aesthetically pleasing.

Ingredients

1 cup (100g) pumpkin seeds (soaked 2-4 hours)
½ red onion, peeled and chopped
½ cup (125ml) olive oil
½ cup (125ml) water
1 tsp purple corn extract
1 tbsp yacon syrup or raw honey
¼ tsp rock salt
2 tbsp apple cider vinegar
350g (12oz) cavalo nero

Serves 4
You need to pre-soak 2-4 hours, then it takes 20 mins to actually make them. They'll need dehydrating 12-18 hours.
You need a blender and a dehydrator

Pre-soak your pumpkin seeds. When they are ready, drain them, and put them in the blender with all the other ingredients, apart from the cavalo nero. Blend for a minute, until you have a smooth cream.

Take your cavalo nero leaves, washing them first if necessary. Snap off any end stems that don't have leaves on. These stems are too fibrous to digest. If you leave stems on, they can act as a handle, kind of like a lollipop stick! When you are eating your Dragon's Spines, once they are done, you will probably find you will have to chew round the middle stems and discard them, like chicken bones.

Take your largest mixing bowl, and put in as many cavalo nero leaves as will comfortably fit. Pour around half the sauce over them, and mix them with your hands, trying to make sure the leaves are evenly covered in the sauce, all over. When you're satisfied, lay them out on a dehydrator tray, placing the leaves side by side. Continue coating more leaves with more sauce until they are all done (depending on the size of your bowl, this will probably take two or three goes). You should have three to four trays laid out. If you have any sauce left, you can use it as a dip or a salad dressing.

Dehydrate for 12-18 hours, turning at around 8 hours if possible to make sure they are crispy on both sides. Once they are crispy, they are done – not before!

Smoked Paprika & Balsamic Vinegar Kale Chips

I was thinking of doing entire book on kale chips at one point, I have so many amazing kale chip recipes. I have made them so many times, and so there's lots of tips and tricks I've learnt about making the best ones. These ones taste like smoky bacon crisps.

Ingredients

400g (1 lb) curly kale
4 tbsp extra virgin olive oil
1 tbsp balsamic vinegar
1 tbsp smoked paprika
1 cup (25g) dulse flakes
2 tsp tamari

Serves 4
Takes 10 minutes to make and 12 hours to dehydrate
You need a dehydrator

I find curly kale works best for kale chips. Other varieties absorb less oil, so if you're using a different variety e.g. cavalo nero, use your judgement to get the oil right. I also find it depends on the quality of oil you use – the better the oil, the less you need.

Prepare your kale by washing it and removing stems. I have found the easiest way to prepare the kale is to keep the leaves whole, rather than tearing them into pieces. Firstly, this is quicker, but secondly, you get much bigger chips to bite into. So, I just remove the thick end stems, and put the leaves in a large bowl.

Once all your kale is in the bowl, pour over all the remaining ingredients – oil, vinegar, paprika, dulse and tamari. Mix it all together with your hands. I don't squeeze it in as I would if I was making kale salad, I just make sure it is evenly covered in the dressing.

Spread it over two trays of your dehydrator. Dry for 12 hours. You don't need to turn it or test it, it will crisp up all by itself.

It is very tempting to eat the whole batch in a single sitting! Kale is THE most nutritious vegetable, and our bodies love us for feeding it to us in large amounts. But I would say 100g kale chips is a good amount to eat in a single sitting. More than that can cause a little, shall we say, ahem, digestive disturbance...

Kate's Kale Krisps

I have written about my love affair with Kale many times. I guess we have so much in common. Just one small "–" between us. Kate, Kale, see. If you wish to join me in my unmitigated adoration of kale, you could purchase a kale necklace from Christy Robinson, or a kale t-shirt from my friend Judita at City & Sea Trading, or get a kale leaf tattooed on your arm, all of which I am proud to say I have done.

Ingredients

400g (1 lb) kale
1 cup (90g) shelled hemp seeds
3 tomatoes
4 sticks celery
2 tbsp extra virgin olive oil
1 lemon, juiced
1 clove garlic
¼ tsp salt

Serves 4
Takes 10 mins to make and 8 hours to dehydrate
Essential equipment: dehydrator and blender

Tear the kale, and remove any excess woody stems. Prepare your tomatoes and celery for the blender, so they are in small enough bits not to get stuck in the blades. Blend up all the ingredients apart from the kale – hemp, tomatoes, celery, olive oil, lemon juice, garlic and salt. You should have a runny cream. Toss the kale in the sauce, so it's coated evenly.

Spread over dehydrating trays – two or three should do it. Dry for 8-12 hours, until crispy. As they taste so incredible, you may want to put a portion aside and eat them as they are, before dehydrating. Or if you eat some when they have been in for just a couple of hours and they are moist and warm, they are mind-blowingly good like that as well.

Kaleola

I stayed with Marketa and Joginder of The Tree of Life, in Birmingham in 2011, and Marketa told me she loves buckwheat so much she even puts it on her kale chips. Inspired, I decided to try it out for myself and found that the addition of buckwheat really grounds out the whole kale chip experience. If you're a kalechipaholic, like me, you'll find that the buckwheat slows you down and makes the kale chips even more of a meal to themselves.

Ingredients

100g (1 cup) buckwheat sprouts
100g (1 cup) sunflower seeds, soaked 2-4 hours
¼ cup (60ml) olive oil
1 lemon, juiced
1 clove garlic
¼ tsp salt
½ cup (125ml) water
300g (10oz) kale

Serves 3
You need to sprout the buckwheat two or three days in advance, and soak your seeds 2-4 hours in advance. They only take 15 mins to make, but then you've got to wait another 18 hours until they are out of the dehydrator.
You need a blender and a dehydrator

Make sure you have some buckwheat sprouts ready, ideally ones that have been sprouting for two to three days. Also soak your sunflower seeds in advance, for at least two hours.

To make the dressing, put your sunflower seeds, olive oil, lemon juice, garlic and salt in the blender. Add the water gradually while the blender is turning, to make a smooth creamy dressing.

Take the kale and remove any excess stems. I have found it best not to tear the kale into tiny pieces but to leave the leaves whole. However, if your kale has long stems, you do want to remove them. I like to use curly kale the best. Put the buckwheat sprouts in the bowl with the kale and mix them together evenly. It's important you do this now because once you pour the dressing on, everything starts to get stuck together. When you're satisfied it's evenly mixed, pour the dressing over and give it another good mix, with a spoon or by hand. It should be just the right amount of dressing to evenly coat the kale and buckwheat.

Spread the kale over two or three drying trays and dry for about 18 hours. It helps to turn the kale after about 12 hours, otherwise it stays soft on the bottom. N.B. this is NOT an excuse to eat half the kale chips, "just to check" if they are ready.

Thai Green Curry Chips

One thing I've noticed when making kale chips is that the amount of dressing you need varies according to the type of kale you're using. Cavalo nero seems to absorb less dressing than curly kale. Green kale needs more than red kale. So bear this in mind when making your chips. Also, if you can't get kale, I've made chips very successfully with spring greens and Savoy cabbage. It works with spinach and chard as well, although you need a lot less dressing as they are so much thinner. I tried chicory (endive) once as well, but that didn't work!

Ingredients

500g (1 lb) kale
5 tbsp extra virgin olive oil
2 tsp Thai green curry paste
juice ½ lemon
¼ tsp salt
2 tbsp nori flakes
2 tbsp pumpkin seeds, soaked

Serves 4
Takes 10 mins to make. You need to pre-soak pumpkin seeds for at least 2 hours, and you'll need to dehydrate them for at least 12 hours.
You need a dehydrator

Soak your pumpkin seeds in advance for at least a couple of hours. Tear your kale into small pieces and place in a large bowl. In a small bowl, mix your dressing ingredients: olive oil, curry paste, lemon juice and salt. I use Geo-Organics Thai green curry paste, which isn't very spicy; you may want to adjust the levels of spice according to how hot the paste you use is. Sprinkle the nori flakes over the kale. Drain the pumpkin seeds and sprinkle those over as well. Toss the kale, so the nori and pumpkin seeds are evenly mixed. Then pour your dressing over and toss again.

When you're ready, put them in the dehydrator. They should cover two or three trays. You're looking at drying them for at least 12 hours, maybe a little longer, until they are proper crispy. As always with kale chips, I'm sorry I can't tell you how well they keep because I have no experience of them lasting longer than a day.

The Best Salt & Vinegar Crisps in the World

Really, honestly, truly, the best. Probably in the entire galaxy, if we are being honest.

Ingredients

400g (1 lb) kale
¼ cup (60ml) extra virgin olive oil
¼ cup (25g) shelled hemp
1 tbsp baobab powder
1 tbsp apple cider vinegar
¼ tsp Icelandic salt

Serves 4
Takes 10 minutes to make and 12 hours to dehydrate
You need a dehydrator

Remove any excess stems from your kale. I find it works best to leave the kale in big pieces rather than tear it into small bits, but you want to make sure you don't have too many woody stems. Put the kale in a large bowl, and add your dry ingredients: the hemp seeds, baobab, and salt. Mix well - with your hands is probably easiest. Make sure the ingredients are easily distributed because once the liquids are poured on it will start to stick together, and you don't want some kale chips covered in baobab, and others totally lacking any. When you're ready, pour over your oil and vinegar, and give it another good mix, making sure all the hemp seeds are coating the kale and not left in the bottom of the bowl.

Spread over three dehydrator trays and dry for around 12 hours. These kale chips don't stay crispy for long once they are out of the dehydrator. If they've been out for a few hours and have started to go soggy, just put them back in the dehydrator and they crisp up in no time – around 15 mins.

Sweet & Spicy Kale Chips

Inspired by Juliano, a legendary LA raw chef. I don't know how he gets his kale chips quite so amazingly gooey and chewy, probably by using more oil and honey than I would dare to. These might not reach the same heights as Juliano's but they are still pretty awesome.

Ingredients

2 tbsp pumpkin seeds, soaked
500g (1 lb) kale
2 tbsp nori flakes
½ cup (125ml) extra virgin olive oil
2 tsp hot chilli sauce or 1 tsp chilli powder
¼ cup yacon syrup or honey
juice ½ lemon
¼ tsp salt

Serves 4
You need to pre-soak your pumpkin seeds for a couple of hours. Then they take 10 minutes to make and 16 hours to dehydrate.
You need a dehydrator

Pre-soak your pumpkin seeds for at least 2 hours.

Tear your kale into little pieces. Remove any excess woody stems. Put it in a very large bowl. Drain your soaked pumpkin seeds and tip them over the kale. Sprinkle the nori flakes over as well. Mix them together well. In a separate bowl, mix the olive oil, chilli, honey or yacon, lemon, and salt. Whisk them together with a hand whisk or a fork, then pour over the kale. Toss well, so the kale is well-covered.

When it's ready, spread over three dehydrator trays. Dry for 12 hours, then flip them over to make sure they get done on both sides. Dry for another 4 hours, then they are ready. Praise the Lord for blessing us with so much kale on this planet and eat to your heart's content (although please try and remember this recipe says FOUR suggested servings. Not, eat in four minutes. Or eat at 4pm. No, it means share between four people. Or at least make them last four days).

Greener Kale Chips

How green can you go? Kale is the most nutritious vegetable, and when you cover it in green powder like this, you are getting such a mega-dose of nutrients that your body may just decide to clone itself just so it can give you a big hug and tell you how wonderful you are for filling it with the most beneficial foods you can find.

Ingredients

400g (14oz) kale
¼ cup (60ml) olive oil
2 tbsp Raw Living Greener Grass powder
2 lemons, juiced
½ large or 1 small red onion

Serves 4
Takes 10 mins to make and at least 12 hours to dehydrate
You just need a dehydrator

Prepare the kale by removing any excess stems. You don't need to tear it into small pieces at this stage, just discard any yellowing leaves. Put it all in a large bowl, and pour the Greener Grass over it. I use Greener Grass because I love it! But you can use any green powder blend. I would think just using a straight green powder such as spirulina or barleygrass would be a bit overpowering though. If you want to do that, I would recommend halving the quantities given i.e. just try it with 1 tbsp powder. Toss the leaves in the green powder so they are evenly coated. Then dice your onion into tiny pieces, and mix that in as well. Finally, pour your olive oil and lemon juice over the kale and give it all another thorough mix.

Put it in your dehydrator: it should fill two or three trays. Don't try and cram it in or it won't dry properly. Dry for 12 hours. Eat and enjoy knowing that you are eating by far the healthiest snack food known to man.

The Myth of 100% Raw

I always talk about how raw is a journey not a destination. Cliché it may be, but the point of doing raw foods is to develop a relationship with your body based on a state of presence and awareness. It is not about reaching a finite point in time when you suddenly are "raw" and can stop trying, and go back to sleep.

Personally, I would say I am 95% raw. I never intentionally eat cooked food, although I am sure I regularly consume food that has been heated over 42°C – the raisins that went in my cookies maybe, or the arame that was in the salad I ate at someone's house. I use non-raw seasonings such as balsamic vinegar and miso. Many of the superfoods I use regularly like chlorella, barleygrass and reishi have been heat-treated in preparation. When I make tea, I am heating my herbs way over 42°.

I know if I were to cook a meal and eat it, I would experience a dip in energy that I do not enjoy. I know just a mouthful of cooked food, such as a piece of steamed vegetable, holds little interest for me. But equally, I have never noticed any negative side effects from a dash of rice vinegar in my sushi, and I certainly feel the benefits of consuming foods such as chlorella far outweigh the fact that they are not raw.

It's important to remember that the idea behind raw foods is that when we cook food over a certain temperature, we kill the enzymes, and the enzymes are basically the life-force in the food. So although we may have destroyed the living energy, many of the minerals, vitamins, proteins, fats etc. still remain in abundance and we can therefore derive plenty of benefits from consuming that food in its non-raw form. If most of your food is raw and delivering a high enzyme content, small amounts of carefully chosen heated foods are not going to have an adverse effect on the body.

I travel around a lot, and am blessed to personally know the majority of raw food chefs, authors and educators in the world. And something I have noticed, is that very few of us are actually 100% raw. I am not going to start giving examples, because that's not the point of the article. Although I would say that it seems to be that the more dogmatic a person is in their approach, the less likely it seems that that's what they do themselves the majority of the time! Most of my friends who are making a career out of sharing the benefits of raw foods take a balanced approach. And most of them eat cooked food regularly. There is no shame in this: it's normal.

I don't know if there is such a thing as a 100% raw-fooder. I think if you examined the diet of even the most committed raw-fooder you would find that some foods they include regularly have been heat-treated. Even the 95%ers like me are very rare. I would say out of all leading raw food educators in Europe and America, 70-80% is where most of them sit.

I love my yoga, and I've been practicing for over thirty years. And at first, you look at all the teachers with their fantastic physiques and calm demeanours and assume that they can achieve the full expression of all the postures with ease and grace. As I have got to know many teachers, I discover that that is not the case. They have stuck areas in their bodies as well, even after practicing for years. They have postures they struggle to achieve, despite their on-going commitment. And that's what makes them yogis and yoginis. Their ability to trust in the process without depending on perfection as a result.

It's the same with raw foods. A raw-fooder is someone who has a commitment to listening to their body and eating with consciousness and awareness. Someone who is engaged in the journey, and who trusts in its unfolding without expecting some idealistic idea of perfection of themselves. It's so much more helpful to be realistic, to let go of the attachment of trying to do something rigidly, and to accept that for 95% of us, 95% of the time, 100% is just a myth.

Some of the raw food classes 2008-2019, including Brighton, Manchester, Cornwall, Scotland, Jersey, France, Iceland, Sweden, Denmark, Goa, Costa Rica, Barbados and more!

153

Ferments

Fermentation is such an art! It's one of those wonderful subjects that truly, the more I learn about it, the less I feel I know. It's been enjoying a massive revival, and I think that's a lot to do with how it's so much about sharing – the culture demands that as it grows, you pass it on, both literally and metaphorically.

The generally agreed-upon modern fermenters' Bible is The Art of Fermentation by Sandor Ellix Katz. Sandor is an amazing man, a Californian who was diagnosed as HIV positive, and has used fermented foods to keep the disease at bay. He is very eloquent on the importance of these foods: he says, a person cannot live a cultured life, without cultured foods. Of course, I am very much of the school of "you are what you eat," so I totally subscribe to the idea that these artisanal foods, that need to be made with so much care and attention, will serve us much better than the mass-produced fare we are standardly served up.

But the real magic of fermentation lies in the bacteria. You may know that we are made up of countless cells, something in the region of 50 trillion. But did you know we also contain more bacteria than cells. Ten times as much! That's right, we think of ourselves as a solid, definable entity, but actually what we are is host to a whole population of uninvited beings. Some of these are friendly and some not so much, and it's the friendly ones we want to cultivate, and that are present in fermented foods.

An emerging field known as neurogastroenterology looks at how intricately connected the brain and the gut are, and how our gut health affects our mental well-being, as well as our immunity. The gut is literally a second brain; in fact, I think it would be more accurate to call it the first brain, as there is more sentient activity happening in the gut than there is the mind. The gut and the brain are inextricably linked, sending signals back and forth constantly. This is why when we improve our diets, one of the most remarkable changes we notice is the improvement in our moods and our outlook. The gut is the seat of good health, it's where it all begins, and getting the right balance there is fundamental: we can't have a healthy mind and body if we don't have a healthy gut. So consuming fermented foods daily is one of the best health practices we can adopt, in order that they can repopulate our guts, and get the whole body system back into balance. There is also a lot of research showing links between the rise in autistic spectrum disorders, and lack of healthy gut bacteria. If you're interested in learning more, a good starting point is the work of Dr Natasha Campbell McBride.

There are many different styles of ferments, but they basically break down into two categories: those that use yeast, and those that depend on lactic acid. The two work very differently in the body, and for health purposes, we want to consider lacto-fermentation. This covers sourdoughs, yoghurts, cheeses, miso and tempeh, all kinds of vegetables, many kinds of drinks, and that's just for starters. What they all have in common is using the presence of the lactobacillus strain of bacteria to start the breakdown of the food. This makes the food more digestible in itself, and also is the ideal way to promote these friendly bacteria in the gut.

One of the reasons that fermentation is so fascinating, is that you can learn all the rules, and yet someone will always come along who is getting results, while breaking them! You could interview ten different people on how to make kefir, and although there would be commonalities, every person would tell you a different thing that you must or mustn't do to make it work. As we are talking about cultivating living organisms rather than soufflé recipes, I think we have to think about it in terms of looking after pets, rather than making dinner, for a successful approach. If you interviewed ten people about how to make a Shepherd's Pie, you're going to get some variation, but if you ask them how to look after their cats, the answers would vary much more wildly. So it is with fermentation. The key is to building up a successful relationship with your cultures. Listen to them, hear what they are telling you. This might sound a little out there, but as mothers you can all relate! It's the same set of skills you apply to looking after your baby. You sharpen your intuition, you focus your intention, and a kind of telepathy develops, a conversation beyond words.

Having said that, here are some of the basic rules that you would be wise to apply.

- **Sterilisation** is key. You want the friendly bacteria to proliferate, not the unfriendly ones. Sterilisation is actually really simple. You can do it in an Aga, if you have one. You can do it in the oven. I do it by pouring boiling water over my utensils. (See! I say to my boys. That's why we don't cook. Boiling water kills everything!) If your equipment isn't clean, your efforts will simply turn to mold.

- **Temperature** makes a huge difference. Most ferments do best in ambient temperatures of around 60-70°F. If it's colder than that, fermentation will slow down. That's why, once your product is ready, you keep it in the fridge. If you are going away and you want to store it, you can freeze it, which will stop fermentation entirely. If it's much hotter than 70°, fermentation will speed up. This might sound like a good thing, but it's not. You need a certain time period for the correct processes to happen properly.

- **Time** is essential. In our time-poor culture, we like to rush things and think that quicker is better. If there's anything I've learnt in this life, it's that the things that demand a long-term investment are the most worthwhile, and the things that are quickly won never ultimately mean as much. Again, as parents that's a concept you must be all too familiar with. We need patience with our little ones when we are helping them to learn how to walk, or read, or tie their shoes, and we need patience with our ferments if we want to get the best out of them.

Finally, I thought it would be helpful to share with you a little on what the most popular lacto-fermented foods are, so that you if you come across them online or in the shops, you will be a little less perplexed.

- The two most popular fermented drinks are kefir and kombucha. Both are sweet, fizzy, and very delicious. Most people have a preference for one over the other – I am a kombucha girl. They are both living organisms or scobys, which stands for Symbiotic Organism of Bacteria and Yeast. Kefir feeds on sugar, kombucha on tea and sugar. Yes, you need sugar! It's the first question every health-conscious person asks. Do I have to use sugar? Yes, you do, the whiter the better! But don't worry, your little friends are going to eat it for you, so as long as you ferment properly there is none left in the finished drink.

- The most well-known of the **fermented vegetables** is cabbage. This is because cabbage naturally contains an abundance of the lactobacillus bacteria which we want to proliferate, so cabbage is the easiest one to start with. But once you're confident, you can ferment just about any vegetable. My favourite is Kimchi, which is a traditional Korean dish, fermented in a red chilli paste. If you're trying Kimchi, make sure you buy it from an authentic Korean store as there are a lot of pale imitations around (and also, vegans, check it doesn't contain fish sauce).

- **Sourdough** is a fermented bread, which doesn't need yeast. A sourdough culture is a mix of water and flour, which is left exposed so that it can pick up wild yeasts, and then be a starter for bread-making. It's not gluten-free, but it is possible to get specific gluten-free cultures made from rice flour.

- **Miso, tamari and tempeh** are all Japanese cultured products that are easy to pick up in the health food store. Just make sure to look for the unpasteurised versions, as these have the enzymes intact, and so are a lot more beneficial.

So I hope that's whetted your appetite, both literally and metaphorically. Fermented foods are a wonderful thing to do yourself, but if you're not quite ready for that, you might just find yourself more inclined to reach for the kombucha or sauerkraut next time you're in the health food store. Lacto-fermentation is a big part of many different food cultures around the world, but strangely not in the UK (we seem to have concentrated on the less healthy yeast-fermented foods like beer and bread), so it's time we changed that and initiated our own Fermentation Revolution, for the health of ourselves and our families.

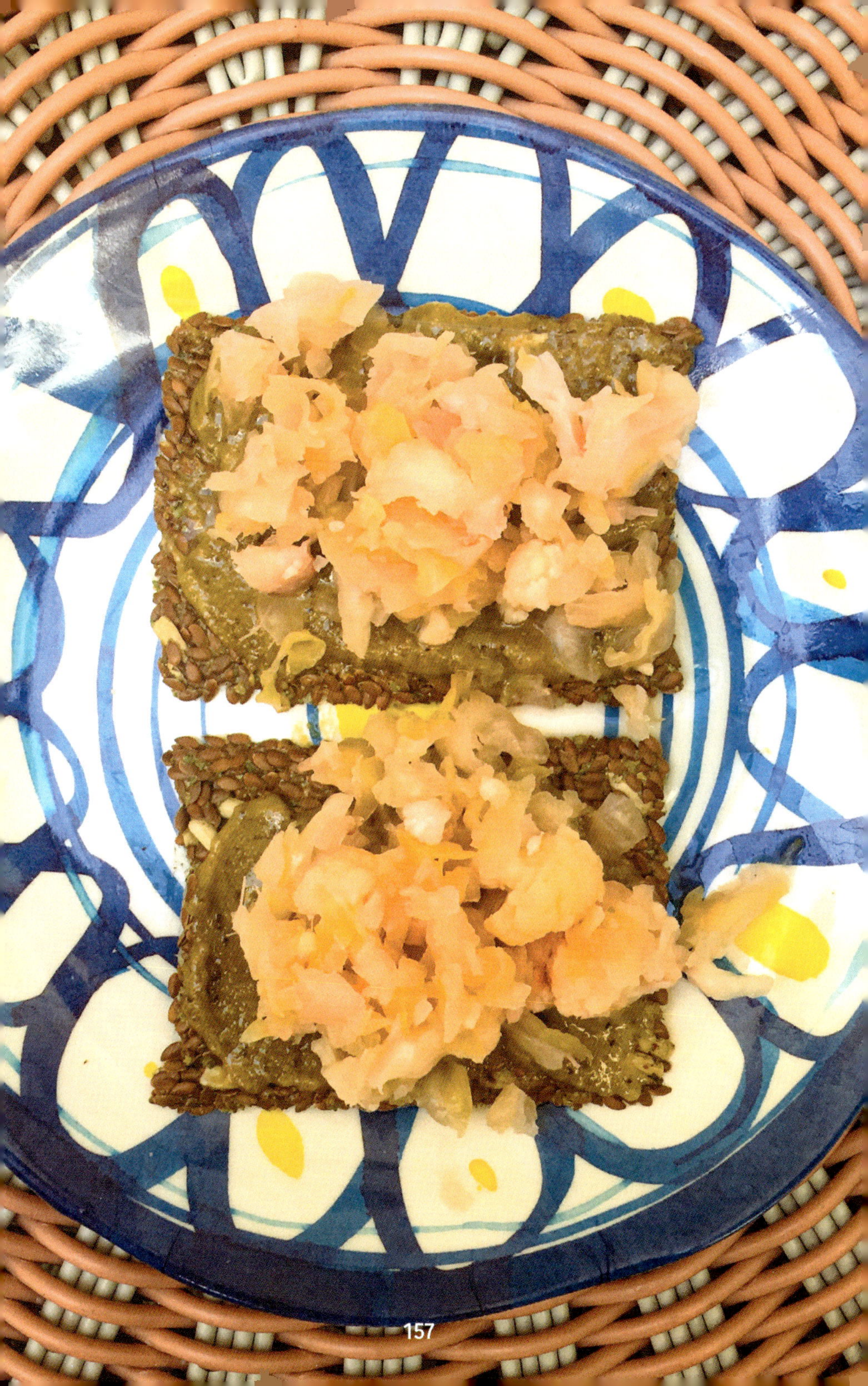

Kefir

I was introduced to Kefir by Ani Phyo, when I stayed with her in her home in LA in 2009. It is a living culture that is used to make fermented drinks. These drinks are known for their probiotic effects, and the huge benefits they can have on the gut and digestion. For this reason, it's best to have kefir first thing in the morning and/or last thing at night. It's also nice to have a small glass after a meal. I find it delicious and very refreshing, and when I started drinking it I noticed how it improved the efficiency in my digestion, and reduced bloating.

You can buy your grains online, or even in some health food stores now, but they are always happiest when they are passed on by a friend. They are very sensitive creatures, and I don't think they like being bought and sold.

Regarding the sugar, everyone asks, do you have to use sugar, and the answer is yes! The whiter and nastier, the better. I compromise by buying organic fairtrade light brown sugar. But coconut sugar, agave, honey, rapadura – none of that works. I heard someone say once, "Don't worry, the sugar isn't for you, it's for the kefir." If you do the process correctly, the grains will digest all the sugar, so you don't have to.

I highly recommend starting to make your own kefir. Once you've purchased the initial grains, it's going to cost you pennies to produce a delicious drink that in the health food stores would cost at least five times the price, come in some kind of packaging you'd need to find a way to dispose of, and probably wouldn't taste quite as wonderful! (Although, having said that, the Purearth brand is quite divine, if you come across it). The only issue is, it is like having a pet, and you have to take responsibility for it; kefir dies easily if you don't give it enough love and attention.

Important points to remember

- Kefir doesn't like metal. You need to use glass, plastic or wood – no metal spoons or sieves.

- I use Kilner jars and I find they are actually very happy with the jar sealed. It makes them bubblier and ferment quicker.

- Water kefir and milk kefir are different strains of grains. You can't interchange them. You can use unpasteurised fruit juice or coconut water with water kefir. I have come across grape kefir and apple kefir on my travels! Milk kefir needs dairy milk.

- Healthy kefir grows – so be prepared to increase the amount you are making, or give it away to a grateful friend.

- The better your water, the happier your kefir. Tap water will kill it. It likes minerals, so a good quality spring water is best.

- Good kefir will be fizzy, and the perfect balance between sweet and sour.

Basic Recipe

½ cup kefir grains
¼ cup sugar
2 figs or dates
1 litre pure water

Put everything into a glass container and stir with a wooden spoon. Leave for a minimum of three days – many people say this is enough, but I would be concerned about the relatively high sugar content. I leave mine for 4-7 days. When you're ready, strain it off with a plastic sieve. Make a second ferment if you wish. Rinse the grains, and start a new batch.

Second Ferment (24 hours)

Try chopped fresh fruit, dried fruit, ginger & turmeric (juice, powder or grated), vanilla pods, Medicine Flower Extracts, or freeze-dried fruit powders.

Kombucha

I love kombucha so much! It's up there with raw chocolate and green juice as one of my go-to panaceas. So here's what I know.

- A happy scoby makes a fizzy ferment! They really respond to the atmosphere in your kitchen and how much attention you give them. I talk to my scobies often and tell them how much I love them.
- As with kefir, no metal allowed, and I use Kilner jars with the lid sealed. Make sure you've got a gap at the top of the jar, don't fill them to the top.
- The kombucha makes babies. One day you will discover where there used to be one scoby now there are two. It kind of splits itself into half, so the baby is as big as the parent. You can either start making more batches, or give it away.
- You can use any kind of caffeinated black tea. I favour the Japanese teas oolong or kukicha.

Basic Recipe

1 scoby
½ cup sugar
2 litres pure water
4 figs or dates
2 tea bags

First, make the tea, and add the sugar. Once the tea is cooled, add the scoby in, along with ½ cup previous ferment (you need this as a starter), and the figs or dates. Many people use more tea than I do, experiment and see what works for you.

Leave for 7-10 days. Strain, bottle for a second ferment, and start again.

Second Ferment

As for kefir.

I also love medicinal mushrooms e.g. chaga, cordyceps, reishi. I use the Four Sigmatic Instants sachets. I think the Cordyceps one tastes like coca cola!

A Note on Jun

Jun is another fermented drink, shrouded in mystery. Even a Google search doesn't reveal much on it. I first had it in California, made by Herbal Junction Elixirs and fell head over heels in love. The story is that the people at Herbal Junction were introduced to it by Tibetan Monks, and it's a rare scoby from Tibet, but I'm not sure if I believe that. I'm not sure why the monks would have particularly blessed some Oakland hippies. Others say that it is just kombucha scoby that has been trained differently, but I don't believe that either, I think it is a slightly different beast. I am fortunate enough to have my own jun scoby and make it at home. It's still very rare, and it's slightly different from kombucha because whereas kombuchas scobies favour black tea and sugar, jun feeds on green tea and honey. If you ever come across the chance to try Jun, seize it, it's very special, the champagne of kombuchas.

Cheese-Making

Although I never liked milk, or eggs, I used to love cheese and yoghurt as a child. As a vegan, I was pretty fond of Scheese. So now I've got the raw vegan cheese thing down, I'm quite pleased with myself, and cheese sandwiches have become a staple part of my diet (we actually make and eat them on the Superstar course that I teach).

Most people do cashew cheese, and I learnt that it's because the high carbohydrate content in cashews lends itself well to the kind of consistency we are looking for. You can do almond cheese, but getting that right involves peeling your almonds, and that's simply not my style. Sunflower seeds are my preferred staple. Sometimes I do pumpkin seeds, but you have to make sure you have the raw pumpkin seeds or your cheese just goes moldy.

Ingredients

2 cups (250g) sunflower seeds, soaked 2-4 hours
½ cup (125ml) olive oil
2 tsp turmeric powder
1 tbsp baobab powder
pinch salt
¼ cup (60ml) kombucha vinegar
water to blend

Makes about 16 servings
Takes a while! Up to a week
You need a milk bag, a blender, and a large bowl with a flat base

I also do blue cheese with a teaspoon of blue-green algae, or a darker cheese with a teaspoon of lion's mane or shiitake powder.

So here are the tricks:

Don't soak your seeds for too long, or your cheese will go off! When they are ready, drain them, and put them in the blender with all the other ingredients.

If you haven't got kombucha vinegar, you can use 1 teaspoon of probiotic powder instead. However, I find I get way better results using the vinegar. Kombucha vinegar is basically just really over-brewed kombucha (well, it is in my house!). It's not fizzy and it's very vinegary. And it makes the best cheese. If you haven't got it, I'm pretty sure old kefir would work, or if you've got the liquid off some proper raw sauerkraut, that would work as well.

The next tricky bit is adding just enough water to get it smooth, but not too much so it's not runny. Try half a cup (125ml) first of all, if your blender isn't so good, you might need more. It's essential it gets smooth at this stage.

When you're happy with the consistency, you need to get your milk bag, and a bowl with a large flat base (or a flan dish will do equally as well). Pour your sunflower seed mixture into the milk bag, and put it in the bowl, ideally a couple of inches high. Fold the bag over so it's covering the top of the cheese. Then you need something heavy to press it down – I use a small Kilner jar filled with water, or a jar of fermenting kraut or pickles. Leave it out for 12-24 hours and liquid should seep out of it, leaving you with a semi-firm cheese. The liquid is very tart, I usually keep it and use it in a salad dressing.

Once you're ready for the next stage, take two plates. Remove the weight, and peel the bag back from the top of the cheese. Turn it onto one of the plates. Then peel the other side of the bag back, and flip the cheese onto the second plate. Wrap it in greaseproof paper to stop any mold forming, and store it in the fridge. Basically, now it's ready, but the longer you leave it, the firmer and tastier it gets. I find it's at its optimum when it's around seven days old, but I find it hard to leave it that long.

My favourite use for it, as I said, is cheese & crackers, and cheese sandwiches. When it's only a day or two old, and not so firm, I may mash some of it up, and use it as a probiotic dressing for kelp noodles or kale.

I Can't Believe It's Not Boursin

In Raw Magic in Costa Rica, we made a blue cheese, and one of the participants, Andrea, said that it tasted like Boursin. Which inspired me to go home and perfect an actual Boursin alternative. I had been making cheese regularly for a few years now, and really getting the knack of it, but I have to say, this recipe takes it to a whole new level. Shaping it into rounds and wrapping it in greaseproof paper is another layer of effort involved, but it makes the cheeses look and taste that bit more professional, and I suspect it makes them keep longer as well. If Boursin isn't something you have in your country, then let me enlighten you: it's a French soft herbed cheese which comes in small rounds. This is just as creamy, just as herby, and just as moreish.

Ingredients

2 cups (200g) sunflower seeds
2 tbsp baobab
½ cup (125ml) kombucha vinegar (or ½ cup water + 5g probiotics)
½ cup (125ml) extra virgin olive oil
½ cup (125ml) water
½ tsp salt
1 lemon, juiced
3 tbsp dried Herbs de Provence

Makes 4-6 rounds
Takes 10 mins to make with 4 hours pre-soaking and 1 week to ferment
You need a blender, a milk bag, a cutter, and some greaseproof paper

Soak the sunflower seeds in advance for 2-4 hours. It's important not to oversoak them or your cheese will spoil. When they are ready, drain them, and put them in the blender with all the other ingredients apart from the herbs. My experience is that using kombucha (or kefir or jun) vinegar makes the best cheese. You just make the vinegar by leaving it fermenting for too long! So it's not fizzy anymore and has a vinegar flavour rather than being sweet. Two weeks should suffice. I use this vinegar a lot in salad dressings and cracker batters as well as cheese-making. However, if you haven't got any, you can just use water and use some probiotic powder to ferment.

Blend everything to a thick cream, and then stir in the herbs by hand. Spoon the mixture out of the blender and into a milk bag. Put the milk bag in a large bowl, and press it down with something heavy; I use a Kilner jar filled with water, or a jar of kraut or honey. Leave it at room temperature for 24 hours.

The next stage is to make the rounds. You need a cookie cutter approx. 7cm (3") in diameter. Tip your cheese out of the bag and onto a large plate. Use the cutter to cut rounds of cheese and transfer them to another plate. You will have a fair bit of cheese left that didn't go into the cutters: you can either squish it together and make another round, or do what I usually do which is store it in the fridge and use as a cheese spread.

Then you need to get your greaseproof paper and cut it into squares large enough to wrap the cheese in. Fold it over neatly and seal it on the bottom with tape. Put your wrapped cheeses in the fridge and ideally leave for a week. At this stage they will be nice and firm and slice really well. There's no harm in eating them sooner, just they won't be as firm. Wrapping it in smaller rounds like this helps preserve it for longer, and I've been able to leave them a couple of weeks and they are still good.

Kimchi

I was definitely Korean in a past life. It's the only possible explanation for how I took to Kimchi like a raw vegan duck to alkalised water. A lot of Westerners say they make Kimchi. What they really mean is they put some chilli in their sauerkraut. Go find an authentic Korean kimchi and you will see what I mean. Just be careful it hasn't got fish sauce in – many of them do, but not all. The secret, I think, is in the method, and also in getting some proper Korean chilli flakes.

Ingredients

2 litres water
2 tbsp salt
1 Chinese leaf
1 mooli
2 carrots
½ cup gojis
50g ginger
25g red chillis
1 tbsp Korean chilli flakes (gochugaru)
1 tsp kelp powder

Makes 12 servings
Timewise it's a little laborious. You need to make the brine, which takes as long as it needs for hot water to cool down. Then you need to soak your veggies in the brine for 12 hours. Actually making the kimchi takes about 30 mins. Then you leave it to ferment for at least a week.
You need a 2 litre Kilner jar, and a large bowl. Plus some disposable gloves.

There are two ways of lacto-fermenting vegetables; the way that kimchi is done involves creating a brine and leaving your vegetables in it to soak overnight. To create the brine, I boil 2 litres water and add 2 tbsp salt to it. I just use plain sea salt. I leave it in a large bowl to cool while I set to work on my veggies. I chop the Chinese leaf into quite large pieces, about 2cm diameter. The mooli and the carrots, however, I try to get really thin. You can use a mandolin, a fine slicing blade on your food processor, or the slicing blade on the spiralizer. You can do it by hand, but you won't get them as thin, they'll be a bit chunkier; I like them like that as well. Put all your veg into a large bowl, and once the brine has cooled, pour that over so it covers them. Find a plate that will fit nicely on top, inside the bowl, not over the edges. Then find something heavy to press the plate down. I use a small Kilner jar filled with water. You want to make sure the veggies are fully submerged in the brine, and you're going to leave them for at least 12 hours.

You can either make your paste now and keep it in the fridge, or leave it until the veggies are ready. To make the paste, soak the gojis for at least 30 mins. When they are ready, add them to the blender with the ginger, the kelp powder, and the chilli flakes. Split the red chillis and remove the seeds, and add them in as well. You can add the goji soak water, or you can drink it separately. You need a few tablespoons of brine as well, just enough so you can blend it to a paste.

Once your veggies are ready, you're going to discard your brine, and pour your paste over them. This is where the gloves come in. If you don't use gloves, your hands are going to really sting from all that chilli. You can use disposable catering gloves, or I use clean washing up gloves and keep them reserved as my kimchi gloves. You're going to massage the paste into the leaf, really thoroughly. This should reduce it down quite considerably, so it's no longer filling the bowl. It should also release the juice from the vegetables, so there's quite a bit of liquid there. After 5-10 mins, when you're satisfied you can't do any more, then you're ready to pack it into a Kilner jar. When it was in the bowl at the beginning, it probably looked like it was enough to fill two large Kilner jars. Actually, you only need one medium sized one. Press the kimchi tightly into the jar, really packing it down. You want to make sure the veggies are fully submerged in the liquid. You also need to leave at least a 1-2cm gap at the top of the jar, because as the kimchi ferments, it bubbles, and you will get red juice dribbling out over your counter tops! I would stand the jar on a dish, just to catch any excess. Leave for at least a week – the longer you leave it, the more pungent it becomes.

Fat Sesame Kimchi

This recipe was inspired by a lady called Freddie Janssen, who is famous for her blue cheese and kimchi sandwiches. Well, you know how much I love my cheese, so I was all over that idea. I was already obsessed with kimchi, but this recipe takes it to a whole new level. The addition of some fat in the form of sesame oil makes it even more umami. I've been making kimchi sandwiches, kimchi wraps, and my favourite is kimchi sushi.

Ingredients

1 Chinese cabbage
1 daikon
2 carrots
2 litres water
2 tbsp salt
1 tbsp coconut sugar

3 tbsp Korean chilli flakes
1 tbsp tamari
1 tbsp miso
60ml sesame oil
1 tsp kelp powder
1 tbsp coconut sugar
2cm ginger
1 clove garlic
3 tbsp sesame seeds (black or white)

Takes 12 hours pre-soaking, 15 mins to make and then one week to ferment

You need a 2 litre Kilner jar

Prepare the brine by boiling 2 litres water. Pour into a large bowl and add 2 tbsp salt, and 1 tbsp coconut sugar. Leave to cool. Once it's cooled, chop your Chinese cabbage, daikon and carrots, and put them in the brine. Slice your carrots and daikon into rounds, as thin as you can. Reserve an outer leaf from the Chinese cabbage, and quarter it lengthways, and then cut those quarters into chunks about ½ cm thick. I like it quite chunky. Reserve the stem for later use. Once they are in the brine, place a plate on top to cover, and something heavy to keep the plate weighted down and the veg submerged in the brine. Leave for around 12 hours.

To make the paste, in a small bowl, mix up the chilli flakes, tamari, miso, sesame oil, kelp powder and coconut sugar. Mince the ginger and garlic and stir those in. At the same time, sterilise your Kilner jar by pouring boiling water over it.

Drain the brine off the veggies, reserving a little in case you need it later. Using plastic or rubber gloves, massage the paste into the veg, along with the sesame seeds. Once it's thoroughly mixed, press it into your Kilner jar. Be sure to pack it down so there are no air bubbles left, and the veg is submerged in the juice. If it's not quite submerged you can add a little extra brine. Cover with the leaf you saved at the beginning, and use the stem as a stopper to keep the veg submerged. Clip the lid down and leave for at least a week for the flavours to develop. Once opened, store in the fridge, will keep indefinitely. What I aim to do is make a fresh batch of kimchi once I open a new one. It can take me a few months to get through a jar, so that way it means the jar that's fermenting gets an opportunity for the flavours to really develop, and I never run out.

Ruby Kraut

Here is my favourite way to kraut it. You can halve the amount given if you want, and use a one litre Kilner jar, but as kraut keeps indefinitely, it makes sense to make more in a batch and save yourself time in the future. The dulse and cabbage combine to make this a beautiful ruby colour once it's fermented, hence the name.

Ingredients

2 red cabbages (approx. 1.5kg)
2 cup (50g) dulse flakes
50g root ginger
2 tbsp salt

Makes approx. 16 servings of kraut
You need a 2 litre Kilner jar and a large bowl
Takes 15 mins and at least a week to ferment

Sauerkraut making is not as tricky as it first appears, trust me. Grate your cabbage; it doesn't matter to the process if you fine grate or thickly grate it, as long as it's uniform. Grate the ginger at the same time as the cabbage. I do it in the Thermomix: you need to do it by hand or in a food processor, a high-power blender won't do it. Put the cabbage and ginger in the bowl with the salt – yes, I know it seems like a lot, but you really do need that much. Reserve the end stalks and a couple of outer leaves of the cabbage – you're going to need those later.

Now you're going to massage it really well. This part will take a good 10-15 minutes. At first, it seems like it's not doing anything. But after a while, it will begin to go squelchy as the action of the salt breaks down the fibre in the cabbage, and releases the juices. You have to be really firm with it, squeeze it really hard. You can tell when it's ready, it changes in texture and becomes soft and swimming in juice. At this point, stir in the dulse flakes, and massage them in for another few minutes.

When it's ready, sterilise your Kilner jar – the easiest way to do this is to pour boiling water over it. This step is essential or you will end up with moldy kraut. Let it cool for a minute, and then pack your cabbage mixture into the jar. Press it down firmly. You want to leave just a 2-3cm (1") gap at the top of the jar to prevent spillage as it ferments. You don't want too big a gap though. It's better to pack a smaller jar and have it full, than underfill a larger jar. If you have some that won't fit in the jar, I usually sterilise jam jars, pack it into those, and give it to friends as gifts. You need to make sure that the cabbage is submerged fully in the juice or it will spoil. Take the cabbage leaves and stems that you set aside earlier, and lie them on top to keep the cabbage pressed down. Seal the lid, and leave at room temperature for at least 2 weeks. The longer you leave it, the more fermented it will be. Two to four weeks is ideal. When you don't want it to ferment more, transfer it to the fridge, where it should keep indefinitely.

Variation:

For a yellow kraut, use white cabbage, omit the dulse, and replace the ginger with turmeric root.

Pickled Cucumbers

I learnt how to make these from my friend Asa in East London, who's quite a fermentation expert. She's Swedish, and it's something her family has always traditionally done, so she's got lots of experience, and expert relatives to refer to. Since I started making them, I am completely hooked. They are so easy to do (much easier than kraut or kimchi). Really hard to mess up. And absolutely wonderful to eat. I put them on a cracker, in a sandwich, or in a wrap or a roll. They have more flavour than the jarred pickles that you buy, plus being fermented they have all those wonderful probiotics. When I crack open my jar, they positively fizz. I love them combined with my Middle Eastern Guac and my Suncheese - in a coconut wrap, or on crackers.

Ingredients

3 cucumbers
1 ½ tablespoons salt
1 tsp chilli powder or fresh or dried herbs

Slice the cucumbers into rounds approximately 1cm thick. I find that a little chunkier is better than too thin. Put them in a large bowl, and pour the salt over them. Toss them in the salt so they are evenly coated. Then find a plate that will sit inside the bowl and cover them. And something heavy to press them down - I use a small Kilner jar filled with water. Leave for 12 hours. Then, like magic, you will find that the water has drained out of the cucumbers and they are swimming in their own juice. Add the chilli (you can omit it if you prefer, or add fresh or dried herbs like parsley, dill, oregano – carrot tops work too!), and make sure the cucumbers are evenly covered. Take a 1 litre size Kilner jar, and sterilise it by pouring boiling water all over the jar and the lid. Leave it to cool for a minute, and then, using plastic or rubber gloves, pack the cucumber down into the jar. Press it right down, and pour any remaining liquid over; the cucumbers must be submerged in the liquid to prevent mold growth. Leave a gap of a couple of centimetres at the top to prevent it spilling up out when it starts fermenting. If I've got leftover liquid I save it for a salad dressing. If I've got leftover cucumbers I eat them straight away! Leave in a warm place - ambient temperature is best, 60-70°F. The longer you leave them, the more fermented they will be. I would say minimum 24 hours, maximum 1 week. You might want to burp the jar a few times in this period to stop gas building up. You can taste them to see how they are doing, just remember to use a clean fork so as to not contaminate the jar. When you're ready, transfer them to the fridge where they will keep indefinitely, as long as the cucumbers are submerged in the liquid and you don't double dip!

Preserved Lemons

This is so fun! Well, maybe my definition of fun isn't the same as everyone else's. But if fun to you means something quick and easy to make that will provide you with months of pleasure in the form of a unique, versatile, and incredibly delicious ingredient, then yes! This is fun.

Ingredients

6 lemons (unwaxed, preferably organic)
1/3 cup salt
sterilise jar (½ litre)
leave 1 month

Makes 1 big jar full
You need a 500ml Kilner jar, that's all
Takes 10 mins and then 1 month to ferment

Sterilise a small (500ml) Kilner jar; the easiest way to do this is to run boiling water over it. Cut the ends off your lemons and slice them into eighths. Coat the lemons in the salt (reserve a tablespoon for later). Then squish them down into the jar. It will look like they won't fit, but keep pressing them down really hard so that they start to release their juices. They need to be covered in their juice. When you can't squeeze them down anymore, sprinkle the last bit of salt over the top of the mixture and seal the lid. You need to leave at least a 1cm (½") gap at the top so it doesn't spill out while fermenting.

Leave them at room temperature for a month, and then transfer to the fridge where they will keep indefinitely. You can use teaspoons of the liquid in recipes, or blend up the peel. You can't use the lemon flesh though as it's super salty – discard that. I love them in this guacamole (p38), or blended into any dip or dressing. They have a wonderful umami flavour – salty, sweet, sour and bitter all at once.

Happiness is a State of Stomach

People get into raw foods for all kinds of reasons. Sometimes it's just intuitive, sometimes it's to cure a minor health issue, often it's something more major. Many people just want to lose weight or have more energy. Whatever the initial motivation it doesn't matter, because we all experience the same thing. We all experience an extraordinary surge in vitality, clarity and enthusiasm for life. You know the most common thing that people say to me? The most universally experienced benefit to going raw? It's happiness. People say time and time again, that they simply just feel happier.

Now why would that be? We all know that sentient activity happens in the brain, that the brain is the site of many neurotransmitters that communicate by electrical impulses and instruct our bodies to operate. In the West, we tend to believe that happiness is dependent on externals, it is something that happens to us. We feel happy when we are with wonderful people, or in a beautiful place. We are encouraged to believe that happiness can be achieved by accumulating material possessions: houses, cars, clothes, shoes, computer games, iPhones. While it is undoubtedly true that we can derive happiness from our external environment, it is false to believe that we are dependent on it. Actually, we can create many of these happy chemicals in the brain ourselves. We can train our minds to react in certain ways, and to keep looking for ways to find joy and appreciation in any situation. With practice, we can squeeze more and more bliss from each moment, so that we don't need to look for it from outside because we are overflowing with it ourselves. Then when something wonderful does happen, we are even more appreciative because we are not waiting on it, expecting it, or even needing it, and it seems like even more of a blessing.

But there is another way, an even more simple way, to find happiness in our lives. Because, there are even more neurotransmitters in our guts than in our brains. There is more sentient activity occurring in the gut than in the brain. Your gut feeling? That's a more powerful tool for understanding the world than your mind. And the two are completely interrelated. They are sending signals back and forth all the time. Your mind is telling your gut what is going on, hence why stress affects the digestion and so many people suffer from IBS and other gut disorders. And your gut is telling your mind what is going on. Which is why foods affect your mood so strongly.

Everyone wants to be happy, right? Everyone wants to feel good. So many of us experience hardships in our lives that make it difficult to achieve that. Most people in this world aren't getting enough love, and most have to work too hard for not much money. Both these things make us sad! So we can work on ourselves, work on our belief systems, and cultivate an attitude of loving positive awareness. This requires consciousness, intelligence, commitment and focus. But it is far more rewarding than chasing externals.

Or even more simply. We can bypass the rational mind. We can skip past the ego that struggles and fights and often seems determined to cling to unhelpful and unproductive thought patterns. And we can go direct to our guts. Put in the happy foods that create happy guts. And lo and behold. Happy guts create happy minds. And happy minds create happy lives.

Candies & Cookies

I'm not a big sweet tooth person, but I know I'm in the minority with that! This section is all about sweets you can eat without a shred of guilt. It goes without saying, there's no compromise on deliciousness: these all taste rich and indulgent, but because they are made with healthy fats and low-glycemic sweeteners, you know that they are only doing you good. And because I follow food-combining principles, they aren't going to give your gut any bother on the way down; these are all simple to digest, so your tummy won't start singing and dancing after you've eaten. These are the best recipes to try out on kids, and some of them are so simple you can even get the little ones involved in making them.

Violet Visions

I can't get enough of these. In fact, I had to make three batches just to get around to taking a picture of them before I ate them all.

Ingredients

3 cups (75g) coconut flakes
1 cup (100g) shelled hemp seeds
1 tsp ashwagandha
10 drops violet Medicine Flower Extracts
2 tsp purple corn extract
1 tbsp coconut oil
2 tsp honey

¾ cup (75g) cacao butter
½ cup (50g) cacao powder
½ cup (50g) mesquite powder
¼ cup (25g) maca powder

Makes 20
Takes 1 hour
You need a high-power blender or food processor

Start by making the centres. Grind the coconut and the hemp together in the high-power blender or food processor. Once you've got them ground to a flour, add in the ashwagandha, violet essence and purple corn extract, and put the machine on again for a minute, to mix those ingredients. Finally, add in the coconut oil (you don't have to melt it first), and the honey, and blend once again. Roll into small balls (probably smaller than you imagine, because once the chocolate is on they will double in size) – you should end up with about 20 balls, each about 1cm in diameter.

Put them in the freezer, while you make the chocolate. Melt the cacao butter. Put the cacao powder, mesquite, and maca in a bowl together. Once the cacao butter is melted, stir it into the powders. Remove the balls from the freezer, and dip them individually into the chocolate. It's important that the chocolate is melted to just the right temperature. If the chocolate is too hot it will be too runny and won't stick to the balls. If it's too cool, it will be too thick and won't coat the balls evenly. Try a few and then decide if you need to heat the chocolate a bit more, or leave it to cool a bit longer. It takes a bit of practice to get them looking pretty, but you won't minding making lots of batches and eating all the ones that don't come out perfect in an attempt to master your craft.

You will probably have some chocolate leftover once you've coated them all, just pour this into molds and make a few extra chocolates. Put your violet candies in the fridge to set – it shouldn't take too long, maybe an hour. Stored in an airtight container in the fridge they will keep for up to a month.

Reishi Candi

These are quite tricky to do, but worth all the effort if you can master it. They make wonderful gifts, if you can resist the urge to devour them all yourself. I have quite a few other flavours that I love, but this one is my favourite so far. It's a good way to get reishi in, as the ginger disguises its bitterness.

Ingredients

For the Balls:
- 3 cups (75g) coconut flakes
- 1 cup (100g) goji berries
- ½" (1cm) ginger root
- 2 tsp reishi extract
- 2 tbsp coconut oil
- 2 tbsp yacon syrup or coconut nectar

For the Chocolate:
- 150g (1 ¼ cup) cacao butter
- 100g (1 cup) cacao powder
- 100g (1 cup) mesquite
- 50g (½ cup) maca
- 1 tsp Etherium Gold (optional)

Makes 20 candies
Takes 1 hour
You need a food processor or high-power blender

First we are going to make our coconut balls. This is the easy bit! In a food processor or high-power blender, grind the coconut, gojis and ginger together, until you have a flour. Then add in the reishi, coconut oil and yacon syrup and process again. It should become one sticky mass very quickly.

Take a spoonful of the mixture from the machine, and roll into walnut-sized balls. You don't want them too big or they will be ginormous once they are coated in chocolate. Make them about two-thirds the size you want them to be once they are done. Once you've rolled them all into balls, place them in the freezer to chill.

Next, we are going to make chocolate. If you're really in a hurry you can melt down chocolate bars; I've done it with my Raw Living Whoosh bars, and it was really good. Whenever you're making chocolate, it's important not to heat the butters, but it's particularly important in this instance. When you melt the butter slowly and at a low temperature, your chocolate is going to be thicker and will coat your coconut balls much more easily. If you over-heat your butter, the chocolate will be runnier and then it's harder to make it stick. As I said, it might take you a good few tries to get this stage of the process right (but don't worry, you won't mind having to eat all the trial batches that didn't come out perfectly).

Melt the cacao butter according to your preferred method. Stir in the mesquite, maca, cacao powder, and Etherium Gold, if you're using it. At this point, I would leave it sitting for 5-10 minutes so it cools down even more, while you tidy up the kitchen a bit. You want it to be liquid, not hard, but thick and ready to set on the balls. Remove the coconut balls from the freezer, and drop one in the chocolate. A fork is easiest to use to swirl it around a little and make sure it is covered. Lift it out with the fork, and put it on a plate to set. Make sure the plate is covered in foil, or it will stick! Or you can use silicon boards or dehydrator sheets. If your chocolate is too runny, it will drip onto the plate and off the base of your ball. Do all the balls like this, one at a time. You will have some chocolate leftover; this is inevitable, or it would be impossible to dip the last few balls. Pour it into molds. Put everything in the fridge to set; it should be ready in an hour or so.

Take care when lifting the balls from the plate; try and ensure you don't leave chocolate behind because then the base of your ball has no covering. It might help to slip a knife underneath as you are removing them. Store them in an airtight container in the fridge. They keep very well, up to two months.

Of course, if you are a busy person or not one for messing around in the kitchen, you could just make the coconut balls and not bother coating them in chocolate; they are delicious and super-energising sweets just as they are.

Roses Grow On You

Do you know what I worked out this time? Make the chocolate first. When you're making any of these candies, I find the trickiest part is to get the chocolate just the right temperature to coat the coconut centre. If the chocolate is too runny, it drips off. If it's too set, it won't coat the balls nicely. Usually, I make the chocolate and then have to wait ages until it's set enough to coat the balls without just dripping everywhere. So this time, I made the chocolate first to give it time to set a little before I used it.

Ingredients

60g (½ cup) cacao butter
60g (½ cup) cacao liquor
60g (½ cup) lucuma
5 drops vanilla Medicine Flower Extract

3 cups (150g) coconut flakes
½ cup (45g) almonds
2 tsp Etherium Pink
1 tbsp freeze-dried strawberry powder
2 tbsp yacon syrup or raw honey
2 tbsp coconut oil
10 drops rose Medicine Flower Extract, or rose essential oil

Makes 18
Takes 45 mins
You need a food processor or high-power blender

First, melt the cacao liquor and cacao butter, either in a bowl stood in a pan of just boiled water, or in a porringer or Thermomix. Once they are liquid, stir in the lucuma and vanilla. Put to one side to set a little. You can put it in the fridge but then it starts to harden too much round the sides, so better to keep it out I feel, where you can keep an eye on it.

For the centres, in a food processor or high-power blender, grind the coconut and almonds together to a flour. Next add the strawberry powder and Etherium Pink and process again. Now it should be a beautiful baby pink hue. Finally, add the syrup or honey, rose flavouring and coconut oil (not melted) and process until it all binds together. Roll the mixture into walnut sized balls.

At this point, if your chocolate still seems a little runny, you can pop your candy centres in the fridge, and clear away as much as you can. When your chocolate is ready (or you've run out of time/patience!), coat the balls in the chocolate. Put them on a plate coated in foil, and store them in the fridge to set. Be careful that they don't touch each other while they are sat on the plate or the chocolate will stick together. When they are done, you can store them in an airtight container in the fridge. They keep well, up to a month.

Spearmint Candies

If you've got loads of time and energy, you could make a batch of these alongside a batch of Reishi Candis, Violet Visions and Roses Grow on You, and have orange, purple, pink and green truffles all alongside each other. You could also include mini Rum Truffles (p199) to make a wonderful presentation gift box, containing more nutrition than the entire Pick 'n' Mix section of Woolworths.

Ingredients

150g (3 cups) coconut chips
2 tsp chlorella powder
2 tbsp xylitol
3 tbsp coconut oil
6 drops spearmint essential oil
2 tsp mucuna (optional)
100g (1 cup) melted chocolate

Note: If you can't get spearmint oil, peppermint oil will do just fine.

Makes 20 candies
Takes 1 hr
You need a food processor

In your food processor, grind up the coconut until it is a flour. Add the chlorella, and give it a quick whizz to make sure it's evenly distributed. Then add the remaining ingredients: the xylitol, coconut oil, mucuna and spearmint oil. Process for a minute until it's formed a paste. Roll it into walnut-sized balls with your hands, and put them in the fridge (on a plate covered in foil) to harden.

If you want to coat them in chocolate, you need about 100g of chocolate to cover them all evenly. Melt the chocolate, or make a new batch and set some aside for your candy coating. Let it harden just slightly so it's thick enough to coat your peppermint balls evenly. There's quite a knack to this, you may need a few practice attempts before you gauge the right thickness of chocolate needed, so it's not too hard to coat the balls, and not too runny that it just drips off. Don't worry, I'm sure you'll have no shortage of volunteers to help you eat the delicious but misshapen failed attempts!

Matcha Mucuna Mints

I first made these for a pop-up dinner party as after-dinner mints. I wanted to do something other than chocolates, so I came up with these – I instantly realised I had created a new favourite. I love using matcha, in small amounts. It's a Japanese green tea, which is very high in a substance called L-theanine. This is an antioxidant which is found in green tea generally, but it's particularly concentrated in matcha. It's also very good for focus and concentration, but as it's a green tea, it's very low in caffeine. It adds a pretty light green hue to your sweets as well – I use it in the Chi Lime Pie recipe (p239) to make it a lime green colour.

Ingredients
150g (1 ¼ cups) cacao butter
130g (1 ⅓ cup) lucuma
1 tbsp raw honey
1 tbsp mucuna
1 tbsp matcha powder

Makes 30 sweets
Takes 15 mins and 1 hour to set
You don't need any special equipment

First, melt the butter and honey together, in a heatproof bowl stood in simmering water. It should take around 7-10 minutes to melt. Once it's liquid, add the powders - lucuma, mucuna, matcha. Stir them in, and then quickly pour the mixture into silicon molds. It should make about 30 little sweets. If you don't have silicon molds, you can just pour it into a tray covered in aluminium foil. Put in the freezer to set in 20 minutes or the fridge in an hour. Once it's set, pop out of the molds, and store in an airtight container in the fridge. They keep really well, up to 8 weeks.

Happy Accident Candy

Another happy accident. In Iceland, I forgot the rum when making rum 'n' raisin fudge. So we improvised with what we had, and came up with this delicious and refreshing sweet treat.

Ingredients

125g (1 cup) coconut oil
100g (1 cup) lucuma powder
5 drops orange essential oil
2 tsp camu powder
2 tbsp baobab powder
100g (1 cup) raisins

Makes 35 pieces
Takes 10 minutes to make and at least an hour to set
You don't need any special equipment

Melt the coconut oil by standing it in a heatproof bowl stood in a bowl of freshly heated water, or in a porringer or a Thermomix. Stir the other ingredients together in a bowl: the lucuma, orange oil, camu, baobab, and dried fruit. Stir the coconut oil in and pour into silicon molds to set. Will take at least an hour in the fridge or just 15 mins in the freezer. Store in the fridge in an airtight container - they will keep for up to two months.

Kids' Lifesavers

When my boys were little, I insisted that they have green powder every day. To my mind, my Greener Grass and Out of the Woods powders are the perfect blends of hemp protein, alkalising grasses, nutritionally dense algaes and adaptogenic herbs. However, when we were out in public, they understandably objected to me turning all their food green. At home, I also tried to get a good dose of maca into them most days in a juice or smoothie, but obviously when we were travelling that's harder to do as well.

In a hotel in Turkey, I hit upon this recipe to make sure they were getting lots of micro-algaes, maca, and the adaptogenic herb ashwagandha, without having to embarrass them in the restaurant. I melted the coconut oil in the sun, stirred it all together in a bowl with a spoon, and then put it in the mini-bar fridge to set. It was such a hit, they still asked for it once we got home.

Ingredients

180g (1 ½ cups) coconut oil
2 tbsp maca
3 tbsp spirulina
2 tsp ashwagandha
100g (1 cup) lucuma
3 tbsp honey

Serves 4
Takes 10 minutes to make and an hour to set
You don't need any special equipment

Melt the coconut oil in a bowl stood in a pan of freshly heated water, or in a porringer or Thermomix. In a bowl, stir together all the other ingredients: maca, spirulina, ashwagandha, lucuma and honey. Once the coconut oil is melted stir that in as well. Pour it into a silicon mold (yes, I do travel with silicon molds, they don't weigh anything or take up any space, and they invariably come in handy), or a tray lined with aluminum foil or greaseproof paper. Put it in the fridge to set for at least an hour. Stored in the fridge, it will keep well, for at least a month.

185

Baobiscuits

These biscuits have a wonderfully complex flavour. Baobab powder adds depth and an unusual taste to any dish it's used in. Buckwheat is very alkalising, so these biscuits make a great grounding and calming snack.

Ingredients

2 cups (300g) dry buckwheat
½ cup (60g) hazelnuts, soaked
½ cup (60g) hazelnuts, ground (optional, see note below)
½ cup (125ml) extra virgin olive oil
½ cup (125ml) water
½ cup (50g) baobab
2 tbsp raw honey
10 drops orange essential oil
10 drops vanilla Medicine Flower Extract

Makes about 40 biscuits
You need to sprout your buckwheat 3 or more days in advance, and soak your hazelnuts 4 hours in advance. The recipe takes about 15 mins to make. It takes 12-14 hours to dehydrate.
You need a food processor, food grinder (or a high-power blender) and a dehydrator.

First, sprout the buckwheat. Soak it for five hours, then rinse well, and leave to sprout for two or three days. Soak half a cup of hazelnuts in advance as well, just for 4 hours or so. Reserve these to use as decoration for your biscuits. When you're ready to get going, grind the unsoaked hazelnuts in a food grinder or high-powered blender. Then put your buckwheat sprouts in the food processor with all the liquid ingredients – the olive oil, water, and honey. Blend to a cream, like a thick porridge. Then add the remaining ingredients – the ground hazelnuts, baobab, vanilla and orange oil. Keep processing until all the ingredients are amalgamated. If it's too much work for your machine, you can transfer the mixture to a bowl and do this stage by hand with a wooden spoon. If it's too thick you may want to add a little more water.

When you're happy that the ingredients are evenly mixed, spread it out on to dehydrator trays. It should cover two trays evenly. Take your soaked hazelnuts and place them at intervals on your biscuits. Press them in firmly so they stay in once the biscuits are ready. You want to get 4 or 5 hazelnuts across and 5 or 6 down. Place the biscuits in the dehydrator and dry for 9-10 hours. Then score them, so there is a hazelnut at the centre of each biscuit, and flip them. If you flip them carefully, most of the hazelnuts should stay where they are. Dry for another 2-3 hours. Stored in an airtight container they will keep for up to a week. If you want to keep them longer, put them in the fridge, where they will keep for 2-3 weeks.

Note: I have made this with and without the ground hazelnuts in. Without the hazelnuts, the recipe makes a moister, creamier biscuit; with them, they are drier and crumblier, more like a digestive.

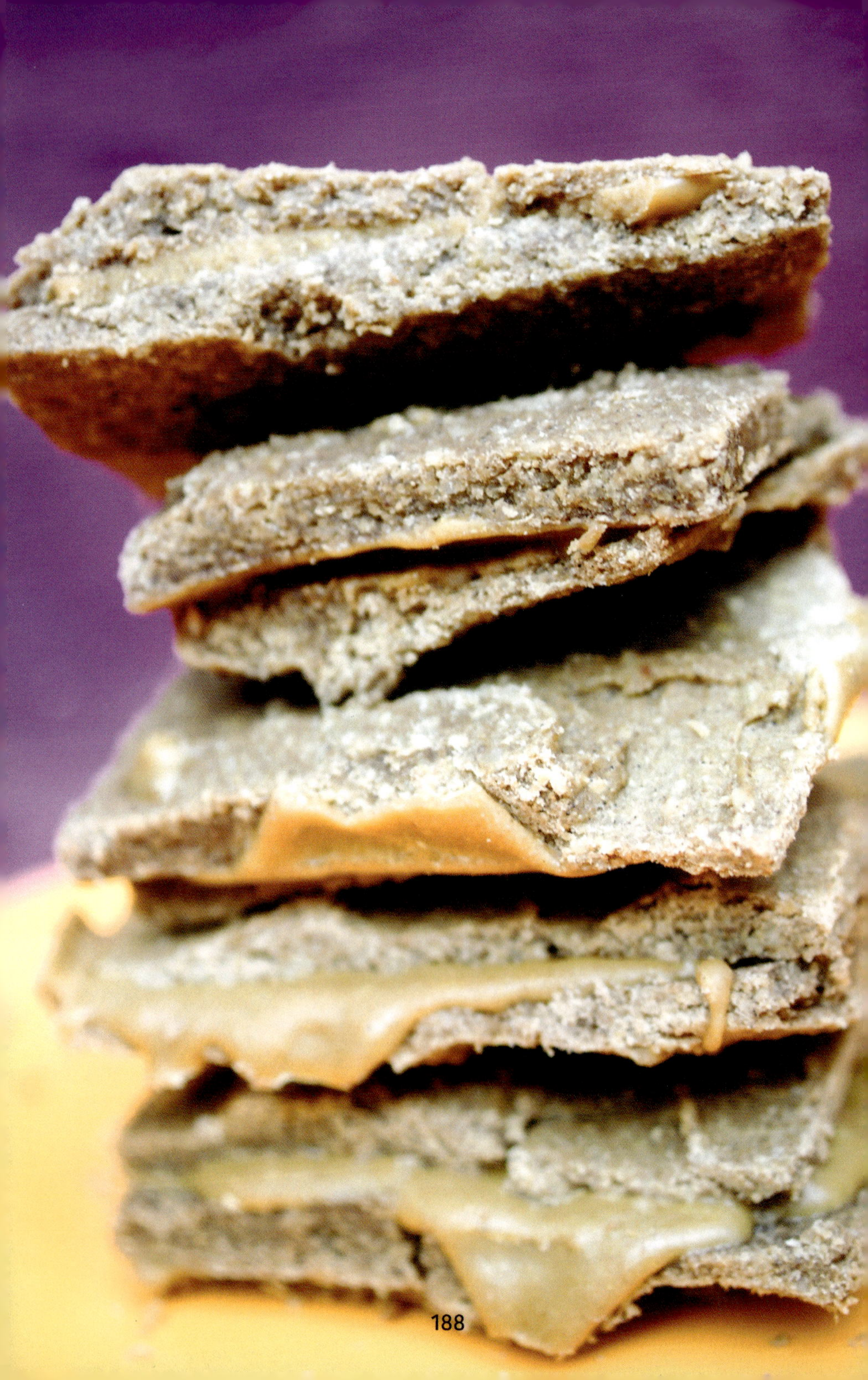

Beyond Custard Creams

We were in Wales, and I actually caught my Auntie trying to feed my boys Custard Creams. They were very tempted, so I promised them raw custard creams. I was always more of a Bourbons girl so maybe I'll make those next.

Note for non-British readers. Custard Creams are apparently the UK's favourite biscuit. You don't really need to know that, just know that these are very, very good.

Ingredients

Biscuits:
1 cup (150g) buckwheat groats, sprouted
1 cup (100g) lucuma
1 cup (250ml) water
½ cup (125ml) extra virgin olive oil
1 tbsp vanilla powder or 10 drops vanilla Medicine Flower Extract
pinch salt
½ cup (90g) coconut sugar or cane juice crystals

Filling:
1 cup (125g) coconut oil
1 cup (100g) lucuma
¼ cup (25g) mesquite

Makes about 25 biscuits
Takes a few days to sprout the buckwheat in advance. The biscuits take about 10 mins to make, and then you need to dehydrate them for 12 hours. Once they are done, it's going to take you another 15 mins to make the filling and assemble the biscuits.
You need a blender and a dehydrator

Make sure to sprout your buckwheat in advance. Buckwheat is tricky. Rinse it well, soak it for 5 hours, NO LONGER, rinse well again, then sprout for 2-3 days.

Put all your biscuit ingredients in the blender or food processor, and blend until you have a smooth cream. Spread the mixture out on a single dehydrator tray, and dry for 12 hours. Score the biscuits into pieces the size of custard creams: about 6 or 8 each way, so you have around 50 pieces in total. Make sure they are as even in size as possible, because you will be sandwiching them together soon. Flip them over, so they get done evenly on both sides, and dry for another 4-6 hours.

Remove them from the dehydrator and make the cream filling when you are ready. Melt the coconut oil and stir in the lucuma and mesquite so you have a thick butter. Spread it on a biscuit, trying to reach the edges as much as possible. Press another biscuit on top so you have a sandwich. Do this with all the biscuits, and you should find you use all the cream, and have around 25 biscuits in total. Keep them in an airtight container in the fridge, and they should keep for a good few weeks.

Marching Biscuits

These are another firm family favourite, that I created back in 2008, and they've never been out of style since. The Aztecs ate chia when they were marching into battle, and I definitely walk faster when I've been eating this wonder seed. So march confidently through your day, with these very irresistible chocolate chia flax crackers. (The other name I had for them was Exciting Biscuits, because paired with some raw chocolate spread, they make a very exciting between-meals snack or breakfast).

Ingredients

250g or 2 cups chia seeds
250g or 2 cups flaxseeds
1 ¼ litre or 5 cups water
100g or 1 cup cacao powder
100g or 1 cup lucuma
180g or 1 cup coconut sugar or cane juice crystals
100g or 1 cup raisins
1 tbsp he shou wu powder
1 tbsp purple corn extract

Makes 50 biscuits
Preparation time: 12 hours pre-soaking, 10 mins to make, 18 hours dehydrating
You need a dehydrator

Soak the chia and flaxseeds together in the water for at least four hours, preferably overnight. When you are ready, stir all the other ingredients into the soaked seeds -this will take a few minutes of patience. When you're satisfied it's all fully mixed, spread them onto two dehydrating sheets. Dry for 12 hours, then score into five by five (25 biscuits on each sheet), flip and dry for six hours more. The end result should be moist and irresistible. (Sometimes I cut a square of chocolate and sandwich it inside a folded in half biscuit, but don't tell anyone, it's so amazingly good I'm sure we'd get told off).

Simplicity & Relativity

When people start on raw food, they can easily become overwhelmed by all the information out there. How much fruit should I eat? How much is too much cacao? Am I getting enough protein? What about B12? And what's this about Vitamin K? Different health educators say different things, and people end up with their heads spinning, wondering if it wouldn't just be simpler to carry on as they were.

I always advise people to simplify it down. Remember when you were doing fractions in maths at school (or maybe you've been helping your kids with their homework like I have!), 228 over 152 looks quite overwhelming, but it actually breaks down to 3 over 2, or 1.5, which is an easy sum to take in. Do the same with your diet. Break it down. Make it as simple as you can. Why are you worrying about this? What got you on this line of research in the first place? For most people, it's the same reasons. A desire to feel better, to have more energy, more enthusiasm for life. So how can you achieve that today? What food choices are going to enable that very straight-forward aim?

I'm going to share with you a very simple, fairly obvious, but highly overlooked fact. If we want to simplify the information as much as possible, where do we look? We go to the root, which in this case is our bodies. And we look at their constituent properties, which are the cells. And we look at how to create the optimum conditions for the cells to thrive. How can we do the very best for our bodies so they are able to perform as efficiently as possible?

We haven't got space here to take a full in-depth look at cellular health. To summarise, the cells need to be in an alkalised and oxygenated environment. Disease cannot thrive in an alkaline environment. The healthy fats are the building blocks of the cells, so we need an abundance of a balance of healthy fats to create healthy cells. And the cells need to be fully hydrated to communicate, and prevent blockages in the system. Obviously, there is a lot more to it than that, but that's the basis of it in a nutshell: hydration, alkalisation, oxygenation, and healthy fats.

The most important fact that we need to focus on today is that of relativity. In terms of cellular health, there is no absolute right or wrong, rather everything is somewhere on a spectrum. Think about anything meaningful in your life: to really affect the fabric of your world in a genuinely transformative and substantial way, you have to work at a thing. Be it your relationship with your children or your partner, your yoga practice or your meditation, your music or your writing, you put in the work day in, day out; you do your practice, you build, and you grow something wonderful. True health is another such lifelong practice. A teacher would never say someone "can't" or "can" do yoga, they would recognise that everyone has different levels of flexibility and strength, and they are working to the best of their ability. Your partner would never say you are "good" or "bad" at loving, they would recognise that you're a human being who has weaknesses and strengths, and in some situations you can be wonderfully kind and compassionate, and in other situations less so! In the same way, the most important precept to achieving cellular health is simply a commitment to the practice. No-one is inherently healthy or unhealthy; only by trying, do you build this relationship with your body and achieve a state of true and lasting health. An earnest desire to listen and learn from this relationship, and to grow from it, is the first and most important condition. And an understanding that this isn't an overnight miracle, but something you are going to need to stay alert to as long as you want it to flourish.

So accept where you are, because that's the starting point to getting to where you want to be. And as long as your commitment is to doing something better than what you were doing yesterday, you're going to be feeling better. If you drop that commitment and let your good habits slide then you will start feeling less than optimum. This is a journey that, if you have the dedication to stick with it, will keep revealing itself more and more with the fullness of time. You won't ever get to a point where you feel you've reached your goal, your path is ended, and you are healthy. Rather, you will enter into a deepening awareness of yourself that becomes more and more rewarding and fulfilling in itself. It's about entering into the present moment within yourself, and being content with all that you find there. Feeling appreciation for the good stuff, and knowing that you, and only you, have the power to change the stuff you don't like so much.

The relativity principle is the main reason why health changes are best made slowly and steadily, and not rushed into. When we start to cleanse and detoxify, we are opening up the cells to receive more information. So if we cleanse for a period, then fall back into old and less positive habits, it can actually cause more damage than if we had never cleansed in the first place, as the negative impact of the less optimum foods takes more of a toll than it did on a system that was clogged and less receptive. Maybe you know the boiling frog analogy? Put a frog in a pan of boiling water and it will leap out to preserve its life. But put the frog in the pan and boil the water slowly, and the frog will boil to death, as it doesn't notice the steady change in temperature. When we do things little by little, our bodies have a chance to gradually acclimatise to the changes. When we jump in at the deep end, we may find the water too hot and leap straight out again!

Whatever changes you are trying to make in life, be it transitioning to raw foods, or changing your lifestyle in any way, remember true and lasting progress is made through gradual and committed implementation. In our current Western culture, we are addicted to the quick-fix approach; we can be demanding and impatient. And although sometimes we can stamp our feet and shout and scream and get what we want straight away, the best things in life are those that we tend and nurture, care for through rain and shine, and allow to blossom in their own gentle time.

Chocolate

Cacao is technically a seed, which comes from a fruit that grows across South America and Africa. The cacao bean is one of the most complex foods known to man: it contains over 300 naturally occurring chemical compounds. I believe there are many factors that contribute to its popularity. Firstly, it has a unique flavour profile: the melting point of cacao is around the same temperature as the human body, so that when we bite into the chocolate it literally melts in the mouth. Secondly, it's a true superfood, full of dense nutrition, including high amounts of the important minerals, sulphur and magnesium. But most importantly, it's the natural mood-boosting chemicals it contains that makes it so special. It's rich in substances such as tryptophan and anandamide, which strengthen our predisposition towards happiness. If a person takes anti-depressants, they affect brain chemistry in such a way that they encourage dependency on the drugs. With cacao it's the reverse: it's encouraging the brain to produce more of these happy chemicals by itself, so strengthening the neural pathways.

If that hasn't persuaded you into trying out some raw chocolate recipes, then I'm not sure what will! I adore raw chocolate, and I eat it pretty much daily, either my own or one of the many delicious bars now available on the market.

Heartcore Chocolate

Maybe not to everyone's tastes this one, but it's super pure and even suitable for diabetics and those on an anti-candida diet.

Ingredients

100g (¾ cup) cacao liquor
75g (½ cup) coconut oil
50g (½ cup) maca
50g (⅓ cup) yacon syrup
5 drops toffee stevia extract
10 drops cherry Medicine Flower Extract (optional)
1 tsp purple corn extract

Makes 25 chocolates
Takes 15 mins and a few hours to set
You don't need any special equipment

Melt the cacao liquor and coconut oil together, either in a heatproof bowl stood in a pan of simmering water, or in a porringer on a low heat, or in a Thermomix. Once it's melted, stir in the other ingredients: maca, yacon, stevia, cherry extract and purple corn. It should be a thick pouring mixture. Pour into silicon molds, or if you don't have them, a tray lined with foil or baking paper. Pop in the fridge to set for a couple of hours. Will keep well in the fridge for a few months. As there is a lot of coconut oil in this chocolate, it's not the best for taking out on day trips, especially in hot weather!

Deviation Chocolate

This is one of my best-loved chocolate recipes. I named it after my friends in London who had the best club night on the planet, and regularly provided me with inspiring and exhilarating fun times for over ten years.

Ingredients

100g (¾ cup) cacao butter
150g (1 ¼ cup) cacao liquor
60g (⅓ cup) coconut nectar
100g (1 cup) mesquite
30g (⅓ cup) maca
10 drops vanilla Medicine Flower Extract
1 tbsp mucuna powder

Makes about 50 chocolates
Takes 15 mins to make and about an hour to set
You don't need any special equipment

Melt the butter and liquor together: either in a porringer, in a heatproof bowl stood in a pan of just boiled water, or in a Thermomix. Once they are melted (this should take about 10 minutes), add all your other ingredients, every single one. Stir them all together, and pour into molds. Silicon molds are best for making chocolate, and so easy to get hold of now. In silicon molds, the chocolate will set as quickly as 15-20 mins in the fridge. In rubber molds, or a tray lined with aluminium foil, this chocolate will set in an hour or so. Keeps for 8 weeks in the fridge, but only if you don't tell anyone else you made it. If you tell everyone else, it keeps for about 8 minutes.

Jing's the Thing

Spirit Jing from RDT Connoisseurs is a wonderful protein blend to add to your milk and smoothies. As it has a naturally sweet flavour, it is ideal to add to chocolate as well. I love this powder because the energy it gives me is very restorative. It feels entirely as if it assists my body in creating new energy, rather than depleting any reserves. As with all superfoods, a little goes a long way, and a bag will last you forever. A teaspoon or two a day is a great maintenance dose. It's fantastic for strenuous physical exercise – if you're training I recommend a tablespoon a day. It's also great for those looking for adrenal support.

Ingredients

75g (¾ cups) cacao butter
50g (⅓ cup) coconut oil
75g (¾ cup) cacao powder
75g (¾ cup) lucuma
25g (¼ cup) Spirit Jing
1 tbsp yacon syrup or coconut nectar

Makes about 25 pieces of chocolate
Takes 10 mins to make and 2-3 hours to set
You don't need any special equipment

Melt the cacao butter and coconut oil first, at a low temperature, either in a heatproof bowl stood in a pan of simmering water, or in a porringer. In a separate bowl, mix together the powders – the cacao, lucuma and Jing. Add the syrup or nectar, and once the butter is melted, pour that in as well, giving it all a good stir. Pour straight into your molds – silicon ones are best. If you don't have silicon, line a tray with foil or greaseproof paper, to make it easy to turn out. Set in the fridge (or in the freezer if you're in a hurry). Once it's hardened (which is much quicker in silicon molds), cut it into pieces. Very energising – don't eat too much and especially not near bedtime!

Chiaji

I had a big chia addiction when I made this recipe. It's such a clean source of energy, when I eat chia, it's always an exciting event. I went through a phase of putting it in everything – drinks, cakes, crackers and chocolates. I love it in chocolate because it makes it all crumbly and moist.

Ingredients

125g (1 cup) cacao nibs
75g (¾ cup) chia
100g (1 cup) gojis
10 drops vanilla Medicine Flower Extract
200g (1 ½ cups) coconut oil
100g (1 cup) lucuma
50g (⅓ cup) yacon syrup or coconut nectar
10 drops orange essential oil

Makes about 36 squares
Takes 10 mins to make and 2 hours to set
You need a blender or grinder

Grind up the nibs, chia and gojis in a high-power blender or grinder. If your machine is not too powerful, you will need to do the gojis separately. Melt the coconut oil in a double saucepan or porringer. Pour it into the blender, and blend it up with the nibs, chia and gojis. Be careful that you haven't got ground chocolate stuck at the bottom of the blender which hasn't mixed in properly, if you do you'll need to dig it out with a fork. Once you've got a good paste, add in your remaining ingredients – vanilla, lucuma, yacon, and orange oil. Blend again, for a good minute, until all the ingredients are fully amalgamated. Transfer to a silicon mold or tray lined with aluminium foil or greaseproof paper.

Will set in the freezer in half an hour, in the fridge in a couple of hours. Once it's hard, turn it out, and cut it into bite-sized squares, six across by six down (or smaller). Stored in the fridge, they will keep for a couple of weeks.

Keep away from airports when you're eating this because you'll be flying so high, air traffic control might mistake you for an aeroplane and try to land you.

New Jamaica

Remember Old Jamaica? It was a Cadbury's chocolate bar sold in the UK in the 70s, which had a picture of a pirate ship sailing off into the sunset on the wrapper. It was rum flavour and it had raisins in it, and it was one of my favourite chocolate bars. Well it's the 21st century, and this is New Jamaica.

Ingredients

60g (½ cup) cacao butter
60g (½ cup) coconut butter
2 tbsp coconut nectar or yacon syrup
50g (½ cup) mesquite
75g (¾ cup) cacao powder
1 tbsp maca powder
20 drops rum Medicine Flower Extract
100g (1 cup) raisins

Makes 35 pieces
Takes 15 mins with a few hours setting time
You don't need any special equipment

Melt the cacao butter and coconut oil in a heatproof bowl stood in a pan of simmering water, or a porringer. In a separate bowl, stir together the cacao powder, maca, and mesquite. When it's all mixed together, stir in the yacon, rum essence and raisins. Finally, pour in the butters. The end result should be a thick pouring consistency. If it's too runny, add a spoonful of maca, that's a great thickener. Pour into silicon molds, and set in the freezer in 15-30 mins or in the fridge in around an hour. If you haven't got silicon molds you can use any type of tray, just line it with foil, cling film, or greaseproof paper. Once it's set, cut into squares and store in the fridge, it will keep for up to eight weeks.

Rum Truffles

Oh yes. Yes yes yessity yes. When I was a kid, there was a baker's at the bottom of our road, and every Saturday, it was the highlight of the week that we could choose any kind of cream cake for Saturday tea. Chocolate eclairs, cream horns, cherry bakewells, jam donuts; you may well recall the standard fare that was on offer in an English bakery in the early 80s. My favourites were the rum truffles, a chocolate and cream affair, coated in chocolate hundreds and thousands. So when I saw the rum Medicine Flavour Extract, my first thought was "rum truffles!" I invented these around the same time as the Shepherd's Pie (p69) and I can't tell you how much joy it gave me to enjoy my Shepherd's Pie along with a rum truffle and a glass of "cherryade" (cherry-flavoured kefir). It evoked all those reassuring and comforting feelings of my 70s childhood, making me feel secure, safe and nurtured.

Ingredients

1 cup (125g) cacao liquor
½ cup (60g) sesame seeds
½ cup (50g) sunflower seeds
½ cup (50g) raisins
½ cup (50g) lucuma
2 tbsp coconut oil
15 drops rum Medicine Flower Extract

2 tbsp cacao liquor, powdered
2 tbsp coconut sugar

Makes about 15
Takes 20 mins
You need a blender or grinder and food processor

Start by melting the cacao liquor. Break it up into tiny pieces, then melt it in a heatproof bowl stood in freshly boiled water, or a porringer, or a Thermomix. While you're waiting for it to melt, grind up the sunflower seeds and sesame seeds in a high-power blender or food grinder. Once they are ground to a powder, add the raisins in and grind again. Once the liquor is melted, you're going to blend everything together. You can do this in a standard food processor or a blender. Once you have a thick cream, add the last three ingredients: the lucuma, coconut oil, and rum extract. You don't need to melt the coconut oil first. Blend to a thick paste.

By hand, remove small lumps of the mixture, and roll into balls, about 30g each. Separately, grind 2 tbsp cacao liquor into a powder, and mix it with the coconut sugar. Roll the balls into this mixture, so it coats them evenly. Store in the fridge.

Sweet Enough

Always on the quest for creating the healthiest chocolate known to man, this is my latest low-glycemic recipe. Not quite as sweetener-free as the Low Down Loretta Brown, but pretty damn close.

Ingredients

100g (¾ cup) cacao liquor
75g (½ cup) coconut oil
50g (½ cup) goji berries
50g (½ cup) maca powder
10 drops vanilla stevia
1 tbsp cinnamon
2 tbsp freeze-dried strawberry powder

Makes about 30 chocolates
Takes 20 mins, with 1-2 hours to set
You need a blender

Start by melting your cacao liquor and coconut oil together. Grate your liquor first, that will make it easier. It takes ten minutes to melt them without heating them too high. Grind your goji berries. Put your gojis in your blender with the melted cacao liquor and coconut oil, and then add in the maca powder, stevia, cinnamon, and strawberry powder. You can sub the strawberry powder for any other of your favourite fruit powders like blueberry or blackberry, but strawberry is the sweetest. Blend it all really well until it's all mixed together smoothly and pour into molds. Silicon molds will set in the freezer in 10 minutes! In the fridge they will take more like 30 mins, and if you don't have silicon molds, allow up to one hour in the freezer or 2-3 hours in the fridge. Keeps in the fridge for at least a month.

The Low Down Loretta Brown

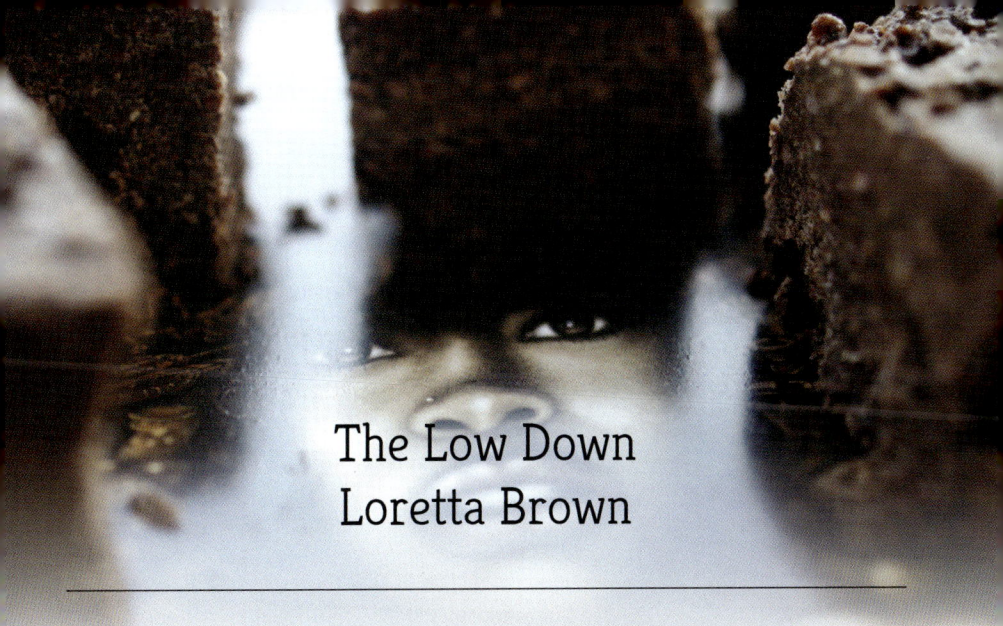

This is my low glycaemic raw chocolate recipe. Maca is a vegetable, with a malty taste, and I don't think anyone would ever accuse maca of being overly sweet. Yacon, as you may know, contains a form of sugar called fructoligosaccharides, which aren't recognised by the body, so yacon is technically sugar-free. This is a great chocolate to eat if you're diabetic, on an anti-Candida diet, or if you're just looking to reduce your sugar intake.

Low Down Loretta Brown is one of Erykah Badu's aliases. Erykah is known for her healthy lifestyle and has been a raw vegan for long periods, so I've named this chocolate after her.

Ingredients

- 200g (1 ½ cups) coconut oil
- 200g (2 cups) cacao nibs
- 100g (1 cup) maca
- 100g (½ cup) yacon syrup
- 10 drops vanilla Medicine Flower Extract
- 1 tsp purple corn extract

Makes about 40 pieces
Takes 10 mins to make and 2-3 hours to set
You need a grinder or high-power blender

Melt the coconut oil in a porringer or in a heatproof bowl stood in a pan of just boiled water. Grind the nibs in your grinder or blender, until they are as fine as you can get them. In a mixing bowl, stir together your dry ingredients: the powdered nibs, maca, and purple corn. Once they are evenly mixed, pour in your yacon syrup, add the vanilla drops, and mix again. Finally stir in your melted coconut oil until you have a gorgeously gooey thick batter, then pour it into your molds. Silicon molds work best for chocolate, but if you don't have them, line a tray with greaseproof paper or aluminium foil.

Put it in the fridge to set for two to three hours, then when it's done, chop into bite-sized pieces and store in an airtight container in the fridge. Maca doesn't keep so well out of the fridge, but in the fridge it should last a good few weeks.

Chiacolate

This makes a beautiful soft crumbly chocolate. Chia is just as energising as chocolate, but not quite so stimulating, so combining the two makes for a lot of fun, and less stress on the adrenals. The maca is also there for adrenal support.

Ingredients

200g (1 ½ cups) coconut oil
100g (1 cup) cacao nibs
100g (1 cup) chia seeds
50g (½ cup) maca
50g (½ cup) lucuma
2 tbsp yacon syrup or raw honey
10 drops orange essential oil

Makes 50 pieces
Takes 2 hours to set
You need a high-power blender or food grinder

Melt the coconut oil in a double saucepan, being careful not to overheat it. Grind the cacao and chia together in a grinder or high-power blender, until it's become a powder. Remove it from the machine, and add it to a bowl with all the remaining ingredients – the maca, lucuma, honey or yacon, and orange oil. Return to the blender, and pour in the oil as well. Give it a good whizz until it's all evenly mixed and then transfer to a silicon mold to set (if you don't have a silicon mold, line a normal baking tray with aluminium foil). Will set in the fridge in 2 hours. Keep stored in an airtight container in the fridge; it should keep for up to eight weeks.

Seasonal Chocolate Truffles

Happy Holidays! These are wonderful. You're going to love them. Make them! That's all I have to say.

Ingredients

1 cup (120g) cacao liquor
½ cup (60g) sesame seeds
½ cup (50g) sunflower seeds
½ cup (50g) raisins
½ cup (50g) lucuma
2 tbsp coconut oil
10 drops orange essential oil
1 tbsp mixed spices
1 tbsp he shou wu

(½ cup) 50g cacao liquor
(½ cup) 50g coconut oil
(½ cup) 50g lucuma
1 tbsp cranberry powder (if you can't find it, just omit it)
5 drops vanilla stevia

Makes about 15
Takes 30 mins, with a few hours setting time
You need a blender or food grinder

Start by melting the cacao liquor. Break it up into tiny pieces, then melt it in a heatproof bowl stood in freshly boiled water, or a porringer, or a Thermomix. While you're waiting for it to melt, grind up the sunflower seeds and sesame seeds in a high-power blender or food grinder. Once they are ground to a powder, add the raisins in and grind again. Once the liquor is melted, you're going to blend everything together. You can do this in a standard food processor or a blender. Once you have a thick cream, add the rest of the ingredients: the lucuma, coconut oil, orange oil, spices and he shou wu. You don't need to melt the coconut oil first. Blend to a thick paste. By hand, remove small lumps of the mixture, and roll into balls, about 25g each. Put them in the freezer while you make the icing.

Melt the cacao liquor and coconut oil as before. Once it's melted, stir in the lucuma, cranberry powder, and stevia. It helps if you leave it to cool a little bit before you start rolling the truffles in it. Clean up or go check your email for 10-15 mins. You want it to be just runny enough to coat them evenly but not too solid it starts to stick. When you're ready, roll the balls into the chocolate, so it coats them evenly, and place them on a plate covered in foil. It's best to do this with your fingers or with a fork. Store them in the fridge.

Easter Eggs

Recently I was teaching a lady who really knew what she wanted. Most of the time, I make dishes and the response is euphoric. But occasionally, someone comes along with a very distinct palate who queries my flavour profiles and wants to do things differently. I love being made to question my assumptions about what works like that, and invited to see things from a fresh perspective.

So when we made chocolate, she asked if we had to use the powders like lucuma and mesquite. Yes, I said, it doesn't work without them. But I realised I had never tried to make chocolate with liquor and no powder, so I actually didn't know how it would turn out. Once I'd got round to having a play, I discovered actually it made silky smooth creamy chocolate, which most definitely did work.

So, here's my simplest raw chocolate recipe ever – just three ingredients.

And if that isn't enough of a story for you, when I posted my Easter Eggs on Instagram, I got such a response – it was my most liked pic on there at the time. So I thought it best to write down the trick to making eggs for you as well.

Ingredients

200g cacao liquor
50g coconut oil
100g coconut sugar or cane juice crystals

2 tbsp tahini
2 tbsp yacon syrup
2 tbsp hemp oil

Makes 6 eggs
Takes an hour
You don't need any special equipment

Grate the liquor into small pieces. Then melt all three ingredients together – in a heatproof bowl stood in a pan of hot water, or in a porringer or Thermomix. Should take the best part of ten minutes to melt – don't rush it.

If you're just making chocolate, that's it – add any flavourings or superfoods that you're into, and pour into silicon molds.

If you're making eggs, you need two sets of egg shaped silicon molds. Pour your chocolate in, but don't fill the mold to the top – leave about 5mm gap. Make the filling by mixing the tahini, yacon syrup, and hemp oil together in a bowl with a spoon. You can add essential oils if you want to make different flavours e.g. peppermint. Using a teaspoon, put this mixture in each chocolate, so that now the chocolate reaches the top of the mold. Be careful to put it in the centre, not round the edge.

Put one set of eggs in the freezer, and the other in the fridge. The ones in the freezer should set in about 15 mins. Once you're sure the chocolate is hard, you can pop those out (carefully, so as not to damage the filling). Then take the others out of the fridge (still in their molds) and press the set eggs down into the semi-set ones. The chocolate should stick together nicely. Put them back in the fridge to set properly.

Once they're set, in another hour or so, carefully press them out and they should stay together. Store in the fridge, they keep quite well, at least a couple of weeks.

Choc Ice

I had this idea in Costa Rica. I don't usually eat bananas in the UK, because they have come so far, and mostly they are hybridised. If I am in a country where they grow, and they have those little baby ones which are kind of meaty, then I will enjoy them occasionally. So Amber, who I was working with in Costa Rica, wanted chocolate made with no sweetener and I thought, how is that going to work! She loves her bananas, so I had the idea of slicing them up and stirring them in to add sweetness. I left it overnight in the freezer to set, and it reminded me so much of choc-ice, I tweaked it a bit to make these. The easiest choc ices you ever made!

(I think some countries don't have choc ices, which is really odd to me; we grew up on them. It's basically an ice-cream bar coated in chocolate. We always had them at the cinema; you had a lady with a tray round her neck who just sold choc ices, and you were allowed to get one in the interval).

Ingredients

75g coconut oil
2 tbsp honey
50g cacao powder
2 bananas

Makes 8
Takes 10 mins to make and a few hours to set
You need bar molds and freezer space

Melt the coconut oil. Stir in the honey and cacao powder. Pour the chocolate into your bar-shaped molds, just enough to cover the base. Slice your bananas into fairly thin slices, about 5mm, then gently place them on the chocolate, with each slice touching each other, and a little space at each end. Pour over the rest of the chocolate so it covers the bananas. Put the molds in the freezer and leave for at least 6 hours (depending on your freezer), until they are frozen. Pop them out of the molds and store them in a ziplock bag. They keep pretty much indefinitely in the freezer.

Magic Bounty Bars

Oh yea! Is the first thing to say about these. Part inspired by my friend Julia Corbett, who used to make the most incredible Diviana Alchemy bars – my favourite was the Golden Kava. Also, a bar version of my candies. They are a little tricky, but that doesn't really matter as they are going to be delicious however they turn out. They have a lot more chocolate than a standard Bounty Bar, but who says that's a bad thing?

Ingredients

3 cups (150g) coconut flakes
3 tbsp coconut oil
3 tbsp coconut nectar or yacon syrup
1 tbsp turmeric powder

100g (1 cup) cacao liquor
50g (½ cup) lucuma
25g (¼ cup) cacao butter
5 drops vanilla stevia
1 tsp Etherium Gold (optional)

Makes 8 bars
Takes 45 mins
You need a high-power blender or grinder, plus some silicon bar molds

Grind up the coconut flakes to a powder. Melt the coconut oil if it's not already liquid. Either in the machine or by hand, stir them together with the coconut nectar and turmeric powder until they've formed a sold mass. Now shape them into fish fingers! Get your bar molds and make the coconut filling just slightly shorter and thinner than the mold. It's going to end up smaller than you expect. Put the fish fingers on a foil-covered plate or silicon board and pop them in the freezer while you make the chocolate.

To make the chocolate, grind or finely chop the liquor and melt it along with the cacao butter. Once it's melted, stir in the lucuma, stevia, and Etherium Gold. Now pour your chocolate into the bar molds, just enough to make a thin layer on the bottom, not too much. Remove your fish fingers from the freezer, and gently place each one in the centre of the molds. Then pour your remaining chocolate over the top, so it covers the coconut. Start in the middle and let it drip off the sides. Put them in the freezer to set – if you're using silicon molds, they should set in 30 mins. Store in the fridge, they keep well for a couple of months.

On the Road

I travelled to over twenty-five countries teaching raw food classes, and became an expert at living out of a suitcase (albeit a very large, rainbow-coloured one). Like everything in life, travelling on a raw food diet is as difficult as you make it. I must admit to often getting a box of superfoods and snacks sent ahead to wherever I was going, but you can do that too, if it makes life easy! Then I knew that as long as I can pick up some local organic veg, source some spring water, and get the WiFi password, I'll survive.

I always carried the following items in my bag (these were standard issue, even if I was only out for the day): Raw Reserve sachets (a green powder blend that I usually added to coconut water), Four Sigmatic mushroom extract sachets (for hot drinks), Gopal's power wraps (for savoury snacking), and a raw chocolate bar.

And this is what I might pack for a weekend away:

- Chia seeds. 250g makes 8 portions of chia porridge. Can be soaked in water and all you need is a bowl, I've even done it in a hotel ice bucket!

- Seaweeds. Nori sheets, kelp noodles, wakame, dulse. Light and easy to pack.

- Chocolate bars for energy

- Flax crackers

- Green powders for sustenance

- Enzymes and probiotics for travel tummy

- Superfoods like hemp seeds, maca, gojis, and chlorella

Hopefully, you will not need to pack your vitamin D supplement because you are going somewhere sunny!

Wherever you go in the world, you should always be able to get local, seasonal fruit and veg, and that should be the bulk of your diet anyhow. If you are going somewhere where vegetables are not commonplace, I would question if you really need to go there! People always worry about how easy it is to eat raw abroad, but fruit and vegetables are found in virtually every corner of our planet, and probably even in the outer reaches of the galaxy as well. If you have some of the extra supplements I have listed above, then you will be doing just fine.

Chia is brilliant because it is so hydrating. The best way to consume chia when travelling is to drink Chia Fresca. Buy a 1 litre bottle of water (or fill up your travel bottle with filter water or spring water if you are lucky enough to have access to it). Drink a few swigs out the top and fill it up with chia – a couple of spoons worth – if you're dextrous you should just be able to pour it straight out of the packet into the neck of the bottle without spilling any. Then add the juice of a lemon – I juice lemons with a fork if I don't have a squeezer. If you're in an airport or a train station, you may have to omit the lemon! This is my favourite travel drink, and is the easiest way to turn a boring bottle of plastic water into a super fun drink. The other brilliant thing about chia is it's very good for keeping you regular, which can often be an issue for people in a different climate, drinking unfamiliar water and breathing unfamiliar air. Chia is the best food I know of for loosening everything up and keeping your gut working efficiently.

Sea vegetables are great to carry, because like chia, once you soak them they grow to up to four times the size. Dulse is a favourite travel snack because it doesn't need soaking and it's so nutritious and grounding. Dulse is generally better soaked, but in this case we eat it dry. We always take a packet of nori sheets because they take up no room at all in your luggage. Other seaweeds are good to take and soak when you arrive at your destination – wakame, hijiki, sea spaghetti, arame, or even kelp noodles, can transform a humble plate of vegetables into a luscious and sustaining meal. A packet of dried sea vegetables makes around four servings, so you only need to take a couple of bags to keep you going for the week.

Next on my travel list are some bulkier, denser foods like flax crackers and chocolate bars. I always prefer to take things that are ready packaged; firstly because it's more convenient, but secondly because when my luggage gets inspected I don't want them wondering what that strange brown slab is in my bag... If you're making your own crackers to take with you, pack them in a ziplock bag or Tupperware and stow them somewhere they won't get smashed to smithereens.

Next we get on to the green powders, which take virtually no space at all, but make all the difference in terms of nutrition and energy levels. I love my salad covered in Spirulina flakes, and have a real taste for it. I realise it's a bit like people who are addicted to salt and need to shake loads of it over their food to make it palatable to them. To me, a dinner doesn't taste right unless it's covered in micro-algae. If I can get some local green leaf, and dress it in loads of green powder and plenty of oil, I'm a happy bunny (and I don't even need a carrot).

Equipment wise, I always pack a juice bag. Again, it takes up next to no space. Not only is it wonderful for making creamy milks, it's the best way to make juice when you're travelling. Blend all your vegetables and/or fruits in your blender, strain through the juice bag, and that twin gear can go eat its big fat juicy heart out. You can also use it as a sieve or a sprouting bag. I usually pack a little travel knife, and if there's no blender at my destination, I'll take a travel blender (I have a Tribest, but Nutribullet is the most well-known brand; it weighs just under 1 kg).

Wherever I land, I seek out the local seasonal fruits and veg, and I look for some good quality oil and spices to make salad dressings. If pre-packaged sprouts (alfalfa is my favourite) are available, I'll stock up on those too. I'll try and get my hands on some raw honey, and whatever other delicacies are local to the region.

So you can see, travelling raw doesn't need to be an issue. Because we are dealing with such nutrient dense foods, you only need to pack a little, and they are going to provide you with days of nutrition. Hopefully, if you pack with a bit of ingenuity, it will be fun for you to explore the local cuisine and not feel you're being deprived.

Cakes

Raw vegan cakes aren't hard to find these days. A quick Google search for "raw cake recipes" just revealed 19 million results. While undoubtedly easier on the body than their dairy and gluten-laden counterparts, the majority of these kind of recipes still aren't optimally healthy. They may well be high-glycemic, filled with dates or maple syrup, and they are very often heavy on the nuts, which aren't the easiest foods for the body to digest, especially when combined with fruits. Mostly, they aren't technically raw either: although they involve no baking, many of the ingredients used will be heat-treated.

The cakes you will find in this section are wonderful to eat AND wonderful to your body. I steer away from nuts and dried fruit, and still produce decadent beauties that transport you into bliss with their sumptuousness. I use ingredients like Irish moss, young coconuts, lucuma, buckwheat and psyllium, which may be harder to find, but are worth tracking down if you are serious about your cakes. I believe cake is a very important food group! Cake is the most affirmative food; when we eat cake, we are declaring to ourselves our intention to be happy and celebrate the moment. The cakes in this section are so truly healthy, they would even make an acceptable breakfast or lunch, on occasion.

Superstar Cake - See page 223

Life is Like a Plate of Cake

You might think that's a fairly obvious thing to say, coming from me, but bear with me, and let me explain.

When you make a cake, you have a basic understanding of what elements you need to include to make it taste good. As we're naturally talking raw chocolate cakes here, we would say we need a substantial amount of lucuma and cacao as the base. We know if we put too much honey in it will be too sweet, and too many nuts will make it too heavy. We add a few drops of essential oil for flavouring, and some superfoods to make it exciting. Really good cake making, achieving just the right balance of flavours, is alchemy, and so is life.

I know I need, for example, exactly one cup of children, one cup of writing time, and one cup of yoga, to create the right base to my day. I know if it spills over into two cups of children it will be too sweet, or two cups of writing and it will be too dry. My cake needs flavouring, so I always get some music in there. It's this that lifts it and brings out all the flavours of the other ingredients. Without it, my cake would be a little tasteless. My cake needs superfoods, something to take it to the next level, but only in small amounts. So I go out dancing, or I get some tattoo work done, or have a colonic. These are things I would never do all day, it would be too intense! But without them, my life would be much less profound.

Of course, there are many, many more elements that make for a happy life than the few I've just listed. It's not the purpose of this article to relate them all, for they are endless. Rather, my intention is to inspire you to think about what ingredients you put in your cake each day, and if they taste good to you.

Most days now, my cake is edible, I am happy to say. But I want my cake to taste amazing every day! So I continue working on the recipe, refining the amounts, trying to get it a little better all the time. I learn new things, and substitute a familiar ingredient with a new more interesting one. I meet new people, and discover different methods for assembling the ingredients in my cake, creating new styles of cake in the process. Understanding the alchemical process helps us understand our lives, and what we personally have to do each day so we can go to sleep with a contented smile on our faces and a happy belly full of delicious life experience.

Triple Layer Chocolate Pie

Yup, I said it. Triplelayerchocolatepie. Part-inspired by Julia Corbett who makes ALL her pies triple layer pies (that girl knows what's going on). First created in the kitchen of Solla, and blessed by an infusion of her talents as well.

Ingredients

Crust:
1 cup (50g) coconut chips
1 cup (90g) almonds
½ cup (50g) cacao nibs
2 tbsp maca
1 tbsp coconut oil
1 tbsp water
1 tbsp coconut nectar or yacon syrup
4 drops peppermint essential oil
pinch salt

Second Layer:
½ cup (50g) cacao powder
½ cup (50g) mesquite
1 tbsp cane juice crystals or coconut sugar
1 tbsp purple corn extract
½ cup (60ml) extra virgin olive oil
4 drops vanilla Medicine Flower Extract
½ cup (50g) buckwheaties
1 tbsp gojis

Serves 8
Takes 1 hour (you need to prepare your Irish moss 3-5 days in advance)
You need a high-power blender, or grinder and food processor

Don't forget to prepare your Irish Moss in advance. You need to soak it 3-5 days ahead of the time you want to use it.

First up, it's crust time. Into a grinder or high-speed blender, please put your coconut chips, almonds and cacao nibs, and grind them to a fine powder. Then either in a food processor, or by hand in a mixing bowl with a spoon, add your maca, yacon, peppermint oil and salt, and mix them in well. Finally, add the coconut oil and water. In the food processor it should all bind together nicely; if it's still a little dry and crumbly add a splash more water. If you're mixing it in a bowl, you need to get stuck in with your hands and press it into a ball of dough.

Get your cake tin ready: silicon molds are best, but if you're using a standard tin, line it with greaseproof paper, cling film or aluminum foil first, so you can turn the cake out nicely when it's done. Press your dough into the base. It's going to be flat, and not line the sides. It should be nice and thick, about 1cm (½"). Put it in the freezer while you make the next layer.

The middle layer is really simple. In a mixing bowl with a spoon, combine the cacao powder, mesquite, sugar, purple corn and vanilla. When they are evenly mixed, pour in the olive oil and make a paste. Once it's nice and gooey, stir in your gojis and buckwheaties (buckwheaties are sprouted and dehydrated buckwheat groats that add a crunchy texture). Remove the base from the freezer, and spoon this sticky crunchy toffee layer over the top. It should be about the same thickness as your base layer. Pop it back in the freezer.

Topping:
28g (1oz) Irish moss
3 cups (375g) fresh or frozen berries
½ cup (50g) cacao powder
2 tbsp lecithin granules
2 tbsp coconut oil
2 medjool dates
1 tbsp suma
½ cup (50g) lucuma powder
1 avocado
1-2 tbsp raw honey

Last bit! Get your Irish Moss from the fridge where it's been soaking for the past few days. Don't rinse it, put it in your blender with all the berries. I've made it with strawberries and blueberries and they both work really well. I tried it with raspberries and it wasn't so good. A high-power blender works best for this, if you're using a standard blender you may struggle a little to get it into a purée. It will still taste good, you're just going to have some lumps in the end result so the texture won't be as good. When you're satisfied it's as puréed as it's going to get, you can start working in some more ingredients: cacao powder, lecithin, lucuma, dates and suma. Blend again, till it's all whipped and creamy. Now add the more liquid ingredients: the coconut oil, avocado and honey. Add honey according to taste: blueberries will probably need more than strawberries. Blend one more time and now you should have a thick whipped cream.

Remove the crust from the freezer and spoon the berry mousse over the top. If you want to really bling it up you can cover the top in more berries; this makes a real extravaganza of a cake. Unless it's a special occasion, I would just leave it without another topping, it's exciting enough as it is! Put it in the fridge to set and leave it for a good 2-3 hours. If you're in a hurry you can put it in the freezer for 30 mins - 1 hour. When you're ready to serve it, it should come neatly out of the mold in one piece - this is where your foil/paper/plastic wrap layer comes in handy, as it should just lift out. The mousse layer should be firm enough to slice without it losing its shape. Transfer onto a plate to serve.

The pie will keep in the fridge for up to a week. If you leave it out of the fridge for too long, the mousse layer will start to melt a little, so don't leave it out for longer than 20 mins or so, or it turns into more of a triple layer chocolate mousse (now there's an idea!)

Teddy's Apple Pie

It was Teddy's birthday and I couldn't go to the party without making a cake. Ysanne was out of town and had left me her LA apartment to stay in for a few days, along with a whole crop of apples she had grown (she is a very skilled gardener). Julia Corbett inspired me again with a recipe for apple pie that has a layer of caramel in. So, events conspired to produce this Autumn recipe, perfect for when you have so many apples you don't know what to do with them.

Ingredients

Crust:
2 cups (100g) coconut flakes
1 cup (100g) lucuma
1 tbsp honey
2 tbsp coconut oil
¼ cup (60ml) water
1 tbsp cinnamon
¼ tsp salt

Raspberry Cream:
2 tbsp maca
1 tbsp freeze-dried raspberry powder
2 tbsp tahini
2 tbsp yacon syrup or raw honey
4 tbsp hemp oil
¼ cup (60ml) water
juice 1 lime

Serves 8
Takes 45 mins to make
You need a good blender and food grinder

Grind up your coconut flakes in a food grinder or high-power blender so you have a flour. Still in your machine, add the lucuma, cinnamon, and salt and mix again for a brief minute. Once it's evenly mixed, add in your wet ingredients: the honey and coconut oil first. You don't need to melt the coconut oil first. Keep mixing, and add the water gradually until you have a solid mixture with no crumbs. It should only just be moist enough to stick together, not too wet, so it creates a good firm base once it's set. Press it into your silicon mold or lined cake tin so it just lines the bottom, not the sides. It should be around ½ cm thick. Put it in the freezer while you make the next layer.

By hand, in a bowl mix together the raspberry layer. Stir together the tahini and honey. When you have a paste, add the hemp oil and stir again. Then add the maca and raspberry powders; by this stage it should be very thick. Add the lime juice, and then the water gradually, until you have a smooth, spreadable paste. Remove the crust from the freezer and spoon the raspberry layer over the top, it should cover it thinly. If you don't have raspberry powder, you can make the recipe just the same without it, it's only for flavour. Pop it back in the freezer while you make the apple layer.

This time you do need to melt your coconut oil in advance. Do this in a heatproof bowl stood in a saucepan of freshly boiled water, or in a porringer, while you prepare the apples for the blender. Slice the fruit so that it's the right size for your machine, removing

Apple Filling:
4 cups apples (about 6)
1 cup (250ml) water
1 cup (125g) coconut oil
2 tbsp lecithin
10 drops vanilla Medicine Flower Extract
2 tbsp coconut sugar or cane juice crystals
1 tbsp ashwagandha

the cores, and any odd brown bits. Put them all in the blender and blend for a minute; they won't purée up at this stage but they will get quite nicely broken down. Next, add the coconut sugar, ashwagandha, lecithin and vanilla, and stir them in by hand to give your blender a head start. While the blender is turning, on a medium setting, add the water gradually. You should now be getting close to a purée. Finally, add the melted coconut oil, and once it's mixed in, blend on high just for 20-30 seconds so it's smooth and creamy. Remove your base from the freezer and pour it over. Return to the fridge to set for at least 2 hours. Keeps well, for up to a week.

Crikey Cake

This is the cake that I made in my food prep classes in 2011. It's a chocolate-free cake, for a change!

Ingredients

Cake:
2 cups (200g) buckwheaties
1 cup (50g) coconut chips
1 cup (125g) sesame seeds
1 ½ cups (150g) lucuma
½ cup (50g) maca
½ cup (90g) cane juice crystals or coconut sugar
1 tbsp suma
1 tsp Etherium Gold
10 drops vanilla Medicine Flower Extract
1 cup (125g) coconut oil
1 cup (125g) cacao butter
1 cup (250ml) water

Icing:
3 avocados
1 tbsp blackcurrant powder
1 tbsp purple corn extract
3 tbsp yacon syrup or raw honey
½ cup (125ml) water
seasonal fruit to decorate

Serves 12
Takes 45 mins to make
You need a high-power blender

Grind up the buckwheaties to a flour (Note: buckwheaties are buckwheat that has been soaked, sprouted and dehydrated. You can't use unsoaked buckwheat, it is indigestible.). Remove the buckwheaties and put them in your large mixing bowl. Grind up the sesame seeds and coconut flakes, and transfer them to the mixing bowl as well. Melt your coconut oil and cacao butter, ready to add in your mixture at the end. Add in all the dry ingredients: lucuma, maca, suma, Etherium Gold, and vanilla. Mix well with your hands, trying to rub air in as you do so; this will make the end result lighter and fluffier. When you're happy you've rubbed as much air in as you can, pour in your cacao and coconut butters. Stir them into the mixture, either by hand or with a spoon, but gently, so as not to remove the air you've previously folded in. Finally, add the water gradually. Sometimes I find I need more water and sometimes less, so be careful while you add it; you just want enough liquid for the cake to hold together nicely, not so it's runny. Put the cake mix in a silicon mold, or a cake tin lined with aluminium foil or greaseproof paper. If you put it in the fridge to set it will take 2-3 hours; if you're in a hurry, put it in the freezer and it should be ready in 30 mins.

To make the icing, it's very simple. Remove the flesh from the avocados and put everything in the blender together: avocado flesh, blackcurrant powder, purple corn extract, honey and water. This recipe is based on average sized avocados, so if you have large avocados use less and small avocados use more! An average avocado is 250g, I feel it's always worth weighing them to get a good idea of how many to use.

Remove the cake from the fridge or freezer and turn it out onto a serving plate. Spoon the purple icing over the top and decorate with your seasonal fresh fruit. Any leftovers will keep in the fridge for up to five days.

Blueberry & Chocolate Chip Cupcakes

I had quite an obsession with cupcakes for a while. They are totally a labour of love, but there is something so fun about the cakes in their individual little cases. I was very inspired by a raw chef called Natalia KW, who had a whole book called Cupcake Heaven. I also loved Caroline Fibaek's book Raw Cakes; I found her recipes a little overly sweet, but her presentation was a total delight.

Ingredients

175g (1 ⅓ cups) coconut oil
250g (2 ½ cups) buckwheaties
200g (2 cups) lucuma
4 tbsp freeze-dried blueberry powder
60g (½ cup) coconut sugar
1 tbsp ashwagandha
80g raw chocolate
250ml (1 cup) water

200g (1 ½ cups) coconut oil
100g (1 cup) cacao powder
100g (1 cup) mesquite
1 tsp purple corn extract
2 tbsp cane juice crystals or coconut sugar

Makes 16 cakes
Takes 45 mins
You need a blender, silicon molds, and an icing bag

Melt the coconut oil in a porringer or a heatproof bowl stood in a saucepan of hot water. Grind up the buckwheaties in a grinder or high-power blender into a powder. In a mixing bowl, stir together the buckwheat flour, lucuma, blueberry powder, sugar, and ashwagandha. Mix all together so they are evenly blended. Grate your raw chocolate into tiny chips, best done with a good knife, and stir them into the mixture. Then stir in your melted coconut oil, and next the water. Add the water gradually to make sure the mixture does not get too sloppy. It should be a dough, with no dry powdery bits left, but not too soft and sticky, and it should be lilac in colour.

You need silicon cupcake molds for this, but they are pretty easy to find. Or you can use paper cupcake cases if you can find quite sturdy ones. Place a handful of your mixture into each cupcake mold: how high is up to you, and whether you want to create fat cupcakes or more delicate ones! I usually fill my molds to about three-quarters full, or about 50-60g per cupcake. Put them in the fridge to set.

Next, we are making the icing. You don't need to pre-melt your coconut oil for this. Put all the ingredients in the blender, and blend to a cream. Then spoon out into a piping bag (without eating it all!).

Clean everything away, to give your cakes another 5-10 mins to set in the fridge. When you're ready, take them out, and turn them out of the molds onto a plate. Use your icing bag to pipe the frosting on, in whatever patterns please you. Decorate with chocolate chips or fresh blueberries, if they are in season, and a sprinkling of coconut sugar.

They should set now in less than an hour. If you need to store them, keep them in an airtight container in the fridge and they will keep for a couple of weeks.

Blackcurrant & Lime Cupcakes

You can make cupcakes straight into paper cases, but you need to get good quality cases; the cheap thin ones won't hold your mixture very well and just collapse. It's easier (and more environmental) to use silicon molds – you can get cupcake shaped ones, or I have hearts and plain circles as well. You also need to master a piping bag to get professional looking cupcakes: again, you can either invest in a good quality reusable piping bag with nozzles, or just pick up some disposable plastic ones at the kitchen store.

Ingredients

175g (1 1/3 cups) coconut oil
250g (2 ½ cups) buckwheaties
200g (2 cups) lucuma
2 tbsp blackcurrant powder
90g (½ cup) cane juice crystals or coconut sugar
1 tbsp he shou wu
100g (1 cup) Incan berries
250ml (1 cup) water

125ml (1 cup) coconut oil
75g (¾ cup) lucuma
125ml (½ cup) water
2 tbsp xylitol or coconut sugar
2 limes
1 tsp spirulina

Makes 16 cakes
Takes 45 mins
You need a blender, silicon molds, and an icing bag

Melt the coconut oil in a porringer or a heatproof bowl stood in a saucepan of hot water. Grind up the buckwheaties to a powder in your high performance blender or food grinder. In a mixing bowl, stir together the buckwheat flour, lucuma, blackcurrant powder, cane juice crystals (or coconut sugar), and he shou wu. Mix all together so they are evenly blended. Mix in your Incan berries. Then stir in your melted coconut oil, and next the water. Add the water gradually to make sure the mixture does not get too sloppy. It should be a dough, with no dry powdery bits left, but not too soft and sticky, and it should be lilac in colour.

You need silicon cupcake molds for this, or of course, you can use paper cases. Place a handful of your mixture into each cupcake mold: how high is up to you, and whether you want to create fat cupcakes or more delicate ones! I usually fill my molds to about three-quarters full, or about 50-60g per cupcake. Put them in the fridge to set.

Next, we are making the icing. If you don't have a high-power blender, you need to melt some more coconut oil, the same way you did before. If you have a high-power blender, and the weather is warm, i.e. your coconut oil is soft, you don't need to melt it first, it will go liquid in the blender. Put all the ingredients in the blender. You want to peel the limes and put the whole flesh in. (Save the peel to use as a garnish). Blend to a cream. Then spoon out into a piping bag.

Clean everything away, to give your cakes another 5-10 mins to set in the fridge. When you're ready, take them out, and turn them out of the molds onto a plate. Use your icing bag to pipe the frosting on, in whatever patterns please you. Decorate with Incan berries and pieces of lime peel.

They should set now in less than an hour. If you need to store them, keep them in an airtight container in the fridge and they will keep for a couple of weeks.

Be the Cupcake
You Wish to See in the World

Next level cupcakes! Based on the Be the Change chocolate bar, the cupcake itself contains the monatomic trace element Etherium Gold, while the frosting contains wild blue-green algae. There's a reason Be the Change was one of the very most popular products on our site (out of over 1000 products), and I'm sure that it's this alchemical combination of gold and phycocyanins that does it.

Makes about 12 cupcakes
Takes 1 hour
You need a high-power blender, silicon molds, and a piping bag

Start by melting the coconut oil and cacao butter together in a heatproof bowl stood in hot water, or a porringer or Thermomix. In a separate bowl, mix the dry ingredients: mesquite, lucuma, cacao powder, coconut sugar, and Etherium Gold. Try and get air into the mixture as you rub them in, so they come out nice and light. Once your butters are melted, stir them in as well, and then add the water gradually to make a dough. Take large spoonfuls of the mixture and either put them into silicon cupcake molds or paper cupcake cases. Try not to press them down too hard in the cases, so that they are still light. Put them in the freezer to set if you have room; if not, the fridge will do.

Ingredients

75g (2/3 cup) cacao butter
75g (2/3 cup) coconut oil
100g (1 cup) mesquite
100g (1 cup) lucuma
50g (½ cup) cacao powder
50g (½ cup) coconut sugar or cane juice crystals
1 tsp Etherium Gold
250ml (1 cup) water

200g (1 ⅔ cup) coconut oil
200g (1 ⅔ cup) cacao butter
200g (2 cups) mesquite
200g (2 cups) lucuma
100g (1 cup) cacao powder
2 tsp Klamath Lake blue-green algae
10 drops peppermint essential oil

1 Be the Change bar

Now, time to make the icing. Melt the cacao butter, but not the coconut. In your blender, blend all the ingredients together. The coconut oil should be soft enough at room temperature that it helps make the icing a good piping consistency. If the mixture is too runny, just leave it on the counter for a while, while you clear up. It's a fine art getting it the right softness to pipe, which really only comes with practice. If you haven't got the time and/or the enthusiasm, you can just ice your cakes without a piping bag. You can also, of course, make them as one big cake if you really can't be hassled with the fiddliness of cupcakes. You will probably have icing left over: you can pour it into molds and eat as chocolate truffles. Once they are iced, cut a Be the Change bar into 12 pieces, four by three, to use as mini-flakes in the top of your cakes. Pop one into each cake. Put them back into the fridge to set for an hour or two. They keep well in the fridge, for at least a couple of weeks.

Strawberry & Baobab Cupcakes

My cupcake fascination continues.... Natalia KW uses coconut flour in all her recipes in her book Cupcake Heaven. I'm a big fan of coconut as you know, and I often use coconut chips ground down into a floury in recipes. The coconut flour is quite different, drier and more floury – you can't just substitute one for the other. I also use it successfully in the Rainbow Cupcakes recipe on KateMagic.com, which you must try.

Ingredients

2 cups (200g) coconut flour
1 cup (100g) lucuma
¼ cup (60ml) yacon syrup or honey
¼ cup (60g) baobab powder
¼ cup (60g) freeze-dried strawberry powder
1 tbsp vanilla powder
1 tbsp ashwagandha
2 cups (250g) coconut oil
2 cups (500ml) water
1 cup (100g) goji berries

2 cups (200g) goji berries
1 cup (100g) mesquite
2 cups (250g) coconut oil
1 cup (250ml) water
2 tbsp baobab powder

Makes about 20 cupcakes
Takes 1 hour to make
You need a blender

Melt the coconut oil in advance, in a porringer, or heatproof bowl stood in a pan of freshly boiled water, or a Thermomix. In a mixing bowl, pour in the coconut flour, lucuma, baobab, vanilla, strawberry powder, and ashwagandha. Once they are evenly mixed, stir in the melted coconut and then add the water gradually. Once you have a dough, stir in the goji berries. Spoon the mixture into cupcake molds – either silicon molds or paper cases work best. I think around 50g is the optimum size per cupcake. If you can make space in the fridge for them to set, while you make the icing, brilliant, if not it's ok to leave them on the side.

To make the icing, you need to melt more coconut oil. Grind your goji berries to a flour, then blend everything together – the gojis, mesquite, coconut oil, water and baobab. You should have a thick orange cream. Spoon this into your piping bag and pipe the top of your cupcakes. Of course, if you haven't got a piping bag or haven't got time to do this, you could just spread the icing on the top, but piping is all the fun of cupcake making! Decorate with dried strawberries or goji berries. Leave in the fridge to set. They keep well in the fridge in an airtight container for up to two weeks.

Superstar Cake

This is the cake we make on the last day of our Raw Magic Superstar Course, that has everyone floating out the door at the end on a cloud of bliss. Irish moss isn't the most straight-forward ingredient to use, but it is well worth the extra effort to get a sublimely light result that you just won't achieve with lots of cashews, avocados or oils as your base ingredients.

Ingredients

1 cup (50g) coconut chips
½ cup (100g) lucuma
½ cup (100g) buckwheaties
½ cup (50g) raisins
½ cup (125ml) water

2 avocados
1 cup (125g) coconut oil
½ cup (50g) cacao powder
½ cup (75g) coconut sugar
1 tbsp mucuna

28g (1oz) Irish moss
1 cup (250ml) water
½ cup (50g) lecithin
2 cups (250g) fresh or frozen berries
½ cup (75g) coconut oil
½ cup (90g) cane juice crystals or coconut sugar

Serves 12
Takes 1 hour to make. You need to pre-soak the Irish moss for 3-5 days. Takes 2-4 hours to set.
You need a high-power blender or food processor

OK, three layers! Are you ready? First up is the crust. We are going to grind up our coconut chips, raisins and buckwheaties in a food grinder or high-power blender. When they are ground to a flour, transfer them to a mixing bowl, or you can do this part in a food processor if you prefer. Add the lucuma to the mix and stir it together so it's evenly mixed. Lastly, stir in just enough water to make it all stick together. Press it into the base of a large silicon mold or lined cake tin. It's not going to line the sides, just make a thin flat base. Pop it in the freezer while you proceed with layer two.

Melt some coconut oil in a heatproof bowl stood in a pan of freshly heated water, or in a porringer or Thermomix. Scoop the flesh out of your avocados, and put them in the blender along with the cacao powder, coconut sugar, mucuna, and melted coconut. Blend to a smooth purée with no lumps. Remove the base from the freezer and pour the chocolate layer over it. Return it to the freezer and move onto layer three.

Melt more coconut oil. Blend up the Irish moss (see preparation instructions here p285) with the water. It won't go to a purée, but break it down as much as you are able. Then add in the lecithin, berries, and sugar, and blend again. Finally, add in the melted coconut oil and blend one last time. By now, you should have a purée with no lumps left. Remove the cake from the freezer and pour the top layer over.

Finally, decorate with fresh berries and put it in the fridge to set. It should be ready in a few hours, and firm to the touch.

Mamacakeshun

One of my most famous cakes is the Dedicakeshun, an overly rich chocolate brownie affair. My son Zachary, in his wisdom, said we should have the Mamacakeshun. So here it is.

Ingredients

Crust:
175g (2 cups) almonds
125g (2 cups) raw oats
100g (1 cup) lucuma
50g (½ cup) cacao powder
250ml (1 cup) water

Filling:
30g (1oz) Irish moss
1 litre (4 cups) hemp milk
30g (¼ cup) lecithin
4 tbsp yacon syrup or coconut nectar
50g (½ cup) cacao powder
60g (½ cup) coconut oil
100g (1 cup) lucuma
1 tbsp vanilla powder
2 tsp suma

Makes a mother of a cake!
Irish moss needs 3 days soaking
Takes about 30 mins to make and needs setting overnight
You need a high-power blender

Prepare your Irish moss first (see p285).

To make the crust, grind up the almonds and oats together in your blender or grinder, till you have a flour. Transfer to a mixing bowl and mix in the lucuma and cacao powder with your hands. When you've got a nice fine mix, pour the water in gradually to make a dough. Use the dough to line a 2 litre cake tin or flan dish – bottom and sides. Silicon molds work best, but if you don't have one, just line a standard tin with greaseproof paper, silver foil or cling film.

When you're ready with your Irish moss, without rinsing it, put the moss in the blender (throw the soak water away, or even better use it to water your houseplants). Add in 1 cup (250 ml) hemp milk and blend for a minute until you have a purée. Don't worry if you have a few lumps of seaweed left, you'll get rid of them in the next round. Add in the lecithin, syrup, cacao powder, lucuma, vanilla powder and suma, and whizz z again. Now it's going to be really thick, and you shouldn't have any lumps. Third time lucky, add in the coconut oil (you can melt it first if you like, it does make it easier but it's not essential) and the rest of the milk. Now it's going to be really runny, like a smoothie. Don't worry, it'll set like a dream. Pour it into your crust and carefully transfer it to the fridge to set. It takes a good six hours I find, but it is soooo worth the wait.

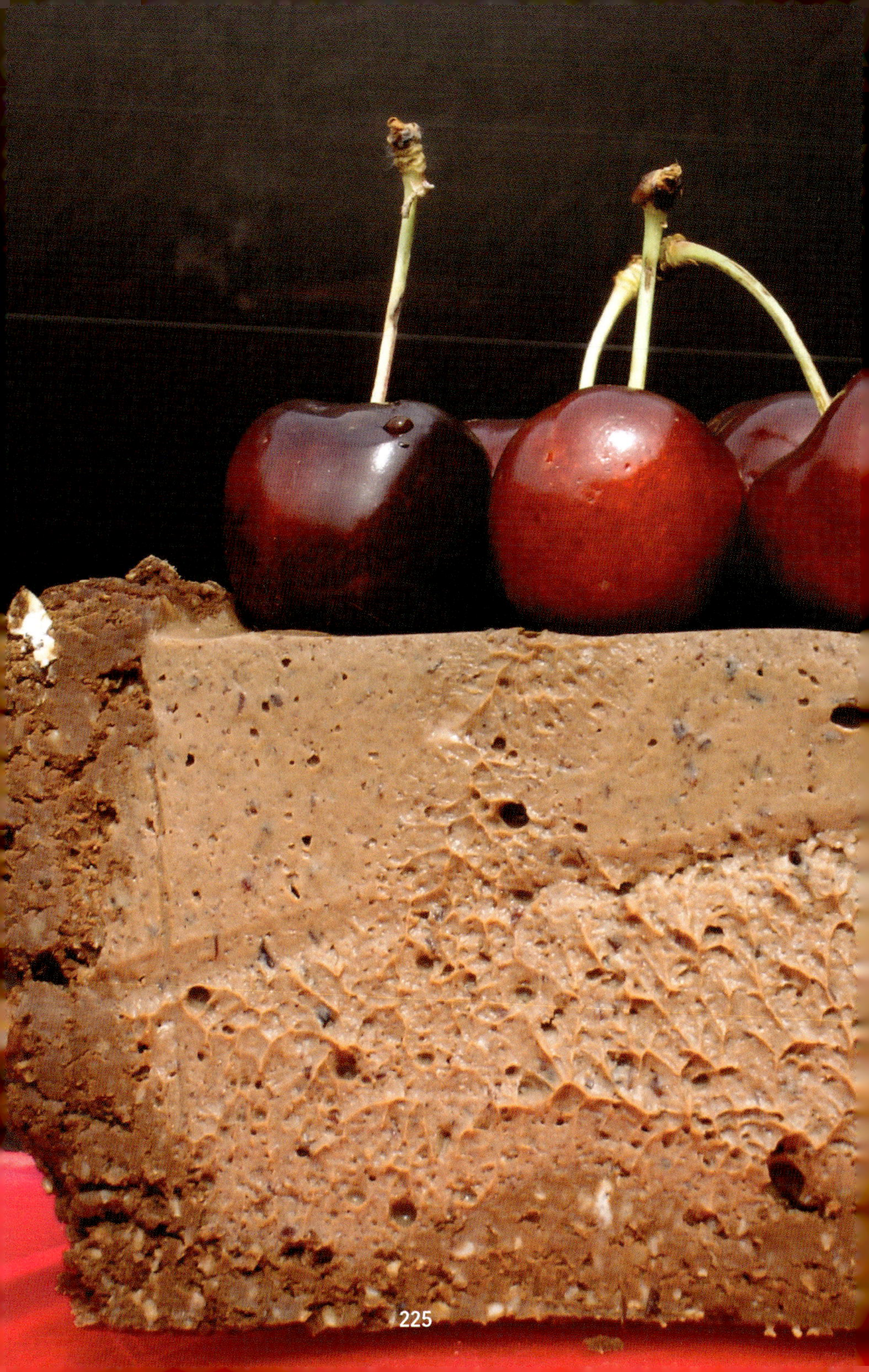

Strawberries & Cream Pie

This is a double layer pie with a goji crust, a layer of vanilla rose cream, and a filling of strawberries and baobab. I made it for a dinner party for my yoga teacher Naomi Clark's birthday and synchronistically she turned up all in red and white, looking like the living embodiment of strawberries and cream.

Ingredients

Crust:
2 cups (100g) coconut flakes
1 cup (125g) sesame seeds
½ cup (50g) goji berries
1 cup (100g) lucuma
1 tbsp honey
2 tbsp coconut oil
¼ cup (60ml) water
1 tbsp cinnamon
pinch salt
1 tbsp ashwagandha

Strawberries Layer:
2 avocados
1 cup (100g) gojis, soaked
4 tbsp freeze-dried strawberry power
1 cup (100g) mesquite
2 tbsp agave or raw honey
125ml (½ cup) water
1 tbsp baobab powder
1 cup (125g) coconut oil
10 drops strawberry Medicine Flower Extract

Serves 12
Takes 1 hour, with 1 hour pre-soaking
You need a blender

Make sure you've pre-soaked your gojis for at least an hour.

First up is the crust. Grind your sesame seeds, coconut flakes and goji berries to a flour. Then (this next bit is best done by hand, but you can use a food processor), stir in the lucuma, salt, and cinnamon. Rub in the honey and coconut oil. Unless your coconut oil is very solid, it should be possible to do this without melting it first. Finally, add the water gradually to make a firm dough. Press the pastry into a cake tin or mold, enough to line the bottom and sides. Silicon molds are easiest to use, but if you haven't got one it's easiest just to line a standard tin with greaseproof paper or aluminium foil.

To make the cream layer, first make sure you've prepared the Irish moss. If you don't have Irish moss, you can omit it, it's not essential, it just makes the cream lighter and fluffier. Then blend together all these ingredients: the shelled hemp seeds, Irish moss gel, lucuma, stevia, sugar, olive oil, water and rose oil. Once you've blended it until it's smooth, spoon it over your base, it should make a thin layer.

Cream Layer:
1 cup (100g) shelled hemp seeds
2 tbsp Irish moss gel
¼ cup (25g) lucuma
5 drops vanilla stevia
¼ cup (45g) cane juice crystals or coconut sugar
½ cup (125ml) extra virgin olive oil
1 cup (250ml) water
7 drops rose oil

Finally, it's filling time. Make sure you've pre-soaked your goji berries. Melt your coconut oil if it's not solid at room temperature. Blend together the avocado flesh, gojis, strawberry powder, mesquite, syrup, water, baobab, coconut oil, and strawberry extract. Once it's smooth, pour into your pie crust, over the top of the cream.

Will set in the freezer within an hour or in the fridge within 2-3 hours. Keeps for up to five days.

Cherry No Bakewell

Just call me Mrs Kipling. You do really need the Medicine Flower Extracts for this to give it that traditional almond and cherry flavour.

Ingredients

Pastry:
1 ½ cup (75g) coconut chips
1 cup (100g) lucuma
1 cup (100g) buckwheaties
1 cup (50g) raisins
½ cup (125ml) water
1 tbsp coconut oil

Jam:
2 cups (200g) gojis pre-soaked 1 hour
2 tbsp freeze-dried raspberry powder
1 tbsp cane juice crystals or coconut sugar

Marzipan:
1 cup (90g) almonds pre-soaked 4 hours
1 cup (100g) lucuma
1 cup (250ml) water
½ cup (125ml) extra virgin olive oil
1 tbsp yacon syrup or honey
10 drops almond Medicine Flower Extract

Icing:
1 cup (125g) coconut oil
½ cup (125ml) water
2 tbsp xylitol
10 drops cherry Medicine Flower Extract

Serves 12
Takes 1 hour, with 4 hours pre-soaking
You need a high-power blender

First, make sure you've pre-soaked the gojis and the almonds (separately). Then we are going to make the crust. In a food grinder or high-power blender, grind up the coconut chips, buckwheaties and raisins. Transfer the ground powder to a mixing bowl with lucuma and mix it all together. Take one tablespoon of coconut oil (you don't need to melt it first unless it's really hard), and rub it into your powders. Then add the water gradually, enough to make a dough, not too sticky, just dry enough to form a single ball of dough. Press the dough into your flan tin, preferably a 12" one. I use silicon molds so it is easy to turn out and doesn't stick. If you don't have a silicon mold, you should line your tin with foil or baking paper so you can turn it out easily. Your dough should line the base and the sides of your tin.

Next up is the jam. Drain your gojis (drink the soak water, don't throw it away, it's absolutely delicious!). Blend them up with the raspberry powder and sugar so that you have a thick jam. Spread the jam over the base of your pie, it should be quite a thin layer.

Third layer is the almond sponge. Drain your almonds, and put them in the blender with all the other ingredients: lucuma, syrup, water, olive oil and almond extract. Blend to a smooth thick cream, with no lumps left. When you're satisfied it's smooth enough, spread it over the jam layer; it's a much thicker layer and makes the bulk of your cake.

Lastly, we've got the icing. In a blender or food processor, blend the coconut oil, water, xylitol and cherry extract. You shouldn't need to heat the coconut first, it should soften in the blender. Once it's liquid, pour it over the top of the cake.

The day I first made this, I went to the health food store to see if I could get organic cherries to decorate it with and would you believe it, they had organic glacé cherries on offer! I would imagine they are pretty hard to get, so you could either use normal glacé cherries and suggest the people who eat your cake treat them as decoration and discard them, or you could depart from convention and use fresh cherries.

Keeps well in the fridge for up to a couple of weeks.

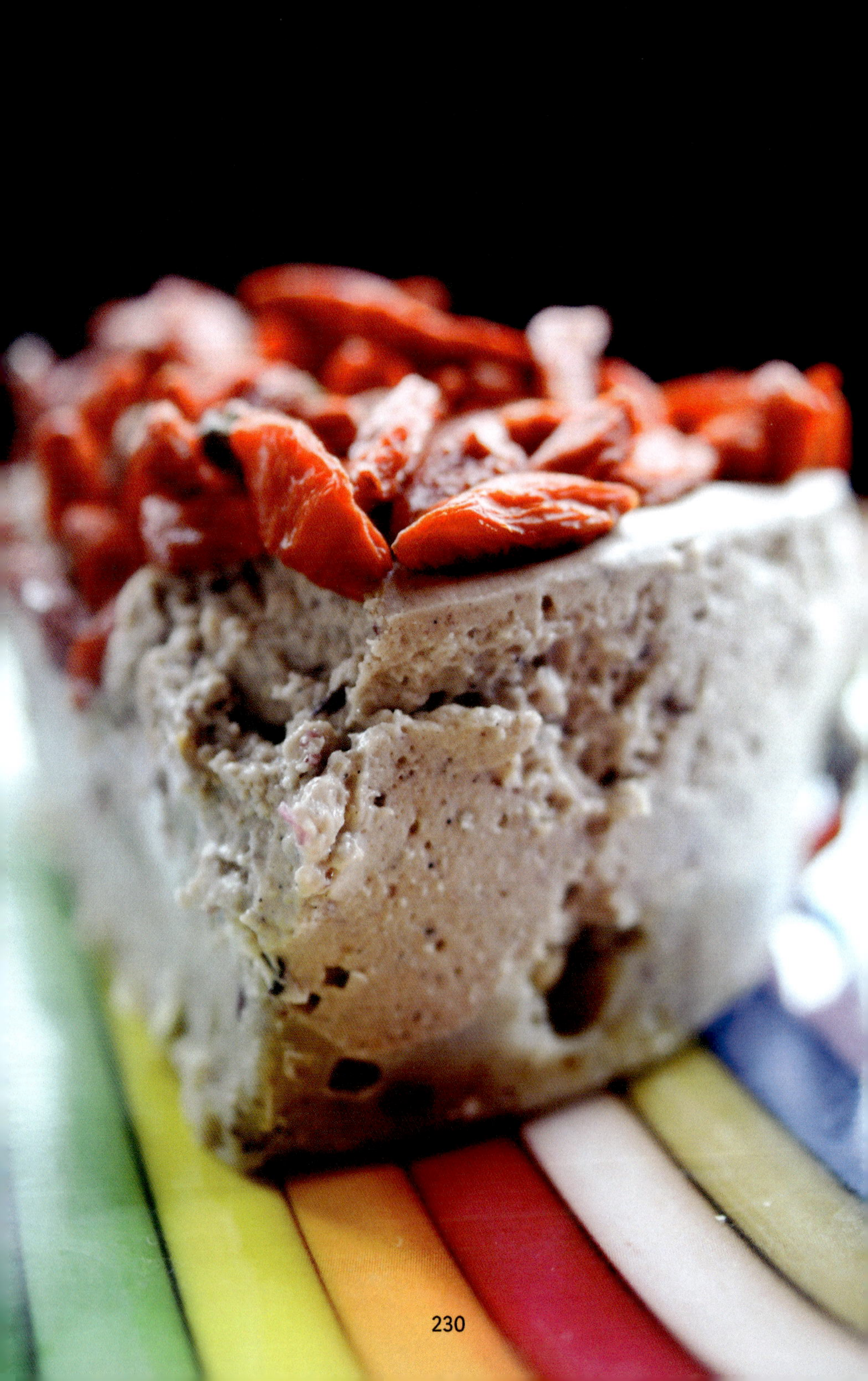

Rosemary's Rose Cheesecake

In honour of my dear friend Rosemary, who always inspires me to create something new and exciting in the kitchen when she comes over. This Irish moss-based dessert is so gorgeously light, you may need to weigh down your pockets with stones after you've eaten it, to prevent you from floating up to the heavens.

Ingredients

Base:
100g (1 cup) buckwheaties
90g (1 cup) almonds
2 tbsp raw honey
60g (½ cup) coconut oil

Topping:
1oz (30g) Irish moss
500ml (2 cups) pure water
125g or (1 cup) raw cashews (pre-soaked 4-8 hours)
10 drops rose essential oil or Medicine Flower Extract
125g (1 cup) coconut oil
50g (½ cup) lucuma
4 tbsp yacon syrup or raw honey
1 tsp Etherium Gold (optional)
Gojis or fresh berries to decorate

Serves 8
Needs 3 days at least to soak the Irish moss, then it will take you about 20 minutes to make the cake and another 2-3 hours to set it.
You also need a high-power blender

Make sure you have pre-soaked your cashews. To make the base, grind the buckwheaties and almonds to a flour. Melt the coconut oil, and stir it into the flour with the honey. Press it into the base of a silicon mold (or cake tin lined with greaseproof paper or aluminium foil). Pop it in the fridge to set while you make the topping.

Prepare your Irish moss according to the given instructions (p285). Blend it for a good few minutes until the moss is broken down as much as possible, and the mixture starts to go light and fluffy. Add all the other ingredients into the blender: the cashews, rose, vanilla, coconut oil, lucuma, syrup, ashwagandha and Etherium gold. Blend for a good couple of minutes. I don't have much of a sweet tooth, so 4 tbsp sweetener tastes perfect to me, but if you do love the sugary sweet stuff, you may want to up the quantities of honey a little. Add the second cup of water (250ml), and blend again until it's light and fluffy.

Pour it out over the buckwheat base and leave to set in the fridge for at least two hours. When its set, it should be light and moussey, but firm enough to slice. Decorate with handfuls of goji berries, or fresh berries such as strawberries if they are in season. Will keep for up to a week in the fridge, if you can stop it ascending up to heaven.

The Pop-Up Cake

I love doing Pop-Up dinners - it's a long held dream of mine to have a chain of restaurants (London, Brighton, LA, NYC, Copenhagen, Reykjavik, and Bali, since you ask), and pop-ups are a great way of testing out what works to make in larger quantities, and what dishes go down the best. Plus I feel, whereas not everyone wants to come to a raw food talk (because they might think they know the information already, or because they find the idea of a talk generally unappealing), everyone wants to go to dinner. And eating an amazing 5-course raw vegan meal is just as powerful a way to convert someone to the wonders of the diet, as spending two hours telling them all the reasons why raw food is beneficial. Maybe even more so. I sometimes plan a menu with a co-chef, and as far as dessert goes, I say, let's be spontaneous! Let's just make it up! But what I realised after half a dozen times or so is that I was "spontaneously" making up the same recipe every time. The Pop-Up Cake. So here it is, evidently what my unconscious mind has formulated as being the most gorgeous and decadent cake to serve to impress guests.

Ingredients

2 cups (100g) coconut flakes
1 cup (125g) sesame seeds
½ cup (50g) goji berries
1 tbsp cinnamon powder
1 cup (100g) lucuma
¾ cup (180ml) water

2 cups (200g) cacao nibs
1 cups (100g) mesquite
1 cup (125g) coconut oil
1 cup (250 ml) water
2 cups (250g) berries
½ cup (90g) coconut sugar

Serves 12
Takes 30 mins
You need a high-power blender

To make the crust, grind the coconut, sesame and gojis together in a high-power blender or food grinder. Transfer to a mixing bowl and stir in the cinnamon and lucuma. Once it's all evenly mixed, add the water gradually to make a dough. Don't let it get too sticky; just add enough water to hold it all together. When it's ready, press it into a silicon mold to line the base and sides. If you haven't got a silicon mold, line a normal cake tin with foil and press it into that. Put it in the freezer to set quickly.

Next step is to grind your cacao nibs to as fine as a powder as you can get them (don't grind for too long or they will start turning to a paste). At the same time as you're grinding, you can be melting your coconut oil in a heatproof bowl stood in a pan of gently simmering water. If you're using a high-power blender at this stage you probably need to remove the cacao nibs or they all get caked up at the bottom. But basically you're going to put everything in the blender and blend it together. Regarding the berries, if they are in season, obviously it's better to get fresh ones, but if they are not, I would go with frozen because they have so much more flavour. You can use strawberries, blueberries, cherries or raspberries, they all work. Better to defrost them before you use them or your mixture can go a funny consistency. So, blend all those ingredients together: the ground nibs, the melted oil, the berries, mesquite, water and coconut sugar. Blend until smooth and then pour into your crust. As the crust has been in the freezer, the filling should set nice and quickly. Decorate with fresh berries, gojis, coconut flakes or whatever you have to hand. If you're in a hurry, pop it back in the freezer and it should set in under an hour. In the fridge it'll take more like a couple of hours.

This cake actually keeps pretty well in the fridge - ideally eat it within a week, but should keep up to two weeks. If you have leftovers, you can always store them in the freezer, they keep for a few months frozen.

Return of the Sun Cheesecake

I make no secret of the fact that I don't really like nuts and I particularly don't like cashews. But this happens to be one of the most popular dishes I make, so what do I know? Clearly there are many, many people in this world who get along just fine with cashews, thank you very much, and this cake is for all of them, which hopefully includes you.

You can vary it with another fruit instead of the blueberries – strawberries, raspberries or mango all work well (I would also omit the purple corn if you're omitting the blueberries, unless you fancy a purple mango tart, in which case go right ahead).

Ingredients

2 cups (100g) coconut flakes
1 cup (60g) sesame seeds
½ cup (50g) goji berries
1 cup (100g) lucuma
1 tbsp honey
2 tbsp coconut oil
¼ cup (60ml) water
1 tbsp cinnamon
pinch salt
1 tbsp ashwagandha

2 cups (250g) cashews, pre-soaked
1 cup (125g) coconut oil
1 cup (250ml) water
2 cups (250g) blueberries
1 tbsp purple corn extract
½ cup (90g) xylitol or coconut sugar

Serves 12
Takes 45 mins, with 4-8 hours to pre-soak the cashews
You need a grinder and a blender

Don't forget to soak your cashews in advance! At least four hours, to make them more digestible.

First of all, we're going to do the crust. You might recognise the crust recipe, it's my current favourite and I use it often. Grind the coconut flakes, sesame seeds, and goji berries together in a food grinder or high-power blender. Then stir in the lucuma, cinnamon, salt and ashwagandha. When they are evenly mixed, add the honey and coconut oil. The coconut oil only needs to be pre-melted if it's very solid. If it's a little soft, you should be able to rub it in. Then add the water gradually until you have a firm ball of dough. Press it into your pie dish, over the bottom and up the sides. A standard 9" (23cm) flan dish works best.

Pop it in the freezer to chill while you make the filling. Melt your coconut oil in a bain marie or porringer. Drain your cashews, and put them in the blender with the melted coconut oil and water. Blend until smooth and then add the blueberries, purple corn and your sweetener of choice. Blend again, and then pour out into your pie crust. It should be a thick pouring consistency. Smooth it out, and decorate with more berries, coconut flakes, or gojis. Pop in the freezer to set in 30 mins, or in the fridge in a few hours. Stored in the fridge, it will keep for up to a week. Or you can keep leftovers in the freezer, these cakes freeze well.

Note: this crust is lovely by itself. You can flatten it and dehydrate it as a cookie. Or my latest discovery is chocolate-coated cookie dough balls! Roll it into balls and coat it in raw chocolate.

Papaya Pie Yea

I am a big fan of using local and seasonal ingredients, as you probably know, so I don't work so much with the tropical fruits. But when I was in Goa, I made this pie, and it's too good not to share. I think the secret lies in using fresh coconut meat. My favourite desserts I ever had were made by Annie Jubb at Life Food Organic in Hollywood, and she used coconut meat as the base in all her pies. It created this blissful creamy but light, melt in the mouth consistency which is my idea of heaven. So if you can get fresh coconut meat, and you're not averse to using tropical fruits, you should give this one a go, you won't regret it!

Ingredients

Crust:
2 cups (100g) coconut flakes
1 cup (120g) sesame seeds
1 tbsp honey
2 tbsp coconut oil
¼ cup (60ml) water
1 tbsp cinnamon
pinch salt

Caramel:
2 tbsp maca
2 tbsp tahini
2 tbsp yacon syrup or honey
4 tbsp hemp oil
¼ cup (60ml) water
juice 1 lime

Papaya Filling:
4 cups papaya
1 cup (250ml) water
1 cup (125g) coconut oil
1 fresh coconut (100g meat)
2 tbsp lecithin
2 tbsp coconut sugar

Serves 8-12
Takes 45 mins
You need a blender

To make the crust, ground the coconut and sesame together. Transfer to a mixing bowl and stir in the cinnamon and salt. Then add the honey, coconut oil and water to make a firm dough. Press it out into a pie tin, just enough to line the bottom, you don't want it to go up the sides. Pop it in the freezer while you make the next layer.

In a medium sized bowl, stir together your tahini, syrup, and hemp oil. Once it's a cream, add your maca; now it will go very stiff. Stir in the lime juice, then the water, so you have a very thick pouring consistency, one that drips off the spoon but only just. Remove your crust from the freezer and spoon this cream over it. Put it back in the freezer while you make the topping.

Melt your coconut oil in a bain marie or porringer. Scoop out your papaya flesh and coconut flesh. Blend them together to a cream. You could just eat this. Yum! But if you can hold back, you need to add some more ingredients to make your final layer. Blend in the lecithin and coconut sugar. Then once that's creamy, add your coconut oil and water. Pour into your pie base. Don't worry if it seems runny, it will firm up in the fridge. Don't put it in the freezer this time, sometimes it makes it go a weird consistency. Leave in the fridge for a couple of hours. Eat within three days.

Inca Redible Cake

I love Incan berries (also known as Golden berries or dried physalis). They have a sweet/sour/fizzy taste just like lemon sherbert. Apparently, they are a great source of bioflavonoids, and an excellent source of pectin. I love to eat them just as they are, or as a trail mix with cacao nibs and bee pollen. Here they are in a cake which you can eat great big slices of and feel nothing but divine.

Ingredients

Cake:
- 2 cups (250g) cacao nibs
- 2 cups (250g) sesame seeds
- 2 cups (200g) Incan berries
- 1 tbsp he shou wu
- ½ cup (120ml) yacon syrup or coconut nectar
- 1 cup (250ml) cold-pressed sunflower oil

Icing:
- 1 cup (150g) melted coconut oil
- 1 lemon, juiced
- 1 cup (100g) lucuma
- 1 tbsp yacon syrup or honey
- 1 tsp purple corn extract

To Decorate:
- 50g Incan berries
- 25g coconut chips

Serves 12
Takes 1 hour, and a few hours for setting
You need a high-power blender

Grind the cacao nibs in a high-power blender or food grinder. Set them aside in a mixing bowl, and grind the sesame seeds. Set those aside, in the same bowl, and grind the Incan berries. With your hands, mix together the cacao, sesame, and he shou wu, so they are evenly mixed. Try to aerate the mix as much as possible. Then add the ground Incan berries and yacon syrup, and mix again, still with your hands. Try and remove lumps as much as possible so you've got an evenly crumbly mixture. Lastly stir in the sunflower oil to bind it together. Put the cake into a silicon mold, if you have one. If you don't, you can use a normal cake tin, but you will have to line it with greaseproof paper or silver foil so you can turn it out easily. Put it in the freezer to set quickly – in a silicon mold it should take just 20-30 mins. In a normal cake tin, you're looking at 45 mins to an hour.

While you're waiting for it to set, clear away, and get ready to make the icing. Melt your coconut oil in a porringer or bain marie. In a mixing bowl, put the rest of the ingredients: lemon juice, lucuma, syrup, and purple corn. Stir them together with the oil, and leave for five or ten minutes so it starts to set a little. This will make it easier to spread on the cake. When you're ready, take the cake out of the freezer, turn it out of the mold and pour the icing over it. Cover the top and just let it drizzle down the sides a little. Press in the Incan berries and coconut chips on the top while the icing is still wet. Leave in the freezer to set for another 30 mins or so, or the fridge for 1-2 hours. Keeps well in the fridge for up to two weeks.

Note: I just recently got hold of some excellent quality raw sunflower oil from Sun & Seed, and I realised sunflower oil isn't used much in raw cuisine. If you can get oil that is definitely raw (cold-pressed itself is not a guarantee), then it makes a tasty alternative to olive oil. If you can't, olive oil works surprisingly well in raw cakes and desserts.

Chi Lime Pie

One of my favourite places I ever ate raw food was Annie Jubb's Life Food Organic, in Hollywood, and one of my favourite dishes there was her Key Lime Pie. I used to dream of it between visits! That and Truth Calkin's Reishi Cappucino. I discovered the secret to the melt-in-the-mouth texture she created was in using fresh coconut meat, so I was eager to try and replicate it with fresh coconuts when they became available in the UK. My 15-year old son loved it, but he wanted to know why it was named Key Lime Pie – where were the keys? And he told me it would be much better as a Chi Lime Pie. So here it is – a pie as full of chi as it is limes.

Ingredients

1 ½ cup (150g) almonds
1 cup (100g) raisins
2 tbsp coconut oil

3 limes
200g coconut meat (2 coconuts)
1 cup (125g) coconut oil
1 cup (250ml) water
½ cup (90g) coconut sugar
1 tbsp matcha powder

Serves 12
Takes 45 mins (plus setting time)
You need a blender

First of all, make sure you've got your coconut meat ready. If you have frozen meat, make sure it's been defrosting for at least 12 hours. If you're using fresh meat out of the coconut, just scoop the flesh out with a spoon. We are going to blend it up, so it doesn't matter how it comes out looking.

To make the crust, ground the almonds in a high-speed blender, spice mill or coffee grinder. Process the raisins in the same way. Melt the coconut oil, and mix everything together in a bowl with a wooden spoon, or in a food processor if you prefer. If it doesn't stick together to form one solid mass, add a little water or more coconut oil until it does. Press the crust into a cake tin. Silicon molds actually work best, but if you don't have one you can use a spring-form or loose bottomed cake tin, or line a standard cake tin with silver foil. Just use the mixture to line the base, not the sides. Pop it in the fridge while you make the next layer.

To make your topping, melt the coconut oil by standing the jar in a pan of simmering water. It will take about 5 minutes to get it liquid. While that's going, peel your limes so you just have the flesh remaining. Add them to the blender with all the other ingredients - the coconut meat, the water, coconut sugar, and matcha powder. Blend to a smooth cream, and pour over your pie crust. Transfer to the fridge for 2-3 hours or the freezer for 1 hour to set. Will keep in the fridge for up to a week, and the freezer for at least a month.

Mucunaroons

Ysanne asked, "Hello love, I'm munching flax crackers, got a bunch of chocolate forming in the freezer, and currently have a big batch of apple rings scenting my house with their sweetness as they dry, but oh no! Coconut macaroons cannot happen unless you can save the day with a tried and tested delicious recipe!

Do you have a fabulous coconut macaroon recipe that doesn't contain cacao please? It's just I can only find ones with cacao in them, and a friend of mine is allergic to it… and you know how I love to make inclusive deserts."

Ingredients

3 cups (150g) coconut chips
½ cup (60g) coconut oil
2 cups (200g) lucuma
2 cups (500ml) water
½ cup (90g) cane juice crystals or coconut sugar
pinch salt
2 tsp vanilla powder or 10 drops vanilla Medicine Flower Extract
1 tbsp mucuna
1 small bar (40g) raw chocolate (optional)

Makes 16-20 cookies
Takes 10 minutes to make and 18 hours to dehydrate
You need a food processor and a dehydrator

Take your coconut chips (or flakes – I mean the long thin dried pieces, not the itty bitty ones) and break them down in the food processor, just a little, so they are more bite-sized. Not so they get as small as rice grains, but so they will mix in easily with the rest of your ingredients. You can't substitute coconut flour as it has a very different texture.

If you have a dough hook in your food processor (that is, an attachment that's going to mix without chopping), you can use that for the next stage. If not, transfer your coconut chips to a mixing bowl. Coconut macaroons are light, so the trick here is to make sure you get as much air as possible in your mixture as you stir it together.

Melt the coconut oil in a porringer, or a heatproof bowl stood in some just boiled water. Stir all your dry ingredients together either in the food processor or by hand – the coconut chips, lucuma, sugar, salt, vanilla and mucuna. When they are properly mixed, add the melted coconut oil – if you're using a food processor, add the oil while the machine is turning. Then, still while the machine is turning add the water gradually, a little at a time. If you're doing it by hand, add half a cup of water, stir it together, and then add another half cup at a time, until it's all done.

Once it's properly and evenly mixed, take spoons of the mix and place them on your dehydrator trays. Don't make them too fat because they won't dehydrate properly, and not too thin or they will be too crispy. Should make 16-20 cookies, depending how big you make them. Dry for 12 hours, flip and dry another 4-6 hours on the other side.

As a kid, I remember enjoying Mr Kipling's macaroons. For some reason, my favourite thing about them was the rice paper underneath them. I used to eat it off the bottom first. I remember getting told off one time for eating the paper and leaving the macaroon. If you want, you could put rice paper on these before you put them in the dehydrator! I didn't do that, but I did drizzle a little chocolate over, just like Mr Kipling used to. I melted one 40g chocolate bar (a Whoosh bar actually) and it was just enough to make a little drizzle on each of my mucunaroons.

Baobab Brownies

I made these when I was first introduced to baobab back in 2011. I won't even try and describe how good these are! Eat them and you'll be left virtually speechless, the only words you'll be able to utter are "mmmmm" and "wow."

Ingredients

2 cups (180g) almonds
1 cup (100g) cacao nibs
½ cup (50g) raisins
½ cup (50g) cacao powder
4 tbsp yacon syrup or coconut nectar
2 tbsp baobab powder
2 tsp cinnamon powder
¼ cup (60ml) olive oil
¼ cup (60ml) water

Makes 12 squares
Takes 20 mins to make and 2-3 hours to set
You need a grinder and a food processor

In a food grinder, grind up the almonds to a flour. Remove them and grind the cacao nibs. Put the ground almonds, nibs and raisins in the food processor and process until the raisins are broken down. Then add in the cacao powder, baobab and cinnamon and process once more, until it's evenly mixed. Next, add your olive oil and syrup in, and process while the mixture starts to get sticky. Pour the water in slowly, while the food processor is on, and the mixture should become a dough.

Press your dough into a square baking tray lined with greaseproof paper or a silicon mold. Leave it in the fridge to set for at least 2 hours. When you're ready, cut it into squares, 3 x 4, or 4 x 4 if you prefer smaller fingers. Will keep well in the fridge in an airtight container, for about two weeks.

Variation: try omitting the baobab and cinnamon, and replacing with 2 tablespoons of blueberry powder and 1 tbsp vanilla powder (or 10 drops vanilla Medicine Flower Extract) for Blueberry Brownies.

Dulsilicious Chocolate Brownies

Don't turn the page! This was one of the most popular recipes on my old website. In my Raw Magic book, there is a recipe for dulse chocolate called Hi-Seas. This is the Brownie version. Just don't tell anyone they have seaweed in and they will never even know!

Ingredients

125g (1 cup) almonds
50g (½ cup) cacao nibs
1 cup (15g) dry dulse
2 tsp vanilla powder or 10 drops vanilla Medicine Flower Extract
100g (1 cup) lucuma
50g (½ cup) cacao powder
1 tbsp mucuna
125ml (½ cup) extra virgin olive oil
2 tbsp raw honey or yacon syrup
180ml (¾ cup) water

Makes 16 squares
Take 20 mins, with a couple of hours setting time
You need a high-power blender

Grind up the almonds, cacao nibs and dulse in your blender or food grinder. Transfer to a mixing bowl along with the other dry ingredients: lucuma, chocolate powder, vanilla and mucuna, and sift together by hand. Then stir in the wet ingredients with a spoon. Add the olive oil and honey first and mix those in, then gradually add the water so you have a gooey dough. Don't use all the water if you don't feel it's necessary. When it's ready press into a silicon mold or a cake tin lined with greaseproof paper or aluminium foil. Leave to set in the fridge for a couple of hours. If you want to ice it, melted chocolate is good. Otherwise, cut into squares (4 x 4) and store in an airtight container in the fridge, they keep well for a couple of weeks.

Zillionaire Shortbread

This is based on the "Tarts for the Tart" recipe in my Raw Magic book, which is definitely one of our personally most made and loved recipes. Still commonly found in our fridge ten years after its original creation – that's how you know a recipe works! But this is the upgrade – a layer of salted caramel to exalt it to the next level.

Ingredients

Shortbread:
175g (1½ cups) coconut oil
200g (2 cups) buckwheaties
200g (2 cups) lucuma powder
75g (½ cup) coconut sugar
250ml (1 cup) water

Caramel:
3 tbsp almond butter
3 tbsp yacon syrup
3 tbsp hemp oil
¼ tsp rock salt crystals

Chocolate:
125g (1 cup) cacao liquor
30g (¼ cup) coconut oil
75g (½ cup) coconut sugar
vanilla – either 6 drops extract or 2 teaspoons vanilla powder

Makes 16 squares or 25 fingers
Takes 1 hour
You need the right shaped silicon mold or baking tray, and a high-power blender or grinder.

Melt the coconut oil first, in a bain marie on a low heat. It should take around five minutes. Grind the buckwheaties into flour in your blender (buckwheaties are buckwheat grains that have been soaked, sprouted and dehydrated, you can buy them from us online or in good health food stores!). Transfer them to a mixing bowl, and add the lucuma, and sugar. Give everything a good mix together, then pour in the melted coconut oil, and stir it in. Add the water and stir that in too. Press into a medium sized rectangular tin. Leave it out on the side while you make the chocolate and caramel layers.

To make the caramel, put everything in a bowl together and stir. As for the salt, I am in love with Saltverk Icelandic pure salt flakes with licorice, and these work perfectly in this recipe. You don't want ground salt because that will be a bit weird! Himalayan salt is also a little bit intense. You want something that's in little chunky crystals. Pour the caramel over the shortbread, and spread it out with a spoon – it makes quite a thin layer. I did try making a thicker layer but it didn't really work when you bit into a square, all the caramel splurged out! So we have to keep it minimal, sorry.

Lastly, we are going to make the chocolate. Melt your cacao liquor and coconut oil together, like you did the coconut oil in the first stage. Cacao liquor takes around ten minutes, don't rush it. Clear up a bit while you are waiting for it! Once it's ready, stir in the sugar and vanilla. Pour it over your caramel layer, and pop it in the fridge to set.

It can go in the freezer if you're in a hurry, but the tricky bit next is to cut it into slices before the chocolate's got really hard. If you take it out the freezer, you'll find it's too solid to cut into neat slices without the chocolate cracking and the caramel going everywhere. When it's in the fridge, it's easier to monitor the right consistency. It's hard to say when that will be I'm afraid, it depends on your fridge and how often it's being opened! I would give it at least an hour. Slice it into four by four (or you can get five by five out, if you would like daintier pieces). Remove the pieces from the mold and place in an airtight container. Keeps pretty well, for at least a couple of weeks in the fridge.

They Call Me Mellow Yellow

This is a triply inspired effort. When I was at Helt Ra in Oslo, Madhu served us a great lemon pie in which she said the only sweeteners were yacon and stevia. Intrigued, I resolved to try creating a lemon pie like that when I got home. You know I am always seeking to create yummy recipes that are also easy on the digestion, and this sounded like a winner. Then I got to Iceland, and Solla was showing me Julia Corbett's book. Julia has a similar approach to me in that she creates superfood-loaded cakes that are true works of art. Her style is very different though, and looking through her book I was hugely inspired to try out her recipes. I saw a lemon pie and remembered Madhu's pie at Helt Ra. So with both these ladies as my muses, I got in the kitchen with Solla.

I love working with Solla because, as a professional restaurant chef for decades, she has an exquisite palate and substantial understanding of how flavours work together in raw vegan cuisine. It was her idea to put the lime leaf and sumac in, and to use herbal tea; I don't think I would have come up with any of that by myself. Of course, you don't need to include these extra ingredients, the lemon pie will be just fine without them, but it's these little touches that will take your pie to a whole new level.

So I got home and did a little tinkering and here we are.
A dessert that I feel is destined to become a classic.

Ingredients

1 cup (50g) coconut flakes
1 cup (120g) sesame seeds
½ cup (50g) gojis
1 cup (100g) lucuma
4 tbsp water
1 tbsp cinnamon
1 tbsp vanilla powder or 10 drops vanilla Medicine Flower Extract

2 lemons
1 cup (125g) coconut oil
1 cup (125g) cacao butter
4 tbsp yacon syrup
2 tbsp maca powder
1 tbsp baobab powder
1 tbsp ashwagandha
1 lime leaf
1 tbsp turmeric powder
1 tsp sumac
2 tbsp lecithin granules
1 cup gynostemma tea (or any other favourite tea - chamomile also works well)

Serves 8-12
Takes 30 mins to make
You need a blender to make this

First, we need to make the crust. Grind the sesame, coconut and gojis in your grinder or high-power blender. Transfer to a mixing bowl and add the lucuma, cinnamon and vanilla powder. Give it all a good mix with a spoon or with your hands, and then gradually add the water to form a dough. Once you have a ball, that is not too sticky, but with no bits of powder left, press it into your cake tin. Use it to form a crust that lines the bottom and the sides of your tin, about 3-4 cm (1-2") high, and pop it in the fridge or freezer while you continue with the filling.

To make the filling, first you need to melt the coconut and cacao butters. Do this in a porringer or a heatproof bowl stood in a larger bowl of freshly boiled water. Take your lemons, remove the peel so you are just left with the whole lemon flesh, and put them in your blender. Add in the yacon syrup, maca powder, baobab powder, ashwagandha, lecithin, lime leaf, turmeric and sumac. Don't start blending until your butters are melted and ready; then pour them in and blend everything together. After a minute, when you have a smooth cream, you can start adding your tea. Pour it in gradually until it is fully blended. Remove your pie crust from where it has been chilling, and then pour your filling in. It should fill it perfectly. Top with berries of your choice; I've made it with blueberries, strawberries, blackberries and redcurrants, all equally delicious. Put it back in the fridge or freezer to set: in the fridge it will take a couple of hours, in the freezer just 30 mins.

This cake keeps quite well in the fridge for up to two weeks. I love it because it is so light and easy on the digestion, and makes a wonderful sweet snack that's not going to unbalance your blood sugar or congest your liver.

California Dreaming Pie

Blueberries don't grow so well in Europe and are a bit of a luxury ingredient (well, organic ones that actually have any flavour are!) When I was in California, I took advantage of their plenitude, and created this blueberry pie. If you don't have access to an abundance of fresh blueberries, you could try substituting figs, blackberries, or perhaps some frozen berries. When I made it as a birthday cake for Ani Phyo, I covered it in melted chocolate, which made it doubly decadent!

Ingredients

1 cup (100g) cacao nibs
1 cup (125g) coconut oil
3 cups (375g) blueberries
1 tbsp lucuma
2 tbsp yacon syrup or honey
1 tbsp cinnamon powder

Serves 12
Takes 20 mins, plus a few hours for setting
You need a blender

Grind the cacao nibs in a high-power blender or grinder. Melt the coconut oil in a porringer, or a heatproof bowl stood in a pan of just boiled water. Put the nibs in the blender with the blueberries, and blend to a paste. Add in the melted oil and blend again. Put in the remaining ingredients, the lucuma, syrup, and cinnamon, and blend one more time. When it's smooth, spoon it out into a serving dish. Silicon molds are best, but if you don't have one, use a standard dish lined with greaseproof paper. Put in the fridge to set for 2-3 hours. If you're in a rush to eat it, pop it in the freezer for 30 mins instead. Tip it out onto a plate and decorate with more berries and dried coconut, or as I mentioned, melted chocolate! This also works well if you make your favourite pie crust recipe first, and press it into that.

This pie will keep in the fridge for up to five days.

Chake

I love the way this cake makes me feel sooooo much. It's VERY low-glycaemic. The actual cake only uses yacon syrup as a sweetener, which has no impact at all on the blood sugar. The icing only contains a small amount of mesquite. The combination of cacao, maca and chia is unbelievably sustaining. I also love the way ground chia swells up in cakes and makes them mouth-wateringly moist.

If you haven't got yacon syrup and you do have a sweet tooth, you can substitute the yacon with honey.

Ingredients

Cake:
2 cups (250g) cacao nibs
1 cup (100g) maca
1 cup (100g) sesame seeds
1 cup (120g) chia seeds
2 tbsp vanilla powder or 20 drops vanilla Medicine Flower Extract
1 tbsp he shou wu
1 cup (250ml) olive oil
½ cup (100g) yacon syrup

Icing:
¾ cup (100g) cacao butter
½ cup (60g) coconut oil
1 cup (100g) cacao powder
1 cup (100g) mesquite
2 tsp gingko powder
¼ cup (50g) yacon syrup
10 drops orange essential oil

Makes 12 slices
Takes 1 hour
You need a high-speed blender or food grinder

In a high-speed blender or grinder, grind the cacao to a powder, and set aside. Put the sesame and the chia in the machine and grind those to a flour also. Put the cacao, sesame, vanilla and chia into a bowl with the maca and he shou wu. With your hands, rub all the powders together, working in as much air as you can, and breaking down any lumps of cacao with your fingers. When your powders are evenly mixed and aerated, pour in the olive oil and yacon syrup and mix with a spoon. You should have a fairly firm, dense cake mixture. Spoon this into a cake mold. I prefer to use silicon molds, but if you don't have one, line a normal cake tin with foil or greaseproof paper. Leave to set in the freezer while you make the icing.

Before you make the icing, clear up everything you've just used, to allow the cake a little extra time to set. To make the icing, melt the butters in a porringer or in a Pyrex bowl sat in a saucepan of simmering water. Pour the cacao powder, mesquite, and gingko into a bowl and mix evenly. Add in the yacon syrup and orange oil and mix again. Once the butters have melted stir them in and you should have a nice thick chocolate liquid.

By this time your cake should be ready to ice. Remove it from the freezer and turn it out of the tin onto a plate. Ice it with the chocolate and decorate it as abundantly as you can. Pop it back in the fridge for an hour or two to set. If you're in a hurry you can put it in the freezer for 30 mins to ready it. Serve with a cup of tea and a big grin.

Fermented Cheesecake

My latest triumph! You may know that I'm not a big fan of nuts. I really don't believe they are an optimum food to regularly consume in large quantities. One of the few recipes I teach that does actually involve nuts is the cheesecake (p234), because until this point I hadn't actually found a way to do a convincing cheesecake without cashews (unless you count fresh coconuts, which aren't easily accessible for most Europeans). But inspired by the trend of people fermenting their cashews before putting them in the cake, I thought I would try it with a sunflower cheese. It really works. It's a bit more time-consuming and fiddly than the usual method, but if cashews are off the menu for you, as they are for me, you'll be glad you made the effort.

Here's two variations for you, a strawberry and a blueberry.

Ingredients

Cheese:
2 cups (200g) sunflower seeds, soaked 2-4 hours
1 tsp honey
¼ cup kombucha vinegar (or probiotics, see below)
¾ cup water
pinch salt

Add
2 tbsp baobab
2 cups (250g) strawberries
1 cup (125g) coconut oil
½ cup (75g) evaporated cane juice crystals or coconut sugar

Or
1 tbsp baobab
1 tbsp purple corn extract
2 cups (250g) blueberries
1 cup (125g) coconut oil
½ cup (75g) evaporated cane juice crystals or coconut sugar

Pie Crust:
Choose between any of the crusts in this book, the one in the Return of the Sun Cheesecake recipe is my favourite (p234)

Makes 12 slices
You need to soak the seeds and make the cheese 24 hours in advance. Then it takes 45 mins, and a few hours to set.
You need a blender, and a milk bag

To make the cheese, first soak your sunflower seeds for a few hours. When you're ready, drain them, and put them in the blender with the honey, vinegar, water and salt. If you don't have kombucha vinegar, replace it with water, and add 10g probiotic powder instead. Blend until you have a smooth cream. Spoon the cream out into your milk bag, and put the milk bag inside a large bowl. Make sure the cheese is fully enclosed in the bag, and put something heavy on the top to weigh it down. Leave it there for 24 hours, then turn it out of the bag, discarding any liquid that has been pressed out. You can leave it at ambient temperatures if you want to ferment a little more, or put it in the fridge until you are ready to use it. You need to make the cheesecake in the next 24 hours or it will start to ferment too much, and the flavours will get too strong.

When you're ready, first make the crust of your choice. Then melt the coconut oil. Blend the cheese with the fruit, baobab, sugar, coconut oil (and purple corn if you're using it). You don't need any extra water or it won't set firmly.

Pour it over your pie crust, and set in the freezer for 2-3 hours. When it's firm, you can remove it from the pie case and store it in the fridge. Doesn't keep long before the flavour of the sunflower starts becoming a little bitter - up to 3-4 days.

Durian Cheesecake

This is just a variation on the Return of the Sun recipe (p234), but it's so good it deserves its own post. If you don't know about durian, it's kind of a legendary fruit from Asia, mostly Thailand and Malaysia. It's got a spikey outer shell, and a very strong aroma – so much so that it's actually banned on public transport in Thailand! People tend to love it or hate it, and most raw-fooders love it. It's my boys' favourite food, and this cheesecake is their favourite cake I ever made. I can't actually eat it, 'cos me and cashews are sworn enemies, but I'm going to make a variation with young coconuts, and I reckon that that will truly be the best cake ever.

Ingredients

Crust:
- 1 ½ cups (135g) almonds
- 1 cup (100g) raisins
- 2 tbsp cacao powder
- 2 tbsp coconut oil

Filling:
- 250g (2 cups) cashews, soaked 4-8 hours
- 4 pillows durian or 2 bags freeze-dried
- ½ cup (90g) coconut sugar or cane juice crystals
- 1 cup (125g) coconut oil
- 1 cup (250ml) water

Serves 12

Pre-soak your cashews for 8 hours. It will take you 30 mins to make the cake, and at least an hour to set it.

You need a blender

To make the crust, grind the almonds to a powder in a high-power blender or grinder. Process the raisins in the same way. Melt the coconut oil, if it needs it, and mix all the ingredients together. Add a little more coconut oil or water if you need to, just enough so that it all sticks together in a solid mass. Press it into your base and put it in the freezer while you make the filling.

Melt the coconut oil. Drain the cashews, and put everything in the blender together – cashews, durian, sugar, melted coconut oil and water. Blend to a cream. Remove your pie crust from the freezer and pour the filling over it. Decorate with chocolate buttons or anything else you fancy. Put back into the freezer to set – will take at least an hour. Once it's set, keep it in the fridge. Durian doesn't keep well – best to enjoy it within a few days, or store it in the freezer.

Value & Abundance

I walked past a well-known pizza chain the other day, and noticed an A-board outside. It was a quote from the editor of Time Out magazine, enticing people into the restaurant. The quote read, "Reliable, Friendly & Great Value." "Great Value" was in the biggest letters. And I thought, since when did value for money become the primary factor to consider when choosing where to eat? There is no mention of either taste or nutrition in that description, because for too many people, those are not even factors that enter into it.

Times are hard, I know. Food and travel prices have gone up by ridiculous amounts in the last few years, while the average wage hardly rises at all (I won't quote a figure as it's likely that by the time you read this the gap will have widened further). As a single parent of three teenage boys, I understand the need to budget and save money where you can as well as anyone. The reality is that it is economically tough right now. But if it's true that we create our own realities, how do we go about shifting the poverty consciousness that is so pervasive?

We need to start with the understanding that everything begins on a cellular level. However we feel deep down in our cells, we project that out into the world. We look inside for guidance on how the world works, and then we use that information to shape our external reality. To give an obvious example, there is the woman whose father was absent as a child, who believes men will always let her down, because that's how the experiences of her early years shaped her. So this woman always attracts untrustworthy men into her life, who validate her view, and she creates a reality where indeed, all men are untrustworthy. We all do it, hold onto patterns from childhood, some of which are minor details, and some of which warp our whole experience of life. And the task in hand is to de-programme, do the work on ourselves, deconstruct these false perceptions of the way things are, and strip them back to find the true authentic self underneath.

This can be scary, when we identify so strongly with the layers and masks that we have built up as adults, and when we have lives revolving around some of these false perceptions that we need to dismantle before we can move forwards. We wonder who will we be and how will we fill our lives without these realities to keep us in our place. Well, the good news is that our authentic self is an infinite and eternal being, and creating reality from the standpoint of being tapped into the limitless power of the cosmos actually presents many, many more opportunities for fun, adventure and growth.

But to get back to my original point, in this time where the money pile is literally diminishing before our eyes, getting squirrelled away by the few as the majority are left with less and less; and our ability to live freely and abundantly is being threatened with every new measure this current government enforces, it's more important than ever that we disengage from the downward spiral that is the "chasing the money" game.

When I speak at events, the topic of how expensive superfoods are nearly always arises. A couple of years ago, someone gave me the best answer ever. He said, yes, superfoods cost more than usual foods, but when I eat them, I feel more abundant. When I eat them, I attract more good stuff to me, and I always find the money I need.

So if we want to shift reality, if we want to find our way out of this current economic downturn, the answer isn't to cut back on the foods that are the best for our bodies. The answer isn't to work longer hours for less pay. The answer is to go within, to tune in, to nourish ourselves body, mind and soul. And when we find that connected standpoint, abundant realities naturally manifest and a natural flow and graceful ease take over.

I believe that the two most vital ways to create this feeling of abundance in the cells are through staying hydrated and eating an abundance of healthy fats. When we are dehydrated, we lose our ability to flow through life; we create a world that is stagnant and dry. When we don't consume enough healthy fats, life loses its richness; we create a world which is stiff and meagre. If on a cellular level, our bodies are being deprived of the most basic nutrients it needs, we create a world that reflects that deprivation, where our most basic needs aren't being met.

Please, don't think that I'm suggesting that if you can't go out and spend $50 on some supplement from the USA then you have a poverty mentality; that's really not my point, and a vast over-simplification. What I'm proposing is that if we want to see ourselves out of this current period of hardship, we need to approach it with a broader vision. We need to begin by realising how the cell picture contributes to our thought patterns, and how we are co-creators to every situation that we find ourselves in. I am a huge believer in the simple modalities being the most profound, and that a glass of water and a spoon of chia seeds might have positive effects in more ways than you imagine.

We are always weaving threads into the fabric of our reality, and if we want to build a new world out of the current one, which frankly is looking more and more like a pile of rubble every day, it's a long term project that will ensue for generations. But we begin by drinking more water and eating more good food, and naturally and effortlessly, over time, we will shed these limiting and constricting patterns of being, and find ways of working that come from an understanding of and connection with the eternal abundance of life.

Desserts

If you haven't worked it out by now, the theme of all my food is light and heavenly. So, think truly angelic desserts, that will whisk you away into food paradise, with no descent into digestive hell afterwards!

Strawberry Coconut Mousse

I was thinking of making this into a pie, but the filling was so good I just wanted it neat. If you set them in cupcake size silicon molds then you can make little individual mousses; I was making heart-shaped ones.

Ingredients

2 cups (250g) fresh strawberries
2 cups (200g) fresh young coconut meat
½ cup (75g) coconut sugar or cane juice crystals
1 cup (100g) lucuma powder
1 cup (125g) coconut oil

Serves 4
Takes 15 minutes, with a couple of hours setting
You need a blender

Extract the meat from your coconuts. The easiest way is to hack the lids off with a machete, and then scoop the flesh out with a spoon. Or sometimes now, you can find frozen meat, which saves you the bother. Melt the coconut oil, in a heatproof bowl over a low heat. Blend everything together: strawberries, coconut meat, sugar, lucuma and melted oil. Once it's a smooth cream, pour it into a silicon mold to set. Leave at least two hours for a melt in the mouth fruity dessert.

Chocolate Chia Trifles

Personally, I'm not a fan of those Instagram pictures with chia pudding and "nice cream" heaped so high that it's pouring out of the jam jar. They look like as soon as you stuck a spoon in the whole thing would collapse all over the table. And the portion sizes look disgustingly huge, like it would take me a week to get through a single serving. The food combining often isn't the best. And they look entirely impractical – how would you ever get to the bottom layer?! They don't tempt me at all. But, never one to miss a trick, here's my own take on a creamy multi-layered chia dessert. My yoga teacher said it was the best she ever tried! It makes a really sustaining breakfast or lunch, and I often serve it as a dessert at dinner parties.

Ingredients

Chia Jelly Layer:
½ cup (60g) chia
2½ cups (625ml) water
½ cup (60g) dried apricots
2 tsp purple corn extract
2 tbsp cacao powder
1 tbsp cane juice crystals or coconut sugar

Goji Pudding Layer:
4 (1kg) avocados
4 tbsp honey or yacon syrup
1 cup (250ml) water
1 cup (100g) gojis

Hemp Cream Layer:
1 cup (100g) shelled hemp
½ up (125ml) water
1 tbsp baobab powder
1 tbsp xylitol
10 drops vanilla Medicine Flower Extract or 1 tbsp vanilla powder

Makes 6
Takes 45 mins with 2 hours pre-soaking
You need a blender

Start by pre-soaking your gojis and your chia in separate bowls. The gojis need soaking in enough water to cover; I always drink the soak-water once I've finished soaking. The chia needs soaking in the water given in the recipe, 2½ cups. Soak both for at least a couple of hours.

When they are ready, start by preparing the chia pudding. Chop the apricots into small pieces with scissors, and stir them in along with the purple corn, cacao powder, and sugar. Stir it really well, and leave to sit while you work on the next stage.

To make the goji layer, scoop the flesh out of the avocados and put it in the blender. Drain the gojis and put them in with the syrup and water, and blend for a minute until it's nice and creamy. Transfer from your blender to a separate bowl.

Next is the hemp cream. Wash out your blender, and put all the ingredients for the cream in together, blending well until smooth.

To assemble your trifles, you need to find six glasses or bowls. I think tall wine glasses look best, but whatever you have that suits. Use your measuring cups, and put half a cup of chia in each receptacle. Then spoon two tbsp of goji pudding onto the top of that, and spread it evenly over the top. Next you want one spoon of hemp cream, and spread that carefully over the top. Then it's two more spoons of goji pudding. Lastly a little more hemp cream – if you've got a squeezy bottle you can use that to make shapes or letters on the top, otherwise just drizzle a little in a spiral or circle with a teaspoon. Decorate with chopped fresh fruit, goji berries, or my favourite, Ombar raw chocolate buttons.

These actually keep fairly well – up to about five days in the fridge.

Autumn Chia

In this pudding I've used traditional Autumn fruits, which soften beautifully when they are soaked in the chia for a few hours. I've added camu and reishi to boost the immune system at the time of year when we need it the most. Plus, maca for a good boost of sustained energy.

Ingredients

4 cups (1 litre) hemp milk
½ apple
½ pear
1 cup (150g) chia seeds
½ cup (50g) raisins
1 tbsp maca
1 tsp camu camu powder
1 tbsp cinnamon
½ tsp reishi extract powder

Serves 4
Takes 10 minutes to make and then needs 2 hours soaking before it's ready to eat.
No equipment needed

Make the hemp milk if you haven't already done so. (Easiest way is just to whizz up 4 tbsp shelled hemp with 1 litre of water). Take the apple and pear, remove any seeds or core, and chop into small pieces, not much bigger than a raisin if you can. Or grate them if you prefer.

Put the chia seeds in a large bowl with the chopped fruit and raisins, and pour the hemp milk over. Stir it well. Then add your powders – the maca, camu, cinnamon and reishi. Stir again to make sure everything is evenly distributed. Leave to soak for at least 2 hours, all day or overnight if needs be. If you are around, stir it once or twice in that time to prevent the chia forming lumps.

The pudding improves with age as the flavours start to marinade. One or two days old pudding is best, beyond that it might start going off. Because the fruit starts fermenting in the hemp milk, it isn't likely to keep past three days.

Tequila Slimmer

Irish Moss makes a wonderful light dessert, which, as long as you don't overdo it with the nuts, is the perfect #eatasmuchasyoulikewithoutanyguilt dish.

I flavoured this pudding with lime and a dash of salt for a wonderfully refreshing treat. And of course, I had to sweeten it with agave, the sweetener that is derived from the same cactus plant as tequila. The addition of some feisty mucuna gives it an extra punch. All the hit, with none of the hangover.

Ingredients

1oz (30g) Irish moss
500ml (2 cups) water
125g (1 cup) cashews (pre-soaked 4-8 hours)
2 limes
½ cup (60g) coconut oil
½ cup (50g) lucuma
4 tbsp agave nectar
1 tbsp mucuna
pinch salt
raspberries to decorate

Serves 4
You need to soak the Irish Moss 3-5 days in advance. You also need to remember to soak the cashews at least 4 hours before you make it. Then it will take 3 hours or so to set.
You need a blender to make this

Prepare your Irish moss according to instructions (p285). Don't forget to soak your cashew nuts in advance too. Once you are ready, put the Irish moss in the blender with one cup of water, and blend to a purée. You might not be able to get it smooth at this stage, don't worry. Peel your limes, and put all the flesh in the blender, along with the pre-soaked cashews, coconut oil, lucuma, agave, mucuna, and salt. Blend it all again for a good minute until smooth. Finally, add the last cup of water and blend once more. By this stage there should be no lumps left. Pour out into a mold or serving dish and leave to set in the fridge for at least three hours.

When you're ready to serve, dish it out into four small dishes or goblets, and scatter with raspberries.

Full of Christmas Chia

The perfect Christmas breakfast. Chia is such an excellent breakfast food because it is so energising and sustaining and very balancing for the blood sugar. But this is Chia with a VERY Christmassy twist. Eat this for breakfast and you'll be satisfying both those urges: to feel fantastic AND festive.

Ingredients

120g (1 cup) chia
1 orange, juiced
½ lemon, juiced
2 grated apples (about 250g/½ lb)
100g (1 cup) mixed vine fruit
60g (½ cup) goji berries or mulberries
30g (¼ cup) dried dates or apricots, chopped
1 tbsp cinnamon powder
1 tsp ginger powder
pinch ground nutmeg or cloves
2 tbsp flax oil
1 tbsp yacon syrup
½ tsp miso
1 litre water

Serves 4
Needs at least 2 hours pre-soaking, preferably overnight
You don't need any special equipment

Put all your ingredients in a large mixing bowl – yes, every single one! Pour the water over it and stir it all together. It should take an hour or two for the chia to swell and absorb the water and make a pudding. You can eat it straightaway, but it's much better if you leave it overnight and allow the flavours to marinade a little. Make it at bedtime and have it for breakfast the next day. If there are any leftovers, they will keep for a few days in the fridge.

If you want to be really decadent, serve with a delicious raw nut cream, and turn it into sundaes.

Red Sky at Night

I don't eat much fruit. I find eating sugary foods makes me feel a bit spacey and drifty, not very focused. Grapefruits I can do in juice, but I can only eat small portions of this mousse. However, it's so light, fluffy and refreshing, it makes a perfect breakfast food. The Hippocrates Health Institute, who advise against eating fruit entirely, say that grapefruits are the best fruit to include if you are going to have some in your diet. Along with lemons, they are also the most alkalising fruit.

Ingredients

Mousse:
2 grapefruits
28g (1oz) Irish moss
1 cup (250ml) water
1 cup (125g) coconut oil
2 tbsp lecithin granules
2 tbsp coconut sugar or cane juice crystals

Cream:
1 tbsp acai
¼ cup (25g) freeze-dried strawberry powder
2 avocados
5 drops strawberry Medicine Flower Extract (optional)
2 tbsp honey
¼ cup (60ml) water

Serves 8
Takes 30 mins, plus you need to prepare your Irish moss 3-5 days in advance. Then there's 4 hours setting time.
You need a blender

Pre-soak your Irish moss according to instructions (p285). When it's ready, blend it up in the blender jug with 1 cup (250ml) water. It won't purée completely, but it should break down quite considerably. When you're satisfied it's as broken down as it's going to get, you're ready to add the remaining ingredients. If it's not warm, and your coconut oil is hard, you're going to need to melt it to soften it a little. If it's already semi-liquid, you don't need to worry. Peel the grapefruits, and put all the flesh in the blender. Add in the lecithin, coconut sugar, and melted coconut oil. Blend it all up to a liquid and pour it into a large serving dish.

Next you're going to make the cream. Put everything in the blender together: the avocado flesh, acai, strawberry powder, strawberry essence if you have it, honey, and water. Blend to a cream. If your avocados are big, you may need extra water. Take spoons of the mixture and cover your grapefruit mousse with splodges of it. As the cream is heavier than the mousse it will sink a bit but that's not a problem. Or if you're very artistic, you could put the cream in a piping bag and pipe it in patterns over the mousse. When you're done, put it in the fridge to set: it will take at least 4 hours. It will keep for up to four days in the fridge.

Chia Leaders

I am always banging on about how good chia is, and one day at a talk, a lady called me a ChiaLeader! So here it is, the ChiaLeader's pudding. Now, where did I put those pompoms...

Ingredients

1 cup (150g) chia seeds
½ cup (50g) raisins
½ cup (50g) Incan berries
¼ cup (25g) lucuma
2 tbsp yacon syrup
1 tbsp cacao powder
40g-100g raw chocolate bar (depending on how much of a chocolate fiend you are!)
1 litre (4 cups) hemp milk

Serves 4
Takes 10 minutes to make, then you need to leave it soaking for a couple of hours
You don't need any special equipment

You need a big bowl so you can soak everything together. Put in everything bar the hemp milk: the chia, raisins, Incan berries, yacon syrup, lucuma and cacao powder. Chop the raw chocolate bar into tiny chunks, as small as raisins if you can, and add that in as well. It's up to you how much chocolate you throw in! Stir it up so it's mixed evenly, then pour the hemp milk over. Stir it well, cover, and leave it to swell for at least a couple of hours. If you're around, you can come back to it intermittently to stir it, to make sure you don't get any lumps of chia. There is no harm in leaving the pudding longer than a couple of hours, say overnight. I find with chia it tastes the best a day or two after its been started, as the flavours marinade in the chia. It will keep for four or five days. Goes great with ice cream!

Yo! Gurt

This happened by accident, playing around with an Irish moss and baobab combination, but to me it is very reminiscent of the little Ski yoghurt pots I used to love as a child. My favourite was black cherry yoghurt! When I went vegan, I still used to enjoy a lot of soya yoghurt; I believe it was my body seeking out the natural probiotics that live yoghurt contains. My favourite way to eat yoghurt was to stir some muesli into it, and so recently I have been enjoying this yoghurt recipe a lot combined with buckwheat cereal, as a stunningly delicious and absolutely sustaining light brunch.

Ingredients

30g (1oz) Irish Moss
3 cups (750ml) water
¼ cup (60g) lecithin granules
½ cup (50g) Baobab powder
1 cup (100g) mesquite powder
2 avocados, stoned and peeled

Serves 4
Takes 30 mins, plus you need to prepare your Irish moss 3-5 days in advance. Then there's 4 hours setting time
You need a blender

Prepare Irish moss according to the instructions (p285). When your moss is ready, blend it up with one cup of water. Blend until it's as broken up as possible, with no bits of moss left. Next add the avocado flesh and lecithin, and blend again, until creamy. Then comes the baobab and mesquite; by now your mixture should be thick and a pudding-like consistency. Once you're happy with it, gradually add the remaining two cups of water while the blender is running. This should make it a thinner, more yoghurt-like consistency.

Stored in the fridge in an airtight container, it will keep for up to two weeks. I like to mix a raw granola into mine, or you can add chopped fresh or dried fruit.

Just Peachy

It's no secret that I'm a big fan of Irish moss. I love my desserts, and I love my sea vegetables, so a dish that combines both is my idea of heaven. And I do think this is the best Irish moss dessert I have yet created.

Ingredients

30g (1oz) Irish Moss
750ml (3 cups) almond milk
1 tbsp honey
2 tbsp baobab powder
2 tbsp lecithin granules
2 tbsp coconut oil
1 cup (100g) lucuma
2-3 peaches
10 drops cherry Medicine Flower Extract (optional)
1 cup cherries, stoned

Serves 4
Takes 30 mins, plus you need to prepare your Irish moss 3-5 days in advance Then there's 4 hours setting time
You need a blender

Soak your Irish moss according to instructions (p285).

Make your almond milk in advance by soaking 2-4 tbsp almonds in pure water for at least two hours. Drain and blend with 750ml water. Strain to remove the shells.

In your blender or food processor, blend the Irish moss with one cup (250ml) of the almond milk. Blend it as much as you can, so the seaweed bits are as broken down as much as you can get them. You don't have to worry too much because it will blend down more in the next stage.

Next add the honey, baobab, lecithin, coconut oil, lucuma, and cherry extract (if you have it). Stone the peaches and put them in as well. Blend to a purée; it should be very thick at this point. Gradually add the remaining 500ml of water, and when it's fully amalgamated, stir your cherries in. You don't want to blend them up, you want to leave them as pieces in the pudding.

Put it in the fridge to set; it will take at least 6 hours to thicken nicely. Keeps in the fridge in an airtight container for up to five days.

Present & Connected

I recently had a raw chef friend from Berlin, Boris, visit. It was interesting to see London through his eyes. He commented on what a vibrant food culture we have here. Who would have thought the English would ever be praised for their cuisine! But when I considered it, I realised how much things had changed in the past decade.

My eldest son went on a PGL holiday last week. I was so worried about his food! We had requested a vegan menu but I was convinced that their version of vegan would be chips and beans and pasta. I was wrong; there were vegetables, and a salad bar at every meal. Reuben said that apparently, until recently, the menus were awful - instant mash and powdered milk - but they've made vast improvements this year.

The fact is that the English, known the world over for our poor culinary traditions, are starting to come home to the virtues of connecting with real food and real food producers. What Boris particularly noticed, was the plethora of local and seasonal options. The City is spilling over with places like Pod, with its "fresh seasonal healthy food in compostable packaging," and Eat, "a family company dedicated to handmade food." Farmers' Markets are no longer a novelty, and places like Borough Market have become popular destinations for local families and tourists alike.

Organic food started appearing in supermarkets a little over 30 years ago. Since then, it has swung in and out of fashion, helped in no small part by the stories that regularly appear in the media telling us that there is no benefit to eating organic produce. Well, I don't know about you, but I can taste the difference every time. From carrots to strawberries to cinnamon, there's never any comparison. I've been buying organic ever since I worked in a wholefoods co-op in 1991 and no media scare stories are going to persuade me to do otherwise.

My first book, Eat Smart Eat Raw, was published in 2002 by Grub Street, a publishing house which only publishes cookbooks and counts luminaries such as Marguerite Patten, Elizabeth David and Jane Grigson as its authors. It was the editor there, Anne Dolamore, who clued me up on the importance of local and seasonal as well as organic. She told me that as well as the superior nutritional content of vegetables that were freshly picked, on balance, the environmental implications of eating local but non-organic foods were preferable to eating organic air-freighted foods.

Since then, I have always made a conscious effort to buy fresh fruits and vegetables grown in the UK. If I can't get UK produce, I'll buy goods that have come across the water from Spain say, or Holland. The only fresh produce I really let myself down with are avocados, because I have three sons who are avocado monsters and there would be a mutiny if I didn't always have a box full in the kitchen. Other than that, if it's not European and organic, I don't buy it.

People often ask me how the superfoods fit in with the local seasonal philosophy. The only popular superfoods that it's possible to get from the UK are wheatgrass, hemp and bee pollen; most are flown in from far away regions such as South America and China. My response is firstly, examine anyone's kitchen cupboards and try and find someone who doesn't have a whole host of produce from China, India and the USA. When you're buying rice or lentils, for instance, they are bulky to transport and something you get through in large amounts, so the food miles add up. But with superfoods, most of the doses I recommend are around a quarter a teaspoon a day! The most anyone would take is a tablespoon in some cases such as maca, and few people would take that much day in, day out. So the impact on the environment by transporting these foods is negligible compared to most household staples.

Secondly, as far as food quality goes, it seems air-freighting dried goods doesn't have the same negative impact as air-freighting fresh goods. Fresh fruit and vegetables really don't like flying – just like humans, they come off the plane dehydrated and tired! Whereas dried goods aren't so affected because they have already been preserved and a lot of the water content has been removed. My recommendation is that a good diet is comprised of around 50% of fresh vegetables, by volume, and up to 15% fresh fruit. So if you're making your diet at least 60% fresh local organic seasonal produce, then I feel with the rest we just need to accept that we live in a less than perfect world, and do the best we can.

Lastly, I don't believe superfoods are a long-term solution. Superfoods are basically nutrient dense foods that help make up for the deficit in the produce that comes from modern agricultural methods. Sadly, the nutrition that's in our fruit and vegetables is at an all-time low. Studies show that there is as little as 20% of the nutrition that there was just 50 years ago. But it's not just the vitamins and minerals that are easily measurable that are lacking. It's the life force in the food. Think about when you have an opportunity to go into the wild and pick berries. How much energy does that food give you? It's an experience totally different from eating a punnet of berries from the supermarket. When the mulberries are in season, I go to Kew Gardens and we pick them straight off the mulberry bush there, which is hundreds of years old. It's virtually a psychedelic experience! The energy you get off those berries is incredible. That's the level of vitality that we should be getting from all our foods.

My ideal is that we would be able to go outside and pick all our food straight from the land. If we were growing our food biodynamically, using permaculture methods, in remineralised soil, and eating it fresh, I don't believe we would need superfoods. But until then, they bridge that gap between what our food offers us and what we need. They are fast-track foods, that give us extraordinary amounts of strength and energy to support us in our work to create balance in this world.

So for now, I would say, as far as fresh produce goes, I would always pick local over organic. So often, small producers can't afford the time and the money it takes to get organically certified. It's always worth trying to connect with your local producer and find out exactly how organic he is. Sometimes, it might just be one pesticide he's using that means he can't call his produce organic. Or it's because of some other minor issue, such as how long the land has been in use. I'm not suggesting in any way that the organic certification process is over-stringent, just that there are other additional factors that need to be taken into consideration when picking our produce. That little organic sticker isn't the be all and end all of quality. For me, eating healthily is all about feeling great in your body. Feeling present, connected and bursting with vitality. And if we are what we eat, that means our food must be present (i.e. as fresh as possible), connected (i.e. as local as possible), and bursting with vitality (i.e. raw!).

Drinks

The one single factor that I personally consider most important for health, is to stay well hydrated. I don't recommend drinking too much plain water, as that acts as a flushing mechanism, and flushes everything through the body, the good stuff as well as the bad stuff. If we've been out on the town the night before, maybe we need a good flush! But when we are eating a good clean diet, drinking plain water all day is not so helpful. Instead I recommend high quality drinks containing an abundance of nutritional information, so the body can process that information with maximum efficiency. You will find consuming these drinks to be much more hydrating than drinking straightforward water. Personally, I typically drink 4-5 litres a day, and that intake would include juices, superfood milks, kefir and kombucha, coconut water, lemonade, smoothies and medicinal teas. Enjoy these recipes and discover for yourself the transformative powers of true hydration.

Kombucha Cocktails

These cocktails are one of my favourite things to drink. I love to serve them at the Pop-Up Dinner Parties I do, and I love them even better with a shot of aloe vera or noni juice. If you can use home-made Kombucha and fresh coconut water then you will be making the best cocktails in the galaxy! Coconut water is so cleansing because it's nearly identical in make-up to human blood plasma, and in the Vietnam war they used it for blood transfusions on the battlefield. Because coconut water is so rich in electrolytes, it's more hydrating than drinking plain water. Kombucha can have a slightly harsh, vinegary taste so by mixing it with coconut water it takes the edge off a little and softens it. An incredible new flavour appears by mixing these two ingredients, which is so much more than the sum of its parts.

Ingredients

125ml kombucha
125ml coconut water

Makes 1 glass
Takes 1 minute
You need no equipment

Pour kombucha first into the glass, because it's fizzy. Then top up with coconut water. Drink with abandon, and know that there's no hangover the next day.

The Chocolate Disco Smoothie

Party in a glass! In 2013, I started a night here in London called The Chocolate Disco, which served up some of London's finest DJs alongside healthy treats such as this, our signature smoothie.

Ingredients

250ml (1 cup) coconut water*
1 banana (preferably frozen)**
1 date (preferably fresh)***
1 tsp tahini
1 heaping tsp cacao powder

Serves 1
Takes 5 mins to make
You need a blender

Blend everything together until smooth. Be prepared for bliss.

*Whichever you choose, make sure it's not from concentrate.

**If you can freeze your bananas in advance, that will make your smoothie thicker. It's a good idea to always have a stock of frozen bananas in the freezer; it's a good way to use them up before they go black as well. Just peel them, break them into chunks, and pop them in the freezer in a sealy bag. They keep indefinitely.

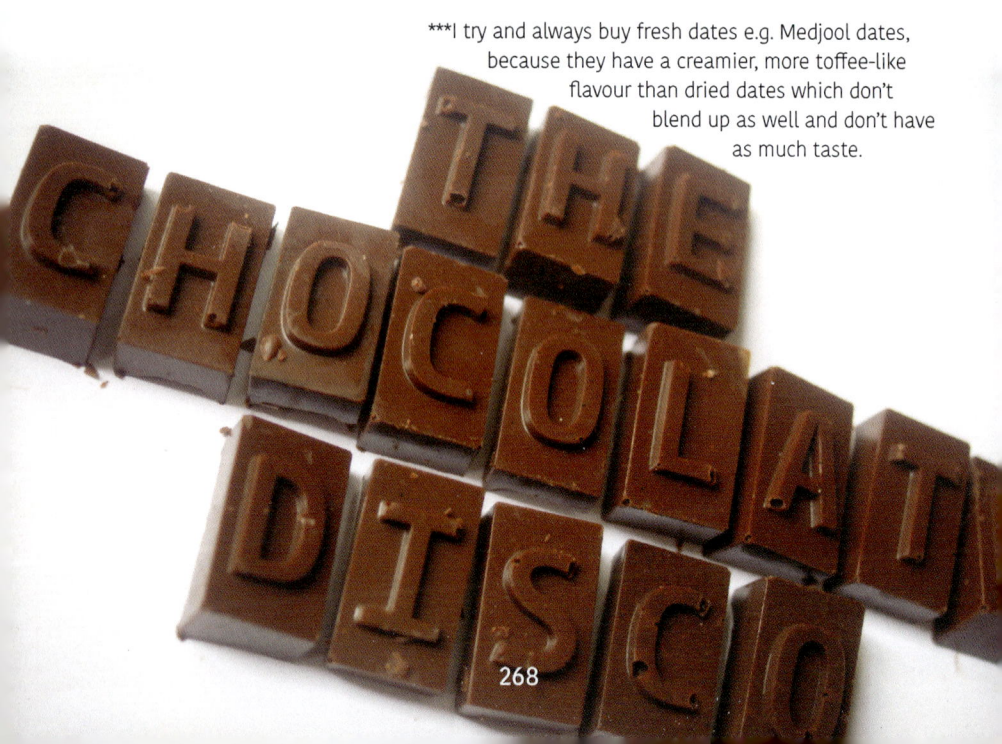

***I try and always buy fresh dates e.g. Medjool dates, because they have a creamier, more toffee-like flavour than dried dates which don't blend up as well and don't have as much taste.

Superfood Mojitos

These are just too good. I've made Bellinis with peaches, and Daiquiris with strawberries, but this is my favourite combination of kombucha and fresh fruit drink.

Ingredients

2 limes
5g fresh mint leaves
1 tbsp coconut sugar or cane juice crystals
5g suma powder
1 litre water kefir or kombucha
5 ice cubes

Serves 5
Takes 5 mins
You need a blender

Remove the peel from the limes. Remove the stems from the mint leaves. Blend up really well with the sugar, suma, and kombucha until its smooth. Then pulse blend in the ice so it's broken down a little. Or pop one ice cube in each glass and pour the lime mixture over the top. Serve immediately.

Magic Milk

This milk doesn't really keep, so you have to drink it all the day that you make it. However, hemp milk is one of the most nutritious drinks you can imagine, so I strongly recommend you make it a regular part of your diet. You can add any sort of flavourings to it that you choose, in order to make it extra delicious: chocolate, or fruit extracts. It's the best way to get superfoods such as spirulina or maca into your diet; just add a teaspoon into the milk once it's made. Use the milk as a base for a smoothie, pour it over cereal, add it to herbal tea, heat it gently and make warm milk or hot chocolate, use it to make chia pudding.... there are no limits!

Ingredients

4 tbsp whole hemp seeds or almonds (pre-soaked 2-4 hours)
5 drops stevia
5 drops vanilla Medicine Flower Extract
pinch salt

Makes 4 cups

Soak the hemp seeds or almonds in advance. Hemp seeds just need 2 hours, almonds need longer as they are bigger, I would suggest soaking them for 4 hours. When they are ready, put them in the blender with all the other ingredients. Blend on a high setting for 30 seconds. Strain into a milk bag. If you don't have a milk bag, you can use a baby muslin, old tea towel, a sieve or even an old pair of tights! However, I would recommend investing in a milk bag, they are inexpensive and very useful. Sit the milk bag over a large bowl or jug, and pour the liquid from the blender in. Squeeze the bag gently; you'll get all the milk in the jug or bowl, and the hemp or almond shell will be left in the bag. Save the pulp, it makes a great exfoliator in the shower! Or you can use almond pulp in raw cakes and breads. Pour the milk and serve.

Sweet Raspberry Milk

My favourite summer smoothie.

Ingredients

500ml (2 cups) coconut water
100g (100g) raspberries
2 tsp maca
4 tbsp coconut yoghurt

Makes 2 glasses
Takes 5 mins
You need a blender

Put everything in the blender together and whizz for a minute. For the perfect summer cocktail, add in 500ml (2 cups) kefir. If you like a kick, add in 1cm root ginger.

Blueberry Almond Milk

When I used to do lots of food prep classes, often at the end I would be left with a handful of soaked almonds, a little bit of lucuma in a bowl, and some berries leftover from cake-making. Never one to let anything go to waste, I would make them into this milk. Which then became one of my favourite recipes! So delicious (Boy George loves it too).

Ingredients

4 tbsp almonds, soaked
1 tbsp lucuma powder
½ cup (50g) blueberries
1 litre (4 cups) pure water

Makes 1 litre of milk
Takes less than 5 mins!
You need a blender

Soak the almonds in pure water for at least two hours, or overnight if you are going to be having the milk for breakfast. Drain the water off, and put them in the blender with a litre of good quality water. Blend for a minute, until your blender has worked its magic on them and ground them down. Pour through a nut milk bag, and strain into a bowl. If you don't have a nut milk bag, you can just use a sieve or an old pair of tights! You can discard the pulp, or save it for another recipe. Put the milk back into the blender and blend with the lucuma, and blueberries.

Serve and drink within 12 hours, this milk doesn't keep well for more than a day.

Secret Lemonade Drinker

I'm pretty obsessed with lemons, especially in the Spring and Summer months. I do a lot of these style drinks, inspired by Annie Jubb's original Electrolyte Lemonade. In a heatwave, it becomes even more of an essential beverage. Here's a simple, and very delicious version.

Ingredients

1 lemon, or more if you can handle it – I use up to 3
2 cups (500ml) coconut water
1 cup (250ml) kombucha or kefir (for the fizz)
1 tbsp flaxseed oil
1 tbsp lecithin
1 tsp turmeric powder

Serves 4
Takes 10 mins
You need a blender

Blend. Keeps in the fridge for 24 hours.

Perfectly Magical Smoothie

The only kind of PMS you need. Shatavari is an Ayurvedic herb known to balance women's hormones, and this recipe is a replenishing drink for any kind of hormonally challenging period; which let's face it, feels like more often than not when we factor in adolescence, pregnancy, breastfeeding and menopause. It contains a hefty dose of maca, but beware, maca is very potent, so if you're not familiar with it, better to start with a teaspoon.

Ingredients

1 banana, peeled or 2 apricots (stones removed)
1 tbsp shelled hemp seeds
1 tbsp flaxseed oil
1 tbsp maca powder
1 tbsp lecithin granules
½ tsp shatavari powder
¼ tsp mucuna powder
1 tsp cacao powder
125ml water
125ml apple juice

Makes 1 large glass
Takes 5 mins
You need a blender

Put everything in a blender and, um, blend. For a minute. It's that easy. Say a positive intention, prayer, or, with your finger, draw a symbol that is special to you on the blender while it's whizzing away to make your smoothie even more magical. I usually reiki the blender and send it love and light.

Magic Maca Hemp Milk

This is the very simplest kind of milk. The addition of lecithin granules makes it creamy without having to add more nuts.

Ingredients

2 tbsp shelled hemp seeds
1 tbsp lecithin
1-3 tsp maca powder
5 drops stevia

Makes 1 litre of milk
You need a blender
Takes less than 5 mins!

Throw all the ingredients in your blender together. Blend for a minute, until the hemp is completely broken down. No need to strain, you can drink straight away.

Serve and drink within 12 hours, this milk doesn't keep well for more than a day.

The Bomb

I have been talking about this a long time, and I've finally started making it. Maybe I wasn't ready before. Are you ready?

This is just about the most powerful blow-your-socks-off combination I could imagine. It contains the holy trinity of anti-oxidant rich plants, chaga, cacao, and matcha. Then you've got the powerful synergy between matcha, mucuna and cacao (L-theanine works synergistically with seratonin and dopamine). Plus the maca is in there for adrenal support.

Way more Bulletproof than that silly coffee stuff.

Ingredients

¼ tsp matcha powder
¼ tsp mucuna powder
1 tsp chaga powder
1 tsp cacao powder
1 tbsp maca powder
2 tbsp coconut butter
sweetener to taste (I use 5 drops stevia)
1 litre hot water

Makes 4 cups
Takes 5 mins
You need a high-power blender

Place everything in a high-power blender. Heat your water in the kettle or a pan (it's better if you don't let it boil, I heat mine to 80°C). Blend together for a minute until its nice and frothy. The trick with blending hot drinks is to allow a bit of air in through the top of the lid, otherwise the steam created in the jug causes the lid to pop off and explode all over your kitchen. You have to use an old tea towel and hold it around the air hole you've created, or it will all splash out that way. Cover it with a towel and it will absorb all the splashes. You can drink it all at once (!), share it with a friend, or keep some until the next day - it's okay for up to 24 hours usually.

Turmeric Latté

Yes, everyone does a Turmeric Latté. But I bet you've never had one quite like mine. I went through the winter of 2016 drinking this every day, the whole litre of it, usually in the afternoon around 3 or 4pm. It gives me the exact energy I'm looking for to push me through the last bit of the working day. The benefits of turmeric are manifold: it's the best natural anti-inflammatory and one of the top natural anti-depressants, for starters. And did you know the addition of black pepper increases the bio-availability of the curcumin content in the turmeric by 2000%? The addition of fats in the form of coconut butter also increases bioavailability, the cinnamon balances the blood sugar, ginger boosts the immune system, and cayenne aids digestion. Truly medicinal!

Ingredients

1 tbsp maca powder
1 tbsp coconut butter
5 drops stevia
1 tsp turmeric powder
1 tsp cinnamon powder
¼ tsp ginger powder
pinch ground black pepper
pinch cayenne powder
1 litre hot water

Makes 4 cups
Takes 5 mins
You need a blender

Put everything in the blender together and blend. I heat my water to 80°C rather than boiling it. You need to take the cover off the hole in the top of your blender, to leave a little gap for the steam to escape, or the blender lid might explode off! Cover with a tea-towel so it doesn't splash everywhere.

Macapuccino

The first incarnation of this recipe happened in 2012. I'd been going to LA and visiting Truth Calkins at the Tonic Bar in the legendary Erewhon. The Reishi Cappuccino they had back when I first tried it in 2009 was something else: maybe it was the quality of the reishi, maybe it was just Truth's magic touch, but it definitely set the gold standard of hot milky superfood drinks, yet to be surpassed. Over the years, I've simplified the recipe, to one that is both easy and delicious enough to make it a staple. I enjoy these kind of hot drinks daily in the winter months. As soon as the temperature starts dropping, usually around early November, until Spring starts peeking out from behind the annual curtains in March, hot superfood drinks are an essential part of my strategy for not letting the cold and the dark get to me. Around 3-4pm, I make a litre, and drink it for the rest of the afternoon, giving me the exact kind of calm and focused energy I need to get me through until the evening meal.

Ingredients

1 litre water
1 tbsp maca powder
¼ tsp reishi extract
5 drops toffee stevia
2 tbsp shelled hemp seeds
1 tsp cinnamon powder
pinch cayenne powder

Makes 4 cups
Takes 5 mins
You need a blender

Heat the water first. I heat it to 80°C rather than boiling it; boiling it destroys the flavour and you only have to let it cool down to around 80°C before you can drink it anyway! Put everything in the blender and blend together. You need to create an escape valve for the steam, or your blender lid might explode off! Blenders usually have a little hole in the top with a cap: lift the cap and wrap it with a tea towel to absorb any splashes. Drink the same day: maca doesn't keep well when added to water.

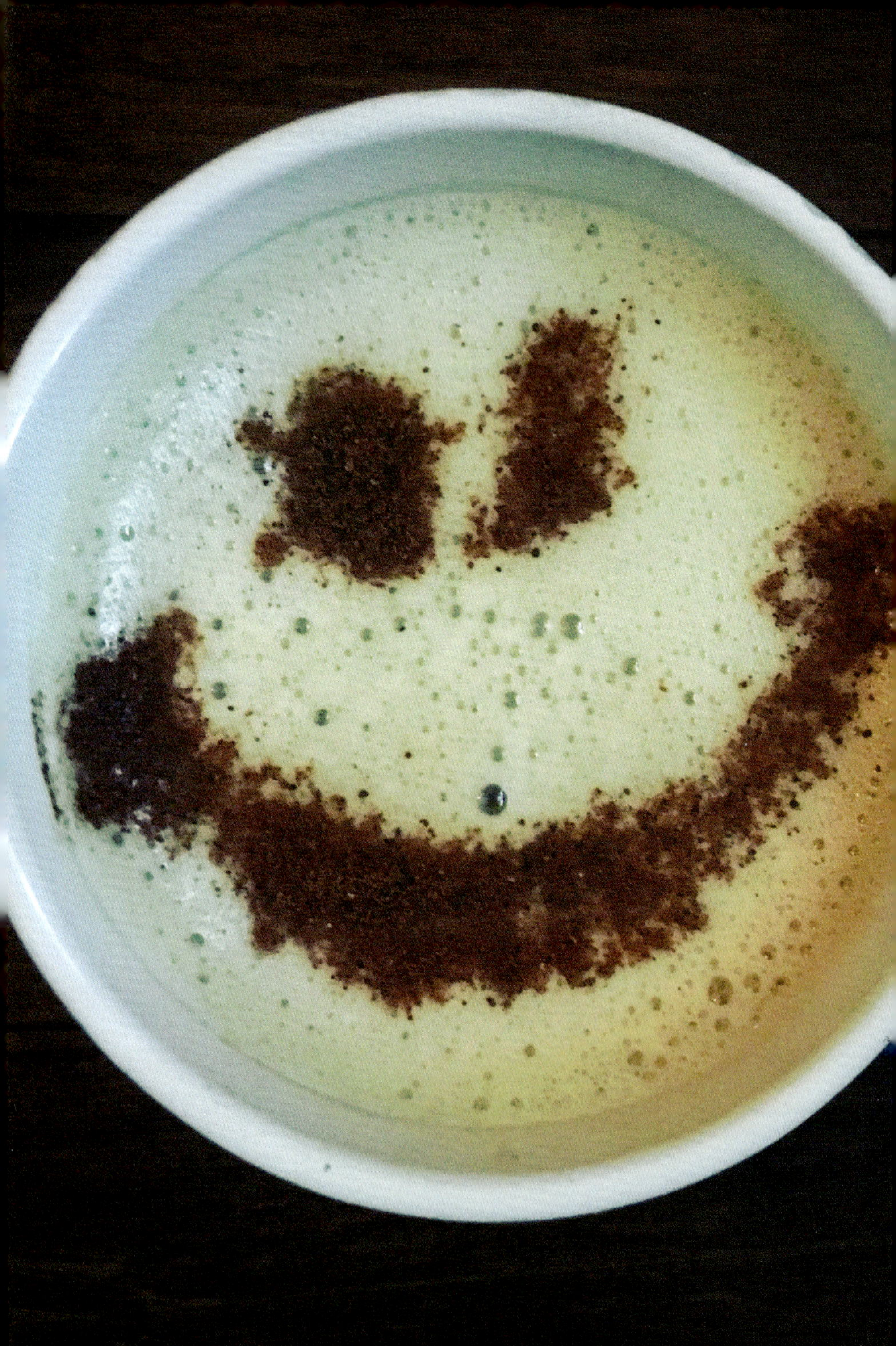

Matcha Latté

Yes, and Matcha Lattés are pretty overdone these days as well. But who else puts mucuna in their matcha lattés? Matcha and mucuna is a very special combination that releases all the right kind of chemicals in the brain to give you drive, focus, and positivity.

Ingredients

1 tsp matcha powder
2 tbsp coconut butter
¼ tsp cayenne
1 tsp cinnamon
1 tsp mucuna powder
1 litre water

Makes 4 cups
Takes 5 mins
You need a blender

Put everything in the blender together and blend. I heat my water to 80°C rather than boiling it. You need to take the cover of f the hole in the top of your blender, to leave a little gap for the steam to escape, or the blender lid might explode off! Cover with a tea-towel so it doesn't splash everywhere.

Black Chaga

Chaga is one of the most wonderful medicinal mushrooms, usually found in Siberia or Northern Scandinavia. It's off the charts in terms of antioxidants, and makes a calming and restorative drink, especially in the winter months. It has a strong earthy flavour that makes it a good coffee substitute. You can't convince me coffee is a health food; I believe adrenal stress is one of the biggest contributing factors to chronic disease, and you can't drink coffee daily without stressing out your adrenals. Any of the hot drinks in this section make a great substitute that will energise you without depleting your precious Jing energy.

Ingredients

2 tsp chaga extract
4 tsp coffee substitute e.g. barleycup, yannoh
1 litre water
sweetener to taste

Makes 4 cups
Takes 2 mins
You need a blender

Heat your water to 80°C. You can either blend everything together in the blender, or it might be simpler to just do it cup by cup: put ½ tsp chaga and 1 tsp coffee substitute in each cup, along with your favourite sweetener. My preference is stevia, and you just need 1 or 2 drops per cup, or you might prefer honey. Pour hot water over the top and stir.

The Mummy Bear Effect

A question that comes up a lot is, "What temperature do we heat our food and drinks to?" It's a subject I find fascinating, and it frustrates me that we don't have more research into the whole area of heating food. We need to know exactly what temperatures we can heat which foods to and for how long. We need to know if dehydrating for 24 hours really does preserve more nutrition and vitality than steaming for 10 minutes (my feeling is, no). We need to know if all the enzymes are immediately destroyed when food gets over 42°C, or if it takes more than a few minutes. We need to know if avocados and coconut are more resistant to heat than strawberries and lettuce, or if everything is affected the same. All sorts of unanswered questions.

For now, the easiest thing to fix in our minds is that we are looking for the Mummy Bear temperature. The temperature that is not too hot, not too cold, but just right. It's no coincidence, that when we heat our food to around 42°C, this is the temperature that tastes just perfect. If you only heat it to around 37°C or 38°C, it tastes lukewarm and not heated enough. Once it goes up to 45°C and above, it starts tasting hot. So it's the temperature that is just warm, without tasting cooked. Apparently, another trick is to put your finger in and count to four. If you can keep your finger in without it starting to burn for four seconds, then it's still raw!

The same with our drinks. I heat my water to 80-85°. If I heat it to 70°C, the tea doesn't brew properly and isn't warming. At 90°C, it's too hot to drink and I need to wait for it to cool down. At 75-85°C, it's just warm enough to drink straight away, and not burn.

So it's clear to me that because these are the temperatures that feel just right for the body, these are the temperatures we should be eating and drinking at. And it's occurred to me recently that the Mummy Bear Effect should be something that we seek in all areas of our lives. In the same way that when we alkalise and consume adaptogens regularly, we find it much easier to stay centred and balanced, when we eat food that is just right, we find it much easier to keep our lives running at a pace and temperature that is just right. If we are putting hot food and drinks into our bodies all the time, our bodies are used to working to adjust and cool ourselves down. We are used to feeling stressed, and having to work to rectify that. So we anticipate stressful situations in our lives, and don't think anything of having to exert energy to de-stress. When we get used to the Mummy Bear temperature, then we expect everything in our lives to go along at a certain pace, because that's what we feel inside. When our food is always just right, we expect our lives to be as well.

Is your life blessed by the Mummy Bear effect? Do you only move into situations that feel just the right temperature? Do you know to move away if something feels too hot or too cold? Or are you still rushing in carelessly, sometimes burning yourself, sometimes getting freezing cold? The Mummy Bear way is to take life one spoonful at a time, constantly checking the temperature, and always being aware that what we are doing feels just right.

Glossary

Acai
I use freeze-dried, powdered, raw acai. It isn't so much sweet, as olive-like in flavour, and has a crumbly melt-in-the-mouth texture. I like to add it to tomato sauces to add a meaty flavour.

Agave
Once upon a time, agave was every raw-fooders' favourite sweetener. Then it had a spectacular fall from grace, as health experts claimed although it was low in glucose, it was high in fructose, so therefore it was still a baddy in the blood sugar department. My stance is that good quality, properly raw (and therein lies the difference) agave in small amounts, is a useful sweetener. Simply because, it's so very sweet, you only need it in small amounts.

Asafoetida
An Indian spice, traditionally used as an alternative to garlic and onions. Also known as hing, it has a similar flavour to garlic, but less of an odour, and according to Ayurvedic practitioners is more conducive to meditation than garlic and onions which are over-stimulating to the brain.

Ashwagandha
One of the most commonly known Ayurvedic herbs, ashwagandha translates as "like a horse." Looking for huge amounts of strength, as well as a supremely noble disposition? Then ashwagandha is the superfood for you. I use it often because it has no flavour, so it's an easy one to sneak into your victims.

Baobab
The South African superfruit which works in absolutely everything you could try it in, sweet or savoury. It has a lemon-like, yoghurt flavour which refreshes and enhances anything it's present in.

Barleygrass
An alkalising green powder with an apple-like flavour, which adds a beautiful pale green hue to your food.

Botija Olives
Sun-cured Peruvian olives which are properly raw, unlike most olives you will buy. As such, they are in a class of their own. Intensely flavoured, a handful make a substantial snack.

Buckwheat
Buckwheat is actually a seed, not a grain, it's not related to wheat and it's super alkalising. Soak it briefly, then sprout without rinsing, to avoid slime. Take it one step further, and dehydrate for 12 hours to make buckwheaties. Buckwheaties can be used in granola, or ground up to make a digestible flour.

Cacao

Cacao butter is the fat of the cacao bean. It's a saturated fat, and quite heavy on the digestion. Good cacao butter has a magnificent aroma, and a higher melting point than coconut oil, so is more stable in your recipes.

Cacao powder has an intense chocolatey flavour; it is the cacao bean with the fat removed. Most cacao powder on the market is not actually raw, even though it may be labelled as such. It's made from the raw bean, but gets heated in the press when they are separating it from the fat.

Cacao liquor or paste is the ground whole bean. It makes a very smooth chocolate.

Cacao nibs are the whole bean broken into pieces.

Camu

A South American berry with an exceptionally high vitamin C content, making it a powerful antioxidant, and a wonderful immune system booster.

Cane Juice

The closest thing I've found to the perfect sweetener. It's raw, low glycaemic, vegan, and high in minerals. The farmers press the sugar cane to make juice, and then dry it in the sun to make crystals. As this means it's basically dried juice, when you add it to cakes and chocolates it dissolves into your recipe beautifully.

Chaga

A medicinal mushroom which is commonly found in Scandinavia and Siberia. As one of the plant foods with the highest antioxidant rating in the world, it is a powerful addition to any dish, sweet or savoury, and adds a fragrant coffee-like note to your dishes.

Chlorella

An oxygenating, rejuvenating micro-algae, which has one of the highest protein contents of any plant food. It isn't as pungent as spirulina, and easier to hide in recipes.

Coconut Butter

Also known as coconut cream, this is the flesh of the coconut, pressed and ground to a butter. I use it for making hot drinks, and add it to chocolate recipes for a mylky flavour.

Coconut Flakes

Also known as coconut chips, these are extremely versatile ingredient in the raw kitchen. Add them to salads as a tropical crouton, combine them with gojis for a superfood trail mix, or grind them to use as a flour in cakes and pastry crusts.

Coconut Meat

The white jelly-like flesh of a young Thai coconut. If you can track down coconuts, it's not as much of a job as you would imagine to hack them open for their precious flesh. Or it's becoming increasingly easy to find the frozen meat, which saves you the job. If you can't find coconut meat for any of the dessert recipes, you could substitute coconut yoghurt; it's not quite as firm, but it will work. Just make sure to get a yoghurt that is pure coconut and not one of the brands that has a lot of starch added.

Coconut Oil

"I have 99 problems and coconut oil solves 98 of them." Of course, you already have coconut oil in your home, in fact, you have two jars, one in the kitchen and one in the bathroom. Just a note regarding measurements: when I say one cup, that's one cup of solid coconut oil, before you melt it. Get out the scales if you're not sure.

Coconut Sugar

Not usually raw! So I don't really understand how it became popular with raw foodies. It is healthy however, being both low glycemic and high in minerals.

Coconut Wraps

These are sold under different brand names, or if you have access to young coconuts, you can easily make your own by blending up the coconut meat and dehydrating it. Use them as a salad wrap. I also make spring rolls with them, and my favourite use for them is as lasagna sheets.

Cordyceps

A medicinal mushroom which is good for physical energy; particularly suitable for athletes and yogis, and beneficial for the lungs.

Dehydrators

I would say that dehydrators are the most essential piece of raw kitchen equipment. Once you have a dehydrator, you can do everything! And leftovers are a thing of the past, just pop leftover salad in and turn it into croutons, or add old veggies into cracker and burger batters. I recommend Excalibur as the best make. Just make sure that you get the paraflex sheets to lay over the mesh sheets. The standard temperature for dehydrating is 110°F (45°C).

Dulse

An easy to use purple seaweed which doesn't need soaking, just rinsing. My favourite is the Icelandic dulse.

Etheriums

These are super potent earth extracts that we use in small amounts. They don't have any flavour, but contain a lot of magic! Etherium Gold is the one I use most commonly, it helps with focus and concentration and it's very good for any kind of creative work.

Fruit Powders

If you use berries when they are out of season, they are sadly lacking in both flavour and colour. In the long months when we can't get fresh juicy organic berries, I like to use freeze-dried powders, which provide a concentrated source of all those yummy nutrients and vibrant colours. We have our own range that I use a lot, and I also love the Scandinavian berries such as crowberries and lingonberries.

Goji Berries

The Chinese say the only side-effect of eating too many Goji Berries is laughing too much. I mostly add them to drinks, hot and cold, or sprinkle them over salads. Wonderfully high in anti-oxidants and B vitamins.

Golden Berries

Also known as Physalis, Chinese gooseberries, or Incan berries, these golden fruits grow across Asia, South America, and South Africa. They have a tangy sweetness that complements cacao well.

Hemp

Hemp seeds come in two forms, shelled or whole. The whole seeds are grey and more nutritious but harder to work with. The shelled seeds are white and nutty and you can use them on everything. I make milks with them almost daily, and sprinkle them as a garnish over salads. The whole seeds I would be more likely to add to a cracker for a bit of crunch.

Hemp is the best source of vegetarian protein, and if it's protein you're after, then cut straight to the chase and buy this powder that has had the fat removed to make it a concentrated protein source. It acts as a good thickener in savoury soups and sauces.

Hemp oil has a delicious nutty flavour. As a polyunsaturated fat high in omega oils, it's delicate and unstable, so never cook with it and store it in the fridge.

Herbamare

Found in the salt section of health food stores, Herbamare is a mix of dried vegetables and salt which has a great taste, and also means you end up using less actual salt. I also like to use seaweed salt for the same reason.

He Shou Wu

Definitely in my top ten superfoods, He Shou Wu is friendly and easy, potent but not challenging like some of them can be. It's one of the most important tonifying herbs in Chinese medicine, so it strengthens your organs and just generally makes you feel better about life. With a coffee-like flavour, it works well in both savoury recipes and desserts.

Himalayan Black salt

Also known as Kala Namak, or more colloquially, eggy salt, this Himalayan sulphurous salt is heavily reminiscent of eggs. Sprinkle a pinch on any dish to conjure up egg mayo or egg fried rice inspired dishes.

Honey

Yes, I call myself vegan, and yes I eat honey. Honey comes from flowers! It's just collected by the bees. I know it's a contentious issue, and I only eat honey that is responsibly sourced. Honey is a wonderful sweetener, rich, round, and full of minerals. I add a teaspoon here and there for its fantastic ability to soothe some of the harsher, bitter notes in a recipe.

Irish Moss

A seaweed which we use as a natural gelling agent. It makes light fluffy melt in the mouth mousses and pies, if you follow these instructions.

Also known as carrageenan, this amazing seaweed makes thick creamy desserts without needing to use excess fats. It takes careful preparation though, so follow the steps meticulously. If you go wrong, you could find your dessert tastes of seaweed, which isn't the desired effect we're going for. Or you could find that it doesn't set and you're left with smoothie not pudding.

Take your moss and rinse it well. Then find an airtight container to house it in (we use our empty 1kg coconut oil tubs), and put the moss and 1 cup (250ml) pure water in the tub. Put the lid on and leave it in the fridge. We find our moss likes a minimum of 24 hours soaking, and a maximum of up to five days.

When you're ready to use it, throw away the soak water, and make sure NOT to rinse the moss again. Blend it up with 1 cup (250ml) of the water. The paste won't go too smooth, but smooth enough to blend into a recipe.

Liquid Aminos

A raw, vegan alternative to soya sauce. Use in moderation.

Kelp Powder

Kelp is the most nutrient-dense seaweed, with a strong fishy flavour. A little goes a long way, in terms of both nutrition and flavour.

Kelp Noodles

Vegan, raw, gluten-free, paleo, soy-free, and extremely versatile, a healthy kitchen is not complete without a couple of bags of kelp noodles in the store cupboard. I eat them at least once a week, in a marinara, with pesto, in a creamy alfredo sauce, as a Thai, Japanese...they never get boring.

Klamath Lake Algae

Nutrient-dense micro-algae which grows in Oregon at the base of the Klamath Falls. Used in small amounts, we include it to up the nutrient profile of a dish while not affecting the flavour profile. E3 Live is the premier brand.

Kombucha

Fermented health drink that is very good for the digestion, the liver, and the immune system. I also make my own Jun, which is a similar drink but made with honey and green tea, where kombucha is made with black tea and sugar.

Lecithin

Lecithin granules are made from soybeans (occasionally, you will come across sunflower lecithin but it's very rare and not always good quality). They are a wonderful raw kitchen ingredient because as well as containing important nutrients in the form of phosphatidyl choline, they make your recipes creamy without having to overdo the fats.

Lion's Mane

A medicinal mushroom, which, while not the most potent, has perhaps the most pleasant flavour of all of them, and is a top nootropic.

Lucuma

A Peruvian fruit, known as the Gold of the Incas, similar to a mango. Lucuma powder is the secret ingredient in raw cake and pastry making to get that wonderful biscuit flavour.

Maca

A Peruvian root vegetable, high in sulphur, and used as a powder for its ability to increase energy and stamina, as well as balance hormones. Maca should be on the NHS for every woman!

Matcha

A Japanese tea, low in caffeine, and high in L-theanine, traditionally used by monks to help with meditation. Good for energy and focus, my personal number one remedy for jet-lag!

Medicine Flower Extracts

Cold-water flavour extracts produced by a botanical aromatherapist in Oregon, these are exceedingly popular among raw food chefs for their potency and ability to enhance your dishes. There are over twenty different flavours, but the ones I always return to are rum, coffee, strawberry, vanilla, caramel, raspberry, and violet.

Mesquite

Mesquite is a Peruvian form of carob, illegal in the EU under the novel foods act, but if you can find it, it will add a sweet caramel flavour to your recipes. You can use our Peruvian Carob from Raw Living, it tastes exactly the same!

Miso

A Japanese soy paste, full of umami flavour and immune-boosting properties. If your miso is unpasteurised, then it's still enzymatically alive. I favour white misos which are less salty than dark misos.

Mucuna

Also known as Kappikachhu, this powder comes from the same Himalayan bean that itching powder is from. It's high in precursors to serotonin and dopamine, so has a powerful effect on brain chemistry, as well as containing traces of DMT. Because of its ability to increase dopamine production, it's used to treat patients with both Parkinson's and Alzheimer's.

Nori

Nori usually comes as sheets, but you sometimes find it as flakes. Nori is one of those items a raw food kitchen can never be without! Make sure you buy dark green, untoasted nori.

Nutritional Yeast Flakes

Not a raw product, but popular among vegans for its cheesy flavour. It's a good source of B vitamins.

Psyllium

A seed husk that comes from the plantain plant, known for its ability to help with colon function, in raw cuisine we use it as a gelling agent, because of its mucilaginous properties i.e. its ability to swell and absorb water and create a gel.

Purple Corn Extract

High in anthocyanins, purple corn is much rarer than blue or yellow, hence more prized. When buying purple corn, make sure you buy the extract; the flour is pointless. Purple corn extract will turn your food an amazing deep purple hue and tastes like Ribena.

Rawmesan

A US product made by a Texan company called Gopal's; yes you could make your own, but they have the flavour perfectly down. I love to sprinkle this over Lasagna, Pizza, or Spaghetti dishes.

Reishi

The number one medicinal mushroom, and contender for the number one superfood (definitely in my top five). Reishi is bitter, so we don't use it for flavour, but for its ability to boost the immune system and calm the mind.

Rice Vinegar

I use Clearspring brand, and add it to my, um, rice dishes.

Salt

I'm not a big fan of Himalayan, as it creates a very dominant note in your recipes. My favourite salt is Icelandic, but any sea salt is good with me. For fermenting, I use Celtic (I would particularly not recommend fermenting with Himalayan).

Shilajit

Basically Himalayan mud, shilajit comes as a resin or in powdered form, and is a great detoxifier. It lends an unsurprisingly earthy tone to your recipes, and also, perhaps obviously, it's very grounding.

Seagreens

The brand name of a wild seaweed that grows in the Outer Hebrides, I love Seagreens for its flavour and nutty texture.

Stevia

Stevia is an exceptionally sweet plant, which means we only need use it in miniscule amounts to add sweetness to a recipe. I favour the drops, and as a rule would suggest 5 drops replace a teaspoon of honey or agave. Suitable for diabetics.

Spirulina

The most well-known of the micro-algaes, spirulina varies a lot in flavour depending where it's grown. Chinese has the most pond-like flavour, while Hawaiian is almost sweet. My favourite way to enjoy it is as spirulina crunchies, which I sprinkle over dinner.

Sumac

My favourite Middle Eastern spice, it's uniquely umami.

Tamari

Unpasteurised tamari is still enzymatically active. Tamari is wheat-free, whereas Shoyu is not, so it's my preference. It's also a little stronger in flavour, so you need less.

Tahini

"You can never have too much tahini!" was actually our motto when we had a raw food shop in Brighton. Tahini is such a staple in the raw kitchen, a jar gets used up in no time at all, so it's always best to stock up. Most tahinis aren't raw; my preferred raw brand is Sun and Seed.

Turmeric

Turmeric you will no doubt know as the number one anti-inflammatory in nature, but did you also know it's a top anti-depressant? Add black pepper to your turmeric recipes to increase bioavailablity by up to 2000% (that's not a misprint!).

Umeboshi

Umeboshi plums are a salt pickled plum from Japan. I adore the paste, and love small amounts in salad dressings, sandwich spreads, and sushi fillings. Ume vinegar is also a good replacement for apple cider vinegar, for those who can't tolerate it.

Yacon Syrup

Along with stevia, the only sweetener I would recommend for diabetics. Yacon contains fructoligosaccharides which taste sweet but have no impact on the blood sugar. Yacon is not overly sweet, but a lifesaver for those on a strict no-sugar regime.

Wasabi

Sadly, most wasabi is actually horseradish – if you find pure wasabi, snap it up! I use Biona wasabi paste or Clearspring wasabi powder.

Wrawps

Zucchini and flax wraps, made in California. These are dense strong wraps that hold their own well, so are great for travelling. I love to use them as Enchilada or Burrito wraps. I also love their pizza bases.

Xylitol

Most Xylitol is not raw; shop carefully in the health food store, rather than the supermarket. Xylitol, I think, is badly named: if they called it fermented birch sugar (for that's what it is) it would be a lot more popular! It has a cooling effect, so works particularly well in mint recipes. It's low-glycemic, and good for the teeth (hence its presence in chewing gum and toothpastes).

Za'atar

A Middle Eastern spice blend of sumac, thyme, sesame and salt.

14 Mushroom Blend

An earthy tasting, all-purpose mushroom blend that I use to add a kind of stock flavour to savoury dishes. I also use 8 Mushroom a lot, which is a more concentrated extract powder. 14 Mushroom is a good introductory product, and as it is less potent, is lower in price.

A Note On Sweeteners:

Cane juice crystals, coconut sugar and xylitol are all pretty interchangeable; use whichever agrees with you the best.

Yacon syrup and coconut nectar are very interchangeable. Honey and agave are interchangeable. Yacon and coconut nectar aren't as sweet as honey and agave, but maybe you prefer to use them.

Mesquite is technically illegal in the UK and Europe, but look for Peruvian carob on the Raw Living website, it is very similar.

Resources

RawLiving.co.uk is our online web shop, founded in 2002. Despite the authorities' best efforts to make health foods inaccessible and kill small business, we've survived for over twenty years and have thousands of glowing reviews from happy customers to attest to the high quality of the products we sell, our ethics and integrity, and the excellence of our customer service.

If there are any strange ingredients in this book that you are wondering where you might find them, we almost certainly have them at Raw Living.

KateMagic.com is my personal website where you can find more recipes, articles, and interviews.

My chef videos are hosted by Vimeo - *https://vimeo.com/ondemand/rawmagicacademy/*

My DJ mixes are on Mixcloud *https://www.mixcloud.com/katemagic/*

I am a certified Functional Nutrition Counsellor with Andrea Nakayama; I completed my Yoga 200hr teacher training with Stewart Gilchrist; I'm a Reiki Level 3 master, a certified QHHT practitioner, and I've completed a Tantric arts training with Shayna Hiller. To book coaching, reiki, yoga, or QHHT, or attend a workshop, course or retreat, visit my website or email *hello@rawliving.co.uk.*

Copyright

Recipes are pretty much impossible to copyright. I have seen my recipes used in restaurants, on TV, shared on social media with no credit, and in other people's books. If there was a way of me receiving royalties for every time one of my recipes was used and sold for commercial gain, I could well be a millionaire! But we don't currently live in a world that respects or protects artistry. As it is, writing books is (in my experience), a below minimum-wage occupation, entirely a labour of love; an act of service.

You could choose to be like countless others before you, and exploit my work. Or you could choose to acknowledge me as the author of the recipe when you post it and change one ingredient; you could offer me payment for the recipe if you intend to use it in a commercial kitchen; you could be transparent, as I do when I get inspiration from other chefs, and tell people about my original recipe when sharing your version of it. I can't tell you what to do, and I have no legal recourse to protect my work in any real way. It's entirely down to your conscience, and besides, karma comes for us all eventually.